9th Workshop on Language Technology for Cultural Heritage, Social Science, and Humanities

(LaTeCH 2015)

Co-located with ACL-IJCNLP 2015

Beijing, China
30 July 2015

ISBN: 978-1-5108-0944-4

Printed from e-media with permission by:

Curran Associates, Inc.
57 Morehouse Lane
Red Hook, NY 12571

Some format issues inherent in the e-media version may also appear in this print version.

Printed by Curran Associates, Inc. (2015)

For permission requests, please contact the Association for Computational Linguistics at the address below.

Association for Computational Linguistics
209 N. Eighth Street
Stroudsburg, Pennsylvania 18360

Phone: 1-570-476-8006
Fax: 1-570-476-0860

acl@aclweb.org

Additional copies of this publication are available from:

Curran Associates, Inc.
57 Morehouse Lane
Red Hook, NY 12571 USA
Phone: 845-758-0400
Fax: 845-758-2634
Email: curran@proceedings.com
Web: www.proceedings.com

LaTeCH 2015

Proceedings of the 9th SIGHUM Workshop on Language Technology for Cultural Heritage, Social Sciences, and Humanities (LaTeCH 2015)

July 30, 2015
Beijing, China

Introduction

The LaTeCH workshop series, which started in 2007, was initially motivated by the growing interest in language technology research and applications to the cultural heritage domain. The scope quickly broadened to also include the humanities and the social sciences. LaTeCH is currently the annual venue of the ACL Special Interest Group on Language Technologies for the Socio-Economic Sciences and Humanities (SIGHUM).

The current, ninth edition of the LaTeCH workshop was organised for the first time in Asia and we were delighted to present humanities research from Indonesia, Singapore, China and Korea, covering topics such as Chinese poetry, Korean History and folktales. We have also witnessed further expansion in the resource and tool development approaches, with works now covering topics ranging from Latin and medieval manuscripts to Minoan, Linear A texts. The submissions were substantial not only in terms of quantity, but also in terms of quality and variety. Acceptance rate for LaTeCH-2015 was 61%.

We would like to thank all authors for the hard work that went into their submissions. We are also grateful to the members of the programme committee for their thorough reviews, and to the ACL-IJCNLP 2015 organisers, especially the Workshop Co-chairs, Hang Li and Sebastian Riedel for their help with administrative matters. Finally, we wish to thank Nils Reiter for volunteering to oversee the workshop local organisation, moderate the annual SIGHUM meeting and chair the workshop sessions.

Kalliopi Zervanou, Marieke van Erp and Beatrice Alex

Organizers:

Kalliopi A. Zervanou (Co-Chair), Utrecht University (The Netherlands)
Marieke van Erp (Co-Chair), VU University Amsterdam (The Netherlands)
Beatrice Alex (Co-Chair), University of Edinburgh (United Kingdom)

Local Organizer:

Nils Reiter, Stuttgart University (Germany)

Program Committee:

Toine Bogers, Aalborg University, Copenhagen (Denmark)
Antal van den Bosch, Radboud University Nijmegen (The Netherlands)
Gosse Bouma, Rijksuniversiteit Groningen (The Netherlands)
Paul Buitelaar, DERI Galway (Ireland)
Mariona Coll Ardanuy, Trier University (Germany)
Thierry Declerck, DFKI (Germany)
Stefanie Dipper, Ruhr-Universität Bochum (Germany)
Milena Dobreva, University of Malta (Malta)
Mick O'Donnell, Universidad Autonoma de Madrid (Spain)
Antske Fokkens, VU University Amsterdam (The Netherlands)
Ben Hachey, University of Sydney (Australia)
Iris Hendrickx, Radboud University Nijmegen (The Netherlands)
Adam Jatowt, Kyoto University (Japan)
Jaap Kamps, University of Amsterdam (The Netherlands)
Vangelis Karkaletsis, NCSR Demokritos (Greece)
Mike Kestemont, University of Antwerp & Research Foundation Flanders (Belgium)
Dimitrios Kokkinakis, University of Gothenburg (Sweden)
Stasinos Konstantopoulos, NCSR Demokritos (Greece)
Barbara McGillivray, Oxford University Press
Gerard de Melo, Tsinghua University (China)
Saif Mohammad, National Research Council (Canada)
Joakim Nivre, Uppsala University (Sweden)
Nelleke Oostdijk, Radboud University Nijmegen (The Netherlands)
Petya Osenova, Bulgarian Academy of Sciences (Bulgaria)
Michael Piotrowski, Leibniz Institute of European History in Mainz (Germany)
Georg Rehm, DFKI (Germany)
Martin Reynaert, Tilburg University (The Netherlands)
Eric Sanders, Radboud University Nijmegen (The Netherlands)
Marijn Schraagen, Utrecht University (The Netherlands)
Eszter Simon, Research Institute for Linguistics (HASRIL) (Hungary)
Caroline Sporleder, Trier University (Germany)
Herman Stehouwer, Max Planck for Plasmaphysics (Germany)
Mariët Theune, University of Twente (The Netherlands)
Takenobu Tokunaga, Tokyo Institute of Technology (Japan)
Cristina Vertan, University of Hamburg (Germany)
Frans Wiering, Utrecht University (The Netherlands)
Menno van Zaanen, Tilburg University (The Netherlands)
Svitlana Zinger, TU Eindhoven (The Netherlands)

Table of Contents

Workshop Program

Thursday 30th July 2015

9:00–10:30 **Session I**

9:00–9:10 *Welcome*
Nils Reiter

9:10–9:40 *Catching the Red Priest: Using Historical Editions of Encyclopaedia Britannica to Track the Evolution of Reputations*
Yen-Fu Luo, Anna Rumshisky and Mikhail Gronas

9:40–10:00 *Five Centuries of Monarchy in Korea: Mining the Text of the Annals of the Joseon Dynasty*
JinYeong Bak and Alice Oh

10:00–10:30 *Analyzing Sentiment in Classical Chinese Poetry*
Yufang Hou and Anette Frank

10:30–11:00 **Coffee Break**

11:00–12:40 **Session II**

11:00–11:30 *Measuring the Structural and Conceptual Similarity of Folktales using Plot Graphs*
Victoria Anugrah Lestari and Ruli Manurung

11:30–11:50 *Towards Annotating Narrative Segments*
Nils Reiter

11:50–12:20 *Ranking Relevant Verb Phrases Extracted from Historical Text*
Eva Pettersson, Beáta Megyesi and Joakim Nivre

12:20–12:40 *Ranking election issues through the lens of social media*
Stephen Wan and Cécile Paris

Thursday 30th July 2015 (continued)

12:40–14:00 **Lunch**

14:00–14:40 **Session III: SIGHUM Annual Meeting**

14:40–15:10 **Session IV: Poster Boosters**

14:40–14:45 *Word Embeddings Pointing the Way for Late Antiquity*
Johannes Bjerva and Raf Praet

14:45–14:50 *Enriching Interlinear Text using Automatically Constructed Annotators*
Ryan Georgi, Fei Xia and William Lewis

14:50–14:55 *Automatic interlinear glossing as two-level sequence classification*
Tanja Samardzic, Robert Schikowski and Sabine Stoll

14:55–15:00 *Enriching Digitized Medieval Manuscripts: Linking Image, Text and Lexical Knowledge*
Aitor Arronte Alvarez

15:00–15:05 *A preliminary study on similarity-preserving digital book identifiers*
Klemo Vladimir, Marin Silic, Nenad Romic, Goran Delac and Sinisa Srbljic

15:05–15:10 *When Translation Requires Interpretation: Collaborative Computer–Assisted Translation of Ancient Texts*
Andrea Bellandi, Davide Albanesi, Giulia Benotto, Emiliano Giovannetti and Gianfranco Di Segni

Thursday 30th July 2015 (continued)

15:10–16:00 Poster Session and Coffee

16:00–17:30 Session V

16:00–16:20 *Integrating Query Performance Prediction in Term Scoring for Diachronic Thesaurus*
Chaya Liebeskind and Ido Dagan

16:20–16:50 *Minoan linguistic resources: The Linear A Digital Corpus*
Tommaso Petrolito, Ruggero Petrolito, Francesco Perono Cacciafoco and Gregoire Winterstein

16:50–17:20 *Lexicon-assisted tagging and lemmatization in Latin: A comparison of six taggers and two lemmatization models*
Tim vor der Brück, Steffen Eger and Alexander Mehler

17:20–17:30 *Closing*
Nils Reiter

Catching the Red Priest: Using Historical Editions of Encyclopaedia Britannica to Track the Evolution of Reputations

Yen-Fu Luo[†], **Anna Rumshisky**[†], **Mikhail Gronas**[*]
[†]Dept. of Computer Science, University of Massachusetts Lowell, Lowell, MA, USA
[*]Dept. of Russian, Dartmouth College, Hanover, NH, USA
{yluo,arum}@cs.uml.edu, mikhail.gronas@dartmouth.edu

Abstract

In this paper, we investigate the feasibility of using the chronology of changes in historical editions of Encyclopaedia Britannica (EB) to track the changes in the landscape of cultural knowledge, and specifically, the rise and fall in reputations of historical figures. We describe the data-processing pipeline we developed in order to identify the matching articles about historical figures in Wikipedia, the current electronic edition of Encyclopaedia Britannica (edition 15), and several digitized historical editions, namely, editions 3, 9, 11. We evaluate our results on the tasks of article segmentation and cross-edition matching using a manually annotated subset of 1000 articles from each edition. As a case study for the validity of discovered trends, we use the Wikipedia category of 18th century classical composers. We demonstrate that our data-driven method allows us to identify cases where a historical figure's reputation experiences a drastic fall or a dramatic recovery which would allow scholars to further investigate previously overlooked instances of such change.

1 Introduction

Histories of nations are reflected in their shifting borders. But the histories of things immaterial, yet no less interesting–concepts, ideologies, reputations of historical personalities–are mapless. This paper describes the progress of the Knowledge Evolution Project (KnowEvo), which investigates the possibility of using historical digitized text to track and map long-range historical changes in the conceptual landscape, and specifically, the history of intellectual networks and reputations.

One of the ways to investigate the change in how ideas and personalities are represented is to use mention statistics from books written at different historical periods. Google Ngram Viewer is a tool that plots occurrence statistics using Google Books, the largest online repository of digitized books. But while Google Books in its entirety certainly has quantity, it lacks structure. However, the history of knowledge (or culture) is, to a large extent, the history of structures: hierarchies, taxonomies, domains, subdomains.

In the present project, our goal was to focus on sources that endeavor to capture such structures. One such source is particularly fitting for the task; and it has been in existence at least for the last three centuries, in the form of changing editions of authoritative encyclopedias, and specifically, Encyclopaedia Britannica. Throughout their existence, encyclopedias have claimed to be well-organized (i.e., structured) representations of knowledge and have effectively served as its (obviously imperfect) mirrors. Each edition of Encyclopaedia Britannica reflected a collective editorial decision, based on a scholarly consensus, regarding the importance of each subject that has to be included and the relative volume dedicated to it. As such, it can be thought of as a proxy of sorts for the state of contemporary knowledge. Of course, institutions such as Britannica, their claims to universality notwithstanding, throughout their histories have been necessarily western-centric and reflected the prejudices of their time. A note of caution is therefore in order here: what this data allows us to reconstruct is the evolution of knowledge representation, rather than of the knowledge itself.

In this paper, we investigate the feasibility of using historical Encyclopaedia Britannica editions to develop tools that can be used in scholarship and in pedagogy to illustrate and analyze known historical changes and to facilitate the discovery of overlooked trends and processes. Specifically, we focus on the history of intellectual reputations. We are interested in whether certain categories of

Proceedings of the 9th SIGHUM Workshop on Language Technology for Cultural Heritage, Social Sciences, and Humanities, pages 1–9,
Beijing, China, July 30, 2015. ©2015 Association for Computational Linguistics and The Asian Federation of Natural Language Processing

people that form an intellectual landscape of a culture can be tracked through time using Britannica's historical editions. We suggest that by measuring changes in the relative importance assigned to a particular figure in successive editions of Britannica we can reconstruct the history of his or her reputation. Thus, each edition can be thought of as a proxy for the contemporary state of knowledge (and reputations in particular), with the history of editions reflecting the history of such states. Continuing previous work (Gronas et al., 2012), we develop a set of tools for cleaning noisy digitally scanned text, identifying articles and subjects, normalizing their mentions across editions, and measuring their relative importance. The data about historical figures and their reputations, based on their representation in different editions of Encyclopaedia Britannica, is available for browsing and visualization through the KnowEvo Facebook of the Past search interface.[1]

We examine the plausibility of using these tools to track the change in people's reputations in various domains of culture. In the current work, we verify the accuracy of our cross-edition normalization methods and conduct a case study to examine whether the discovered trends are valid. As a case study, we look at the reputations of 18th century classical composers. Many of 18th century classical composers had utmost importance for western classical music and exerted far-reaching influence during the following centuries. We looked at the reputation changes between the 11th edition (1911) and the 15th edition (1985–2000), thus covering most of the 20th century.

The results of our case study suggest that our methods provide a valid way to examine the trends in the rise and fall of reputations. For example, the case study revealed that in the course of the 20th century, among the major composers, Handel's reputation underwent the biggest change, as he dropped from being second most important composer (after Johann Sebastian Bach) in the beginning of the century to the fifth position, well behind Gluck and Haydn. Meanwhile, Mozart dethroned Bach, who moved from the first to the second place. Some of the lesser composers (Lotti and Gaensbacher) disappeared from encyclopedia-curated cultural memory altogether; whereas the familiar name of Telemann owes its familiarity to a recent revival. Another notable shift, empirically revealed during the case study, was the change in Vivaldi's legacy. The author of "The Four Seasons", known to his contemporaries as the red priest (due to his hair and profession, respectively) was completely forgotten towards the beginning of the 20th century and then rediscovered and joined the canon in the second part of the century. For a student of musical history these facts are not surprising. However, they have been obtained through an automatic method which can be used in other, less well known areas of cultural history and on a large scale.

2 Related work

A big data analysis of large textual datasets in humanities has been gaining momentum in recent years, as evidenced by the success of Culturomics (Michel et al., 2011), a method based on n-gram frequency analysis of the Google Books corpus, available via the Google Ngram Viewer.

Skiena and Ward (2013) recently applied similar quantitative analysis to empirical cultural history, assessing the relative importance of historical figures by examining Wikipedia people articles. They supplemented word frequency analysis with several Wikipedia-based measures, such as PageRank (Page et al., 1999), page size, the number of page views and page edits. Their approach is complementary to ours: whereas they are interested in the reputations as they exist today, we seek to quantify the dynamics of cultural change, i.e. the historical dimension of reputations, rather than a contemporary snapshot.

A culturomics-like approach applied to large structured datasets (knowledge bases) is advocated in Suchanek and Preda (2014). Our approach is somewhat similar in that the corpus of historical editions of Britannica can be considered a knowledge base, with an important difference being a chronological dimension, absent from such knowledge bases as YAGO or DBpedia. An example of mining a historical corpus for trends using the frequentist approaches to vocabulary shifts as well as normalization to structured sources can be found in the recent work on newspaper and journal historical editions such as Kestemont et al. (2014) and Huet et al. (2013).

Disambiguation of named entities to structured sources such as Wikipedia has been an active area of research in recent years (Bunescu and Pasca, 2006; Cornolti et al., 2013; Cucerzan, 2007; Hof-

[1] http://knowevo.cs.uml.edu

fart et al., 2011; Kulkarni et al., 2009; Liao and Veeramachaneni, 2009; Ratinov et al., 2011). Our approach to diachronic normalization between different editions opens the door to time-specific entity disambiguation, which would link the mentions of a particular person in a historical text to the time-appropriate knowledge base, which in this case would be the encyclopedic edition from the same time period.

3 Methods

In order to track the change over time, we collected several historical editions of Encyclopaedia Britannica, including the 3rd, the 9th, the 11th, and the 15th editions. The first three editions are OCR-scanned version but the 11th edition is partially proofread by Project Gutenberg.[2] Encyclopaedia Britannica, Inc. gave us the authorization to use the electronic text of the current 15th edition for research.

Our text-processing pipeline includes article segmentation, people article extraction, and article matching. For the case study presented in this paper, we rely on our automated matching of articles between the 11th and the 15th edition. Published in 1911, the 11th edition was a fully reworked version of the encyclopedia which represented a substantial change in the state of knowledge from the last 19th century edition, and which remained mostly unchanged over the next several editions. We use edition 15 (the last paper edition of Encyclopaedia Britannica, converted to electronic form, 1985–2000) to represent the state of encyclopedic knowledge at the end of the 20th century. We normalize the 15th edition Britannica articles to their Wikipedia counterparts, and use Wikipedia categories as the proxy for different domains of culture.

Our framework relies on identifying the corresponding articles about the same historical figure in different editions, which are then used to form the representation for the stream of history. In the following subsections, we describe in detail the approach we used to extract the matching people-related articles, as well as the obtained estimates for system performance on different subtasks of the pipeline.

3.1 Article Segmentation

We developed a set of simple title heuristics to identify article titles in the historical editions. We look for uppercase words at the beginning of a line preceded by an empty line and followed by at least one non-empty line; the first word should be at least two characters long, and excludes frequent words such as "OCR", "BIBLIOGRAPHY", "FIG.", and Roman numerals.

For example, the following are the first sentences of the articles for Giorgio Baglivi in the 3rd and 9th editions, respectively:

```
BAGL1V1 (George), a most illustrious physician
```

```
BAGLIVI, GIORGIO, an illustrious Italian physician,
```

Note that OCR errors in the first word of article are quite common, as seen here in the 3rd edition title.

In addition, we used metadata regarding the titles present in each volume. For example, articles in the first volume are from A to Androphagi. Therefore, for the first volume, we use the regular expression that extracts potential titles that begin with "A" to "AN". We developed the heuristics for article segmentation in an iterative process which used the fact that article titles in the encyclopedia are sorted alphabetically. Article titles that appeared out of order were examined to refine the heuristics at each step.

The 11th edition of Encyclopaedia Britannica contained the total of 29 volumes, including the index volume. We obtained a digitized copy from Project Gutenberg. The errors caused by the OCR process were corrected manually by distributed proofreaders on the first seventeen volumes available from Project Gutenberg. However, the 4th, 6th, 14th, and 15th volumes are not complete. Therefore, we performed the article segmentation on the original fourteen OCR-Scanned and thirteen revised volumes. We also collected article titles from Project Gutenberg for segmentation and evaluation.

3.2 People Article Extraction

We use the 15th edition gender metadata to identify and extract articles about people from the current edition. In order to identify people articles in the historical editions, we use the Stanford CoreNLP named entity recognizer (NER) with pre-trained models,[3] on the first sentence of the article. The common format of a person name is "last name, first name" in the 9th and 11th edition and "last name (first name)" in the 3rd edition. The first token always serves as the article title and is prone to OCR errors, since it is usually all-capitalized, and in some editions, uses a special font.

[2] http://www.gutenberg.org

[3] http://nlp.stanford.edu/software/corenlp.shtml

For most historical figures, the encyclopedia gives both the first name and the last name. Typically, the first name which is not a part of the title is much more accurately recognized by the OCR. We therefore first check if the third token (which corresponds to the first name) was recognized as a person entity by Stanford NER. In cases when it is not recognized as such, we also check the first token. This is done in order to identify historical figures that do not have last name emperors, royal family members, mythological figures, ancient philosophers, etc. However, we observed that Stanford NER often mis-identifies locations as people in the first position. We therefore employ several heuristics to filter out the non-person articles, including checking for the presence of keywords such as 'he', 'his', 'she', 'her', 'born', and date or time mentions in the full text of the article.

3.3 Article Matching

We use two complementary strategies to match the articles that refer to the same person across different editions. The first matching method, pairwise matching, relies on the assumption that it is easier to match articles between consecutive editions, since for most articles, the text is likely to have undergone fewer changes. For each person article in a given edition of Encyclopaedia Britannica, we try to find a matching article about the same person in the next edition. If we fail to identify a matching article, we back-off to matching the same article directly to Wikipedia.

The pairwise matching results are concatenated to produce "chains" of matching articles between the four editions of Encyclopaedia Britannica. The last article of each chain is linked to the corresponding Wikipedia article. If the pairwise matching strategy fails to link together the matching articles in two adjacent editions, multiple incomplete chains may be generated. If several incomplete chains are linked to the same Wikipedia article, they are merged.

Figure 1 illustrates the article matching process using Dante Alighieri as an example. In this case, matching from the 3rd edition to the 9th edition fails, but the back-off strategy finds a matching article in Wikipedia. At the same time, pairwise matching between editions 9 and 11 and between editions 11 and 15 succeeds, and the article in edition 15 is successfully matched to Wikipedia. Since the article from the 3rd edition and the article from

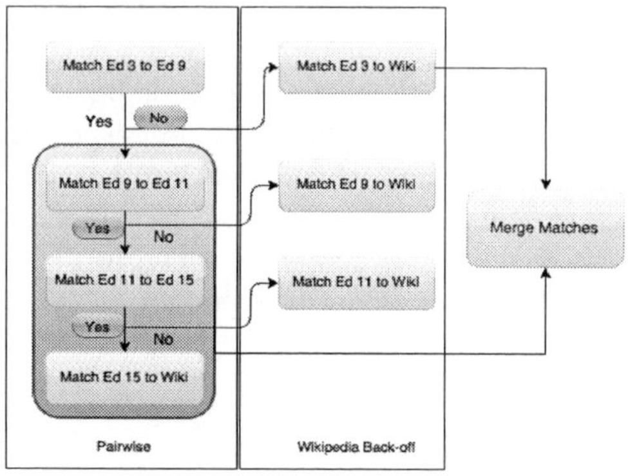

Figure 1: Article matching for *Dante Alighieri*.

the 15th edition are matched to the same Wikipedia article, the two incomplete chains ("Ed. 3–..." and "...–Ed. 9–Ed. 11–Ed. 15") are merged.

Both matching strategies first identify a set of possible matches (a *confusion set*), and then select the best matching candidate using a set of thresholds which were selected using the matching precision obtained on the development set. Two development sets were manually created by one of the authors: (1) 50 randomly selected people articles from 9th edition were matched to the 11th edition, (2) 50 randomly selected people articles from 15th edition were matched to Wikipedia. We describe the two strategies below.

3.3.1 Pairwise Matching of Historical Editions

Note that some people featured in the older edition may not appear in the newer edition at all. Also, some of the people in the later Britannica editions may not have been alive and/or sufficiently known to be included in the encyclopedia when the previous edition was published. Therefore, the pairwise matching process proceeds from the earlier editions to the later editions. We first match the 15th (current) edition to Wikipedia, then the 11th edition to the 15th, the 9th edition to 11th, and finally, the 3rd edition to the 9th edition.

The matching methods are similar for each pair of historical editions. To use matching between the 11th and 15th editions as an example, we match the people articles from the 11th edition to the corresponding articles in the 15th edition by first identifying a set of potential matches (the confusion set) using a heuristic-based search on article titles. We then find the best matching article by computing the cosine similarity (Baeza-Yates et al.,

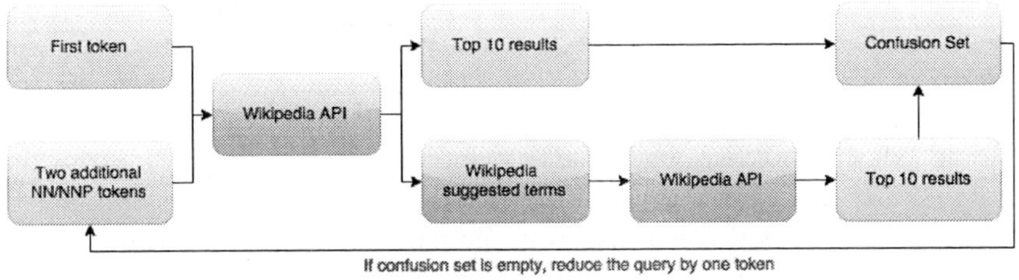

Figure 2: Deriving the confusion set with Wikipedia back-off strategy.

1999) between the original 11th edition article and the candidate article from the 15th edition. We use "bag-of-words" Boolean features on the full text of the article to compute cosine similarity. We then filter out the articles that do not have matches by applying a 0.2 threshold for minimum similarity.

In the present implementation, the confusion set is obtained by searching for all the 15th edition people articles that have the same first word. The resulting set of candidate matches contains all the articles about people with the same last name. We found that for people articles that do not contain last names (such as royalty, ancient writers and philosophers, etc.) searching on the first title word still produces a reasonable confusion set.

However, the first title word may also contain OCR errors. We are currently working on an OCR-correction system specifically tailored to the encyclopedic text. In the present implementation, we use the following solution. If no people with the same last name (first title word) are found, we take all the people with the longest matching prefix of the first title word. For example, due to the longest matching prefix, "Elme", "Elmes, James" in the 11th edition is compared to "Elmen, Gustav Waldemar" in the 15th edition. In this example, the cosine similarity between Elmen and Elmes is 0.07 and our method reports that no corresponding article exists in the 15th edition. However, if an article with the longest matching prefix is a correct match, the cosine similarity measure is likely to be above the selected threshold.

3.3.2 Matching to Wikipedia as a back-off strategy

Using the articles with the longest matching prefix allows us to identify the correct match in case when the OCR error occurs far enough from the beginning of the word. If the misspelling occurs in the very beginning of the first word, the best match for the resulting confusion set will be filtered out by the similarity threshold. For those cases, we use a back-off strategy that attempts to reprocess the articles with no matches by obtaining a new confusion set from Wikipedia API. In order to query the Wikipedia API, we use the first token and two additional tokens with NN, NNP, NNS, or NNPS part-of-speech tags (if any), identified using the CoreNLP part-of-speech module. We use this query to retrieve the top 10 search results from Wikipedia. Wikipedia API also suggests a possible correction to the query. We use the suggested query to retrieve the top 10 search results (if any), which are then used to expand the candidate set. If no results are retrieved using the original and the suggested query constructed from three keywords as described above, the first two keywords are used to repeat the above steps. The process of obtaining the confusion set is illustrated in Figure 2.

In order to reduce processing time, we set up Java Wikipedia Library (JWPL)[4] to access all information in Wikipedia locally. Wikipedia page titles of the candidate set are used to retrieve plain text of Wikipedia article from JWPL. Cosine similarity is then calculated for each candidate article to find the best match. We use "bag-of-words" TF-IDF (Salton and Yang, 1973) scores on the full text of the article to compute cosine similarity. We then filter out the articles that do not have matches by applying a 0.13 threshold for minimum similarity. As mentioned above, the threshold was selected based on the matching precision for the development set. Note that using boolean features for pairwise matching between historical editions effectively reduces the noise caused by the OCR errors. The back-off matching strategy uses TF-IDF features for cosine similarity calculation, since the clean electronic text is available for Wikipedia.

Since the 15th (current) edition is available in electronic form, correct and complete names

[4]https://code.google.com/p/jwpl/

can almost always be retrieved from the metadata. We therefore use the complete names, rather than the first three noun tokens, to retrieve the Wikipedia articles with the same title. The candidates are retrieved using both JWPL functionality and Wikipedia API. If several namesakes are present in Wikipedia, the best match is selected using cosine similarity.

3.4 Importance Measure

In the current implementation, we use a simple z-score as an importance measure, with the following formula:

$$importance(a) = (L(a) - average(L))/stddev(L)$$

where a is a particular person article, L is the article length (i.e. the number of words in that article), and average and standard deviation are computed for all articles in a given edition (Gabrovski, 2012).

Note that importance can be measured in a number of ways, for example, using the number of times a person is mentioned in other articles, or using a PageRank on an article graph constructed for each edition. An article graph can be constructed by treating person mentions or "see also" references in a historical edition as edges between the article nodes, making a historical edition more similar to Wikipedia, in which hyperlinks added by the users serve as connecting edges. However, OCR errors make any methods relying on person mentions less robust.

3.5 Gold Standard Data

System performance on article segmentation, people article extraction, and article matching was evaluated on a gold standard data created by an independent annotator. An evaluation set of 1000 randomly selected articles was created for each historical edition separately using the article segmentation produced by the system. The articles were divided into 20 equal-size bins, and 50 consecutive articles were picked from each bin. The annotator was asked to go through the 1000 articles for each edition, and perform the following tasks for each article: (1) check if the article segmentation is correct, (2) check if the subject of the article is a person, and (3) for person articles, find the matching articles a) in the next historical edition and b) in Wikipedia. For the 15th edition, 1000 articles were selected using the segmentation provided by the electronic edition, and the annotator performed only the tasks of people extraction and matching to Wikipedia.

Our preliminary pilot annotation experiments conducted during annotator training indicated that annotator error was highly unlikely for these tasks. We therefore created the gold standard using a single annotator whose work was spot-checked for correctness by one of the authors. Table 1 shows the results of annotation for people article extraction and matching. System segmentation accuracy is shown in Table 2.

	Ed. 3	Ed. 9	Ed. 11	Ed. 15
Total # of person articles in evaluation set	137	368	407	335
Person articles with matches in the next edition	75	337	232	n/a
Person articles with matches in Wikipedia	124	364	403	327

Table 1: Person articles in gold standard data.

4 Results

Table 2 shows the results of evaluation for article segmentation, extraction of articles about people, and the matching of corresponding articles across different editions.

4.1 Article Segmentation

Segmentation accuracy is the percentage of articles the system segmented correctly. According to the annotation results, the segmentation accuracy for the 3rd, the 9th, and the 11th editions are 92.2%, 96.5%, and 99.9%, respectively. Since the 15th edition is available in XML format, it is excluded from segmentation evaluation.

4.2 Person Article Extraction

We estimated the number of person articles in each of the historical editions using the number of articles about people identified in the 1000 articles reviewed manually by the annotator. Table 2 shows the estimate for number of person articles in each edition, as well as the number of articles identified by the system.

The recall and precision for person article extraction for each edition are computed as the ratio of the number of person articles identified correctly by the system to the total number of person articles identified by the annotator (for recall), and the total number of person articles extracted by the system (for precision). Person article recall for all historic editions is around 70%, so there are about 30% of person articles not recovered. This can likely be addressed by developing additional name patterns or annotating Britannica to retrain CoreNLP NER models. For the 15th edition, the articles that contain gender information in the metadata are identified as person articles by the system, which fails to recover approximately 10% of person articles.

4.3 Article Matching

Person article pairwise precision is the percentage of article pairs between adjacent historical editions that are identified correctly, relative to the total number of matches identified by the system. Since the 15th edition is matched directly to Wikipedia, it is excluded from this evaluation. *Person article matching precision* is the percentage of person articles for which the matching articles in Wikipedia were identified correctly, relative to the total number of matches identified by the system. The *pairwise recall* and *matching recall* are computed accordingly, with the percentages reported relative to the total number of matches identified by the annotator.

	Ed. 3	Ed. 9	Ed. 11	Ed. 15
Segmentation Accuracy	92.2%	96.5%	99.9%	n/a
Estimated # of Person Articles	2654	5910	14823	27465
System-detected # of Person Articles	2089	4600	10702	26230
Person Article Precision	80.0%	94.7%	93.8%	100.0%
Person Article Recall	67.2%	72.6%	74.0%	91.3%
Person Article Pairwise Precision	88.2%	99.6%	96.2%	n/a
Person Article Pairwise Recall	57.7%	89.6%	92.6%	n/a
Person Article Matching Precision	81.0%	96.1%	93.3%	96.5%
Person Article Matching Recall	40.0%	82.6%	83.6%	91.3%

Table 2: Evaluation results for segmentation, person article extraction, and matching.

Note that the last two rows in Table 2 show the matching precision and recall obtained by two complementary strategies described in Section 3, giving the estimates of the overall quality of the matching algorithm. Note that precision and recall improve progressively for the later editions, and with exception of edition 3, we obtain the precision above 90% and recall above 80%. Edition 3 recall is substantially lower due to the diminished quality of the OCR scan, and the differences in the fonts and the formatting conventions. One should also keep in mind that the matching precision and recall are computed over the articles that have been recognized as person articles, therefore in order to get the estimates for the actual number of articles matched correctly, one should factor in person article recall.

5 Use Case Study

We applied our approach to the Wikipedia category of the 18th century classical composers in order to investigate whether the output of our algorithm can be used to identify valid trends in the rise and fall in reputations of historical figures. Wikipedia uses collaboratively created categories to group articles based on a variety of classificatory principles.

We investigated the change in the reputations of the 18th century classical composers using the corresponding Wikipedia category. Currently, there are 109 composers in this category. We evaluated manually the matching accuracy for the articles in this category, obtaining 95.5% and 89.1% matching accuracy for the 15th edition and 11th edition respectively, with the lower matching accuracy for 11th edition mainly caused by segmentation errors.

We used Web-based Analysis and Visualization Environment (WEAVE)[5] to visualize and analyze the relative importance, rank, and its change over time for the historical figures in this category. Figure 3 illustrates the change in importance. The legend on the left lists the composers alphabetically. The top two bar charts are their rank in the 11th and 15th editions, respectively. The bottom bar chart shows their reputation change from 11th to 15th edition, sorted on its absolute value.

6 Discussion

Table 3 shows the relative ranking for the most important 18th century composers in the 11th and 15th editions of Britannica. Each composer's importance score is shown in parentheses, with the higher relative importance score corresponding to a higher rank. Interestingly, while the top five composers remained the same, the order of importance underwent a significant change. In the 15th edition, Mozart replaced Bach at the top of the hierarchy, a change potentially brought on by the era of sound recording which led to classical music reaching a wider audience; this may have proved detrimental to Bach's difficult polyphonies, while Mozart's light melody lines with suitable harmonic accompaniment rose in popularity.

[5]http://www.oicweave.org

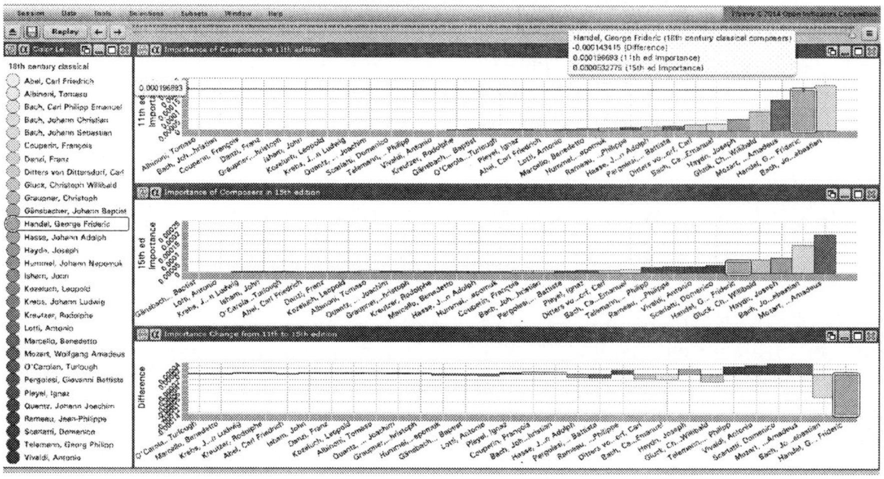

Figure 3: Biggest "movers and shakers" among the 18th century composers.

1911 (11th edition rank)	1985-2000 (15th edition rank)
1. Johann Sebastian Bach (2.2×10^{-4})	1. Wolfgang Amadeus Mozart (1.9×10^{-4})
2. George Frideric Handel (2.0×10^{-4})	2. Johann Sebastian Bach (1.4×10^{-4})
3. Wolfgang Amadeus Mozart (1.5×10^{-4})	3. Joseph Haydn (7.5×10^{-5})
4. Christoph Willibald Gluck (9.2×10^{-5})	4. Christoph Willibald Gluck (6.6×10^{-5})
5. Joseph Haydn (5.6×10^{-5})	5. George Frideric Handel (5.3×10^{-5})

Table 3: The rank of top five 18th century composers. The importance score is shown in parentheses.

The most drastic change within the top 5 composers was Handel's drop from the second to the fifth place. A possible explanation may lie in the history of genres: in the 20th century, the genres of the archaic Italian opera and oratorio that defined Handel's oeuvre lost their popularity and were, in general, less frequently performed and recorded.

These trends seem to be confirmed by the frequency plots for the names of these composers obtained from the Google Ngram Viewer (Figure 4). For the first decade of the 20th century Bach is the most frequently mentioned composer, with Handel and Mozart sharing the second position; towards the end of the century, the mention frequency for Mozart approaches and sometimes surpasses Bach, while the mention frequency for Handel falls.

Two composers that did not even have a dedicated article in the 11th edition, but ranked quite high in the 15th edition are Georg Philipp Telemann and Antonio Vivaldi, aka "the red priest". Their 20th century rediscovery is a well known fact. Importantly, our algorithm has been able to "catch" these two comebacks automatically.

The reverse case is the Venetian Antonio Lotti (1667-1740), a composer who according to our algorithm, was considered rather important in the beginning of the 20th century but lost his stature towards its end. Lotti's rare fans should not be discouraged; he may well be due for rediscovery in the 21st.

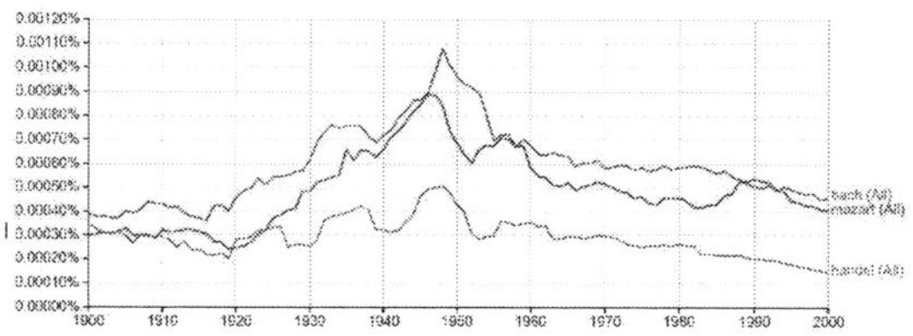

Figure 4: Google Books mention frequency for Mozart, Bach, and Handel.

7 Conclusion and Future Work

We have developed a method for matching and comparison of articles about people in historical editions of EB, as well as mapping category information from Wikipedia to EB. Our analysis has shown that the automated comparison between the historical editions of EB can be used to detect and track the historical changes within selected domains of culture. In the future, we plan to extend the pipeline to other editions of EB, thus widening the chronological scope of our research, and scale up from a few selected categories to a wider range of categories encompassing different domains of cultural and political history.

References

Ricardo Baeza-Yates, Berthier Ribeiro-Neto, et al. 1999. *Modern information retrieval*, volume 463. ACM press New York.

Razvan C Bunescu and Marius Pasca. 2006. Using encyclopedic knowledge for named entity disambiguation. In *EACL*, volume 6, pages 9–16.

Marco Cornolti, Paolo Ferragina, and Massimiliano Ciaramita. 2013. A framework for benchmarking entity-annotation systems. In *Proceedings of the 22nd international conference on World Wide Web*, pages 249–260. International World Wide Web Conferences Steering Committee.

Silviu Cucerzan. 2007. Large-scale named entity disambiguation based on wikipedia data. In *EMNLP-CoNLL*, volume 7, pages 708–716.

Aleksandar R. Gabrovski. 2012. *Knowevo and Gravebook: Tracking the History of Knowledge*. An undergraduate thesis, Dartmouth College, Hanover, NH.

M Gronas, A Rumshisky, A Gabrovski, S Kovaka, and H Chen. 2012. Tracking the history of knowledge using historical editions of encyclopedia britannica. In *Workshop on Adaptation of Language Resources and Tools for Processing Cultural Heritage Objects. LREC*.

Johannes Hoffart, Mohamed Amir Yosef, Ilaria Bordino, Hagen Fürstenau, Manfred Pinkal, Marc Spaniol, Bilyana Taneva, Stefan Thater, and Gerhard Weikum. 2011. Robust disambiguation of named entities in text. In *Proceedings of the Conference on Empirical Methods in Natural Language Processing*, pages 782–792. Association for Computational Linguistics.

Thomas Huet, Joanna Biega, and Fabian M Suchanek. 2013. Mining history with le monde. In *Proceedings of the 2013 workshop on Automated knowledge base construction*, pages 49–54. ACM.

Mike Kestemont, Folgert Karsdorp, and Folgert Karsdorp. 2014. Mining the twentieth centurys history from the time magazine corpus. *EACL 2014*, page 62.

Sayali Kulkarni, Amit Singh, Ganesh Ramakrishnan, and Soumen Chakrabarti. 2009. Collective annotation of wikipedia entities in web text. In *Proceedings of the 15th ACM SIGKDD international conference on Knowledge discovery and data mining*, pages 457–466. ACM.

Wenhui Liao and Sriharsha Veeramachaneni. 2009. A simple semi-supervised algorithm for named entity recognition. In *Proceedings of the NAACL HLT 2009 Workshop on Semi-Supervised Learning for Natural Language Processing*, pages 58–65. Association for Computational Linguistics.

Jean-Baptiste Michel, Yuan Kui Shen, Aviva Presser Aiden, Adrian Veres, Matthew K Gray, Joseph P Pickett, Dale Hoiberg, Dan Clancy, Peter Norvig, Jon Orwant, et al. 2011. Quantitative analysis of culture using millions of digitized books. *science*, 331(6014):176–182.

Lawrence Page, Sergey Brin, Rajeev Motwani, and Terry Winograd. 1999. The pagerank citation ranking: bringing order to the web.

Lev Ratinov, Dan Roth, Doug Downey, and Mike Anderson. 2011. Local and global algorithms for disambiguation to wikipedia. In *Proceedings of the 49th Annual Meeting of the Association for Computational Linguistics: Human Language Technologies-Volume 1*, pages 1375–1384. Association for Computational Linguistics.

Gerard Salton and Chung-Shu Yang. 1973. On the specification of term values in automatic indexing. *Journal of documentation*, 29(4):351–372.

Steven S Skiena and Charles B Ward. 2013. *Who's Bigger?: Where Historical Figures Really Rank*. Cambridge University Press.

Fabian M Suchanek and Nicoleta Preda. 2014. Semantic culturomics. *Proceedings of the VLDB Endowment*, 7(12):1215–1218.

Five Centuries of Monarchy in Korea: Mining the Text of the Annals of the Joseon Dynasty

JinYeong Bak
Department of Computer Science
KAIST
Daejeon, South Korea
jy.bak@kaist.ac.kr

Alice Oh
Department of Computer Science
KAIST
Daejeon, South Korea
alice.oh@kaist.edu

Abstract

We present a quantitative study of the Annals of the Joseon Dynasty, the daily written records of the five hundred years of a monarchy in Korea. We first introduce the corpus, which is a series of books describing the historical facts during the Joseon dynasty. We then define three categories of the monarchial ruling styles based on the written records and compare the twenty-five kings in the monarchy. Finally, we investigate how kings show different ruling styles for various topics within the corpus. Through this study, we introduce a very unique corpus of monarchial records that span an entire monarchy of five hundred years and illustrate how text mining can be applied to answer important historical questions.

1 Introduction

Historical documents are usually studied qualitatively by researchers focusing on a close reading of a small number of documents. However, for a large corpus of historical texts, qualitative methods have limitations, thus quantitative approaches have been introduced recently (Moretti, 2005; Jockers, 2013). There is also research in applying text mining and natural language processing methods to identify patterns in a corpus of large and longitudinal documents (Mimno, 2012). In this paper, we introduce a unique corpus of historical documents from the written records that span almost five hundred years from the fourteenth century up to the late nineteenth century within the Korean peninsula. We apply text mining to this corpus to show the power of a computational approach in answering historical questions.

We first introduce *The Annals of the Joseon Dynasty* (Chunchugwan, 1863). Joseon is the last monarchial nation in the Korean Peninsula from its founding in 1392 up to 1910. The Annals of the Joseon Dynasty are a series of books of historical facts, recorded almost daily during the Joseon dynasty. Whenever a king abdicated the throne, the Chunchugwan (office for annals compilation) updated the Annals for that king from all related official and unofficial documents. The Annals contain political, economic, social and cultural topics during the corresponding time periods.

To illustrate the application of a text mining approach, we analyze each king's ruling style from the Annals of the Joseon dynasty. Being a monarchial system, almost all decisions within the government are confirmed by the king, where the king can make the decision on his own, or after discussing it with the government officials. We identify the patterns of each king's decision making and compare the patterns among the kings. The results show interesting patterns of the kings' ruling styles, including the tendency to make arbitrary decisions of the kings who were later dethroned because of tyranny. Additionally, we apply a topic model to the corpus and analyze the kings' ruling style for each topic.

2 The Annals of the Joseon Dynasty

In this section, we describe the details of *The Annals of the Joseon Dynasty* (from here referred to as the AJD) (Chunchugwan, 1863) and our process for building a corpus of the AJD. In its entirety, the AJD consists of records from twenty-seven kings over 519 years. However, the last two kings' (Gojong, Sunjong) books are usually excluded from research by historians because many facts are distorted. We follow that convention and use the books of the first twenty-five kings. These records, in their original Chinese text and in the Korean translations, are available publicly through

Proceedings of the 9th SIGHUM Workshop on Language Technology for Cultural Heritage, Social Sciences, and Humanities, pages 10–14,
Beijing, China, July 30, 2015.

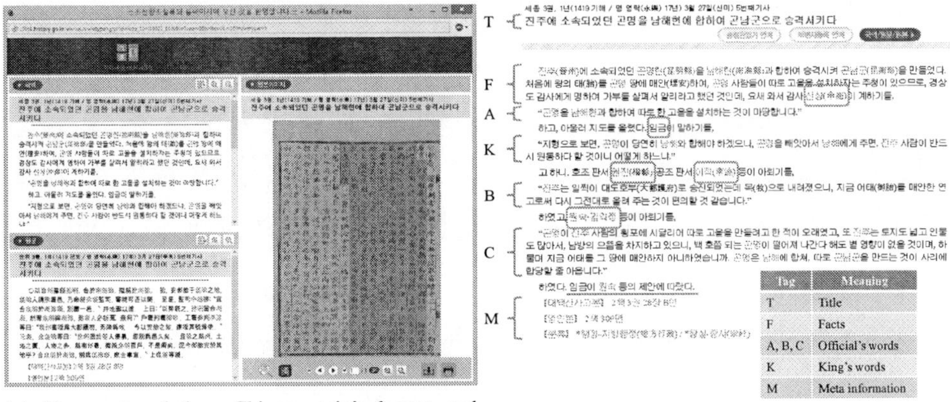

(a) Korean translation, Chinese original text and scanned image

(b) Structure of the article

Figure 1: Screenshot and structure of an article in the annals of the Joseon dynasty

King name	Period of reign	# months	# articles
Taejo	1392-1398	81	2,387
Jeongjong	1398-1400	24	624
Taejong	1400-1418	220	10,331
Sejong the Great	1418-1450	391	30,969
Munjong	1450-1452	27	2,670
Danjong	1452-1455	40	2,534
Sejo	1455-1468	165	10,832
Yejong	1468-1469	17	1,503
Seongjong	1469-1494	311	32,443
Yeonsangun	1494-1506	146	12,009
Jungjong	1506-1544	474	39,653
Injong	1544-1545	8	671
Myeongjong	1545-1567	272	15,044
Seonjo	1567-1608	438	26,712
Gwanghaegun	1608-1623	187	22,121
Injo	1623-1649	325	16,046
Hyojong	1649-1659	125	5,431
Hyeonjong	1659-1674	189	9,295
Sukjong	1674-1720	568	24,209
Gyeongjong	1720-1724	54	2,744
Yeongjo	1724-1776	639	36,731
Jeongjo	1776-1800	302	17,681
Sunjo	1800-1834	425	15,529
Heonjong	1834-1849	182	3,986
Cheoljong	1849-1863	180	5,771
Gojong	1863-1897	536	27,939
Sunjong	1907-1910	38	4,858

Table 1: Name, period of reign and the number of months and articles for 27 kings in Joseon dynasty

a website[1]. We build our corpus by crawling all articles from that website[2], and this corpus comprise 1,893 books and 380,271 articles covering 472 years (1392 - 1863). Table 1 shows the basic statistics of our AJD corpus including the period of reign and the number of articles for each king.

Each *article* on the website consists of the transcription of the original Chinese text, the Korean translation, and the scanned images from the original books. Figure 1 shows an example article[3]. For this paper, we analyze the Korean translated text (Figure 1b), though we refer to the Chinese version to understand the meaning of some words that are not currently used in the modern Korean language. Each Korean article has a title (marked T in the figure) that is created by the translators, the body text (A, B, C, F and K in the figure) and the meta information (M) including the source, page, and tags of the article.

3 King's Ruling Style

Joseon was a monarchy, but a king could not make all decisions by himself. Instead, Joseon adopted a government system that most of the public issues are discussed with the government officials (Park, 1983; Kim, 2008) before the king made the decisions, which are all recorded in the AJD. Hence, by analyzing the decision making process in the AJD, we can understand each king's ruling style.

3.1 Categorizing ruling style

In Joseon dynasty, the king was the final decision maker. Even when the government officials discussed the public issues, a king's approval was needed. We can categorize each king's decision making process into three types. First, a king can order directly without discussion, which we call Arbitrary Decision (AD). Second, a king can discuss an issue with the officials and then direct his

[1] http://sillok.history.go.kr

[2] We crawl and investigate the AJD from the site legally, because it is opened to the public by Korean government.

[3] Article URL: http://sillok.history.go.kr/viewer/viewtype1.jsp?id=kda_10103027_005

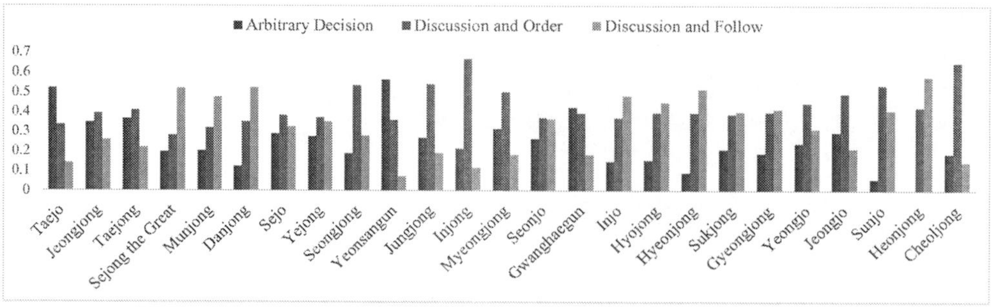

Figure 2: Joseon king's ruling styles. Each king shows quite different ruling style ($p < 0.001$).

Decision	Words
Order	명하다, 하교하다, 전교하다, 命, 傳教, 下教
Approve	윤허하다, 허락하다, 允
Disapprove	불허하다, 허락하지 않았다, 不允
Reject	따르지 않았다, 듣지 않았다, 不從, 不聽
Follow	따르다, 따랐다, 從之, 依啓

Table 2: Example verbs for identifying king's decision in the AJD. Words are written in Korean and Chinese alphabet.

order, which we call Discussion and Order (DO). Third, a king can discuss an issue with the officials and then decide to follow the officials' suggestion, which we call Discussion and Follow (DF). The difference between DO and DF is that in DO, the king acts aggressively with his own opinion.

From these observations, we ask two research questions: 1) Can we identify and categorize kings with different ruling styles? 2) Do kings' ruling styles differ depending on the topic?

3.2 Method

To understand each king's ruling style, we first identify relevant articles that contain the king's decision making because many of the articles describe non-governmental affairs, such as the weather, or simple status reports. These relevant articles contain direct quotations of the words of the king or the government official. The original texts do not contain any quotation marks, but translators added them to distinguish explicit quotations, which we can use to identify these relevant articles. Its size is 126K, 36% over all articles.

Each article contains who said what for an issue, and king's final actions are written mostly in the last part of the article. For example, the underlined last sentence in Figure 1b says that the king followed the official's suggestion. Hence, to identify king's action for each issue, we focus on the last sentence in each article.

First, we identify that the setence subject is the king, because some issues are dealt by others. For example, Sunjo, Heonjong and Cheoljong's mother or grandmother ruled as regent, so her decisions are recorded in the AJD. To identify the part of speech in Korean, we used HanNanum (Choi et al., 2012). And, we investigate the verbs that indicating decisions including order, follow, approval and reject. We use sixty verbs that describe king's decision specifically, and table 2 shows example words. Finally, we classify these decisions into three types: 1) the king orders without discussions with the officials, and we label them as AD, 2) the king orders, approves, or rejects verbs in which their original Chinese characters show active decision making by the king, and we label them as DO, and 3) the king follows or discusses verbs which show passive submission by the king, and we label them as DF.

To identify topics, we use a Bayesian topic model, LDA (Blei et al., 2003). We implement it using Gibbs sampling (Griffiths and Steyvers, 2004), set 300 topics, and optimized hyperparameters after 100 iterations (Asuncion et al., 2009). We remove stopwords and words with document frequency of 30 or smaller.

3.3 Results and Discussions

We investigate the difference of ruling style between kings. We run multinomial test (Read and Cressie, 1988) between king's ruling style distributions. Result shows that almost all kings are different significant from others ($p < 0.001$). It means that each king has his own ruling style.

Figure 2 shows the distribution of each category of ruling style. Overall, many kings do not act arbitrary. They discuss about many of the national affairs with officials. But, Taejo who is the

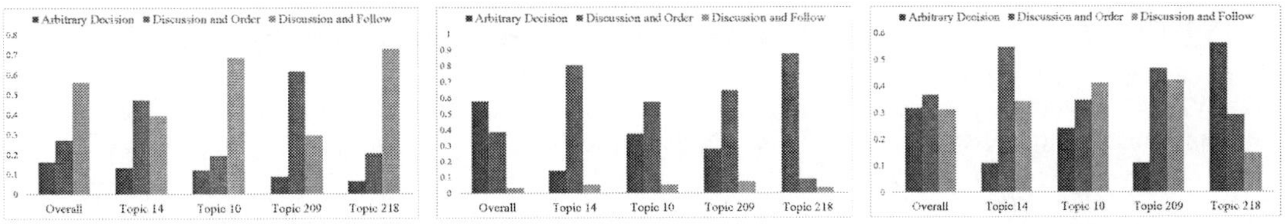

(a) Sejong the Great (b) Yeonsangun (c) Gwanghaegun

Figure 3: King's ruling styles given a topic. It differs from overall ruling style (leftmost bars) ($p < 0.01$).

14	10	209	218
retirement	**agriculture**	**remission**	**grants**
vassal	grain	sin	a roll of cloth
retire	village	law	a piece
position	a piece	majesty	royal grant
person	storehouse	engage	saddle
capable	people	forgive	a piece
job	rice	favor	a part
duty	save	rebel	tiger skin
duties	bad year	person	epidermis

Table 3: Example of different topics ($p < 0.01$) from overall ruling style distribution

founder of the Joseon dynasty shows high value of AD. And Yeonsangun and Gwanghaegun who are evaluated as a tyrant also show high value of it. So we can imagine that tyrants tend to act arbitrarily.

We also identified those kings whose ruling style differed most from other kings. We use JS divergence which is the symmetric measure of the difference between two probability distributions. We compute JS divergence with each king pair's ruling style distributions. Result shows that Heonjong (0.1220) and Yeonsangun (0.0998) have highest distance value. It means their ruling style are quite different from other kings. Because Heonjong's grandmother governed the Joseon each year, so his actions are quite few. But, unlike Yeonsangun, Gwanghaegun (0.0454) who is known as a tyrant has similar value mean distance from other kings (0.0434). It means his ruling style is quite similar to other kings, and this result supports previous results in Korean historical study (Kye, 2008) that re-evaluate his reputation.

We investigate the difference of king's ruling style based on the topic. We run multinomial test (Read and Cressie, 1988) between king's overall ruling style distribution and specific distribution given a topic. Results show that some ruling styles given a topic are different significant from overall ($p < 0.01$). It means that the king's ruling style when the topic is given is different from his usual style. Table 3 shows examples of topic. Figure 3 shows four kings' overall ruling style and specific one given a topic. Comparing with the leftmost bars which is overall ruling style of the king, each ruling style given a topic is different from it. And, we can see that kings show similar/different ruling style for a topic. For example, kings tend to discuss and order (DO) to officials for retirement and remission topics. And, Sejong the Great and Gwanghaegun discuss and follow (DF) officials' words for agricultural topic. But, for grants topic, Yeonsangun and Gwanghaegun act more arbitrarily (AD) than overall ruling style, and Sejong the Great follows more official's opinions (DF).

4 Conclusion and Future Work

We introduced long and large historical documents, *The Annals of the Joseon Dynasty*. It contains lots of topics such as political, economic, social and cultural over 500 years. We looked at the ruling style of kings in Joseon dynasty and its difference by topics by computational methods.

This is ongoing work, and we are looking to find more hidden structures in the AJD. Currently, historians evaluate the king's reputations (Park, 2004; Lee, 2010). This evaluation is done by many aspects, but one of the important feature is king's ruling style (Kim, 2008). So we are looking to improve methods for analyzing ruling style more specifically. For example, we will look at the relationship with officials, especially who can make the king follows his opinion. This approach can be used to measure king's leadership.

Acknowledgments

We would like to thank the anonymous reviewers for helpful comments, and National Institute of Korean History for checking legal issues. This work was supported by ICT R&D program of MSIP/IITP. [B0101-15-0307, Basic Software Research in Human-level Lifelong Machine Learning (Machine Learning Center)]

References

Arthur Asuncion, Max Welling, Padhraic Smyth, and Yee Whye Teh. 2009. On smoothing and inference for topic models. In *Proceedings of the Twenty-Fifth Conference on Uncertainty in Artificial Intelligence*, pages 27–34. AUAI Press.

David M Blei, Andrew Y Ng, and Michael I Jordan. 2003. Latent dirichlet allocation. *Journal of Machine Learning Research*, 3:993–1022.

DongHyun Choi, Jungyeul Park, and Key-Sun Choi. 2012. Korean treebank transformation for parser training. In *Proceedings of the ACL 2012 Joint Workshop on Statistical Parsing and Semantic Processing of Morphologically Rich Languages*, pages 78–88. Citeseer.

Chunchugwan. 1863. *Joseonwangjosillok (The Annals of the Joseon Dynasty)*. The name of the publisher.

Thomas L Griffiths and Mark Steyvers. 2004. Finding scientific topics. *Proceedings of the National Academy of Sciences*, 101(suppl 1):5228–5235.

Matthew L Jockers. 2013. *Macroanalysis: Digital methods and literary history*. University of Illinois Press.

Jeong Ki Kim. 2008. A study on the policy decision-making process of the chosun era: Focus on mandarins' participation function. *Korean Public Administration History Review*, 23(1):161–186.

Seung B. Kye. 2008. The causes for the coup of 1623 and their adjustment in choson korea. *NAMMYONG STUDY*, 26(1):439–478.

Dukil Lee. 2010. *Say about Joseon King*, volume 1. WisdomHouse.

David Mimno. 2012. Computational historiography: Data mining in a century of classics journals. *Journal on Computing and Cultural Heritage (JOCCH)*, 5(1):3.

Franco Moretti. 2005. *Graphs, maps, trees: abstract models for a literary history*. Verso.

Munok Park. 1983. *Discussion about new Korea government*. Shincheon.

YoungKu Park. 2004. *Reading though a book about The annals of the Joseon dynasty*. Woongjin ThinkBig.

Timothy RC Read and Noel AC Cressie. 1988. *Goodness-of-fit statistics for discrete multivariate data*. Springer New York.

Analyzing Sentiment in Classical Chinese Poetry

Yufang Hou **Anette Frank**
Institute for Computational Linguistics, Heidelberg University, Germany
(hou|frank)@cl.uni-heidelberg.de

Abstract

Although sentiment analysis in Chinese social media has attracted a lot of interest in recent years, it has been less explored in traditional Chinese literature (e.g., classical Chinese poetry) due to the lack of sentiment lexicon resources. In this paper, we propose a weakly supervised approach based on Weighted Personalized PageRank (WPPR) to create a sentiment lexicon for classical Chinese poetry. We evaluate our lexicon intrinsically and extrinsically. We show that our graph-based approach outperforms a previous well-known PMI-based approach (Turney and Littman, 2003) on both evaluation settings. On the basis of our sentiment lexicon, we analyze sentiment in the Complete Anthology of Tang Poetry. We extract topics associated with positive (negative) sentiment using a position-aware sentiment-topic model. We further compare sentiment among different poets in Tang Dynasty (AD 618 – 907).

1 Introduction

Classical Chinese poetry is a precious cultural heritage. Among its over 3,000 years of history, the Tang Dynasty (AD 618 – 907) is widely viewed as the zenith of the art of classical Chinese poetry. The Complete Anthology of Tang Poetry, edited during the Qing Dynasty (1644 – 1911), contains over 42,860 poems in 900 volumes by more than 2,500 poets. The collection provides a magnificent insight into all aspects of social life of that period.

Research on sentiment/emotion and imagery analysis of Tang poetry is an active subfield in Chinese philology, with a vast literature (Watson, 1971; Kao and Mei, 1971; Kao and Mei, 1978). In this paper, we seek to analyze the sentiment (i.e., *positive* or *negative*) of textual elements in Tang poetry from a computational perspective. Specifically, we propose a novel graph-based method to create a sentiment lexicon for classical Chinese poetry. Such a lexicon is a valuable resource for other computational research on classical Chinese poetry, such as semantic analysis (Lee and Taksum, 2012) or poetry generation (He et al., 2012; Zhang and Lapata, 2014).

Turney and Littman (2003) propose a PMI-based algorithm to estimate the *semantic orientation* or *polarity* of a word. The semantic orientation of a given word is calculated by comparing its similarity to positive reference words (e.g., excellent or beautiful) with its similarity to negative reference words (e.g., poor or bad). Instead of calculating the similarity between a given word and each of the positive (negative) reference words separately, we apply Weighted Personalized PageRank (WPPR) to measure the similarity between the given word and all positive (negative) reference words **simultaneously** in a lexical network that we build from a poetry corpus. Our graph-based method is able to find globally optimal solution because the lexical network is analyzed as a whole (Section 3).

We evaluate our poetry sentiment lexicon intrinsically and extrinsically. For the intrinsic evaluation, we compile two test datasets. The first dataset contains 933 words (532 positive and 401 negative) taken from three Chinese sentiment lexicons[1]. The second dataset contains 55 words taken from literature of imagery analysis for Tang poetry. These words reflect the common imageries in classical Chinese poetry and have certain fixed emotional connotations. For instance, the character "猿" (ape) often relates to sadness, anxiety and distress, while the character "荷" (lotus)

[1]Although these lexicons are for contemporary Chinese, some words keep the same meaning and polarity as in classical Chinese poetry.

Proceedings of the 9th SIGHUM Workshop on Language Technology for Cultural Heritage, Social Sciences, and Humanities, pages 15–24,
Beijing, China, July 30, 2015.

is the symbol of beauty, love and rectitude. We show that our method outperforms the very competitive PMI-based approach when evaluating on both datasets (Section 4.1). Our method also outperforms the baseline on an extrinsic evaluation task of predicting sentiment orientation of classical Chinese poetry (Section 4.2).

On the basis of our sentiment lexicon, we analyze sentiment in the Complete Anthology of Tang Poetry. We first analyze topic distributions under positive/negative sentiment in Tang poetry using a position-aware sentiment-topic model (Section 5.1). We then compare sentiment among different poets in Tang Dynasty (Section 5.2).

The main contributions of our work are:

- We propose a graph-based method to build a sentiment lexicon for classical Chinese poetry. Our method is weakly supervised and does not rely on existing lexical resources (e.g., WordNet). It can be easily ported to other domains/languages.
- We evaluate our sentiment lexicon systematically and demonstrate that it can be utilized to analyze sentiment orientation of classical Chinese poetry.
- We analyze sentiment in Tang poetry on the basis of our sentiment lexicon. We apply *a position-aware sentiment-topic model* to extract themes which are tightly associated with positive/negative sentiment. Our model builds in specific assumptions that characterize sentiment expression in classical Chinese poetry. It assumes that lexical items from the same region are generated from a single sentiment-topic pair. We compare sentiment among different famous poets and show that our results are in accordance with studies in Chinese philology.

The poetry sentiment lexicon described in the paper as well as all test datasets are freely available at `http://www.cl.uni-heidelberg.de/~hou/resources.mhtml`.

2 Related Work

Sentiment lexicons. In recent years, considerable attention has been given to the creation of large polarity (positive and negative) lexicons, including various corpus-based approaches (Turney and Littman, 2003; Kanayama and Nasukawa, 2006; Kaji and Kitsuregawa, 2007; Kiritchenko et al., 2014) and dictionary-based approaches (Kamps et al., 2004; Esuli and Sebastiani, 2005; Mohammad et al., 2009; Baccianella et al., 2010). Unlike previous graph-based approaches which create sentiment lexicons based on existing lexical resources (e.g., WordNet, thesauri) (Takamura et al., 2005; Rao and avichandran, 2009; Hassan et al., 2011), there are no such lexical resources for classical Chinese poetry. Therefore, we choose a corpus-based approach.

While our approach for building sentiment lexicons is domain independent, in this paper we apply it to classical Chinese poetry. This is not a trivial task. There are a variety of reliable resources for English sentiment analysis. However, only a few sentiment lexicons for Chinese are available. In particular, these lexicons are for contemporary Chinese. Moreover, given that these lexicons are developed for contemporary Chinese, they will only have partial coverage for classical Chinese poetry. There might also be divergences due to the change of language over several thousand years. To improve sentiment analysis for Chinese, one line of work seeks to leverage rich English sentiment resources through machine translation (Wan, 2008; Wan, 2009; He et al., 2010). These approaches depend on the quality of machine translation and translation of classical Chinese poetry to English is hard even for professional translators. Our work is similar to Zagibalov and Carroll (2008) in the sense that both approaches are weakly supervised. They build a sentiment lexicon iteratively, starting from a small set of seed items and several lexical patterns (negated adverbial constructions) which can indicate lexical polarity. However, such lexical patterns (e.g., 不 (not) 很 (quite) + 满意 (satisfied) (target word)) are not applicable in classical Chinese poetry.

Computational analysis of classical Chinese poetry. There has been previous work focusing on classical Chinese poetry generation (Zhou et al., 2010; He et al., 2012; Zhang and Lapata, 2014). Lee and Kong (2012) develop a dependency treebank for the Complete Anthology of Tang Poetry. On the basis of this corpus, Lee and Tak-sum (2012) quantitatively analyze the semantic content and word usage in the Complete Anthology of Tang Poetry. Voigt and Jurafsky (2013) find that the classical characters of Chinese poetry decreased across the century by comparing classical poetry and contemporary prose.

There are only a few works trying to analyze sentiment in classical Chinese poetry. Hu (2001) proposes "similarity search" by using word association measures. For instance, given typical emotional words such as "悲伤 (sadness) 哀 (sorrow)", the system can find words (e.g., 南浦 (southern shore, a place often used to hold farewell parties in ancient China)) associated with sad emotions. However, he does not analyze sentiment in classical Chinese poetry quantitatively. Based on manually annotated data, Luo (2009) analyzes the sentiment of classical Chinese Song poetry among different poets. To the best of our knowledge, there is no publicly available sentiment lexicon for classical Chinese poetry.

3 Building a Sentiment Lexicon for Classical Chinese Poetry

In this section, we briefly introduce Weighted Personalized PageRank (WPPR). We then detail how we construct a lexical network and how we apply WPPR over the lexical network to build a sentiment lexicon for classical Chinese poetry.

3.1 Weighted Personalized PageRank

The original PageRank algorithm was first introduced by Brin and Page (1998). It is a link-based algorithm for ranking the vertices in a graph. Later, various extensions have been proposed. Weighted PageRank (Xing and Ghorbani, 2004) takes into account the importance of both the inlinks and the outlinks of the vertices when distributing rank scores based on the popularity of the vertices. Personalized PageRank (Haveliwala, 2002; White and Smyth, 2003) computes the importance of vertices in a graph relative to one or more root vertices. It has been successfully applied in other NLP tasks, such as word sense disambiguation (Agirre and Soroa, 2009).

Here we combine Weighted PageRank and Personalized PageRank to measure the similarity of lexical items in a lexical network relative to sentiment seeds. Let G be a lexical network with N vertices $v_1, \ldots, v_n \in V$ and w_{ij} be the weight associated with the edge from v_i to v_j. Let M be a $N \times N$ transition probability matrix, where $M_{ij} = w_{ij}$ if a link from v_i to v_j exists, and zero otherwise, let S be a set of sentiment seeds where $S \subseteq V$. Then the Weighted Personalized PageRank vector R over G can be calculated as follows:

$$R = \alpha MR + (1 - \alpha)P, \quad (1)$$

where α is the *damping factor* and its value usually set in the $[0.85..0.95]$ range. P is a $N \times 1$ vector, where $P_i = \frac{1}{|S|}$ for $v_i \in S$, and zero otherwise, i.e., all vertices in the sentiment seeds have equal prior probability.

Equation 1 can be viewed as the result of a random walk process starting from the seed nodes, where the random walkers can jump back to the seed nodes S with a given probability $1 - \alpha$. The final rank of vertex v_i, biased towards the set S (the bias is encoded in P), represents the probability of a random walk over the weighted graph (weights associated with edges are encoded in M) ending on vertex v_i, at a sufficiently large time.

3.2 Lexical Network Construction

To create a sentiment lexicon for classical Chinese poetry, we first build a lexical network on the basis of the Complete Anthology of Tang Poetry[2]. Since poetry is imbued with emotions, we assume that: (1) each lexical items in the lexical network bears positive or negative sentiment; and (2) lexical items within a small window are more likely to share the same sentiment. Therefore, by applying WPPR on the basis of a small set of positive (negative) lexical items, we can trace how positive (negative) sentiment information is distributed over the whole lexical network.

The lexical network G is a directed weighted graph, where each vertex v_i is a lexical item. We define a lexical item as a word containing one or two characters. Classical Chinese poetry is typically written in a highly compressed style, where each line normally has a fixed five or seven characters. As a result, each character itself or words containing two characters are expressive and can be used as the main semantic units. Instead of carrying out word segmentation, we simply use a frequency threshold to extract lexical items: a lexical unit is extracted as a lexical item if it appears at least x times in the corpus (x is ten for single-character unit and 50 for two-character unit).

We then create an edge from v_i to v_j, if v_i and v_j co-occur within a window of five characters, i.e., v_i occurs within a window of five characters before or after v_j. Let f_{ij} be the number of times

[2]The corpus can be downloaded from http://datatang.com

that v_i and v_j co-occur in the whole corpus, we set the weight of the edge from v_i to v_j as follows:

$$w_{ij} = \frac{f_{ij}}{\sum_{k=1}^{N} f_{ik}} \quad (2)$$

Alternatively, w_{ij} can be viewed as the probability of lexical item v_j occurring nearby, given the lexical item v_i.

As a result, we construct a lexical network containing 8656 lexical items (4779 are single-character items, 3877 are two-character items) and 8,832,234 edges. This lexical network contains the word co-occurrence information in the Complete Anthology of Tang Poetry.

3.3 Sentiment Lexicon Creation

We compile a small set of sentiment seeds, which contains six positive lexical items and six negative lexical items (see Table 1). These lexical items are frequent single characters in the Complete Anthology of Tang Poetry and carry strong sentiment. Similar to Turney and Littman (2003) who use 14 sentiment seeds (seven positive words and seven negative words), we only focus on a small number of sentiment seeds to study whether we can build a reasonable sentiment lexicon from weak supervision.

	Characters
positive seeds	香 (fragrant) 爱 (love) 欢 (happy) 贤 (virtuous) 喜 (delight) 瑞 (lucky)
negative seeds	寒 (cold) 愁 (anxiety) 孤 (lonely) 苦 (painful) 悲 (sorrow) 怨 (resentment)

Table 1: Positive and negative sentiment seeds.

We apply WPPR (Section 3.1) twice over the lexical network described in Section 3.2, initialized with the positive seeds and negative seeds respectively. We follow the common practice of setting the *damping factor* to 0.85. Consequently, we get two PageRank vectors Rp and Rn. They can be seen as a measure of similarity of lexical items to all positive seeds and all negative seeds respectively. Finally, we calculate the sentiment vector as follows:

$$Rs = Rp - Rn \quad (3)$$

A lexical item i has a positive sentiment orientation if its corresponding entry in vector Rs (hence Rs_i) is positive, and a negative sentiment orientation if Rs_i is negative. The value of Rs_i can be viewed as the strength of the sentiment orientation associated with the lexical item i.

4 Sentiment Lexicon Evaluation

We evaluate our poetry sentiment lexicon intrinsically and extrinsically. For the intrinsic evaluation, we utilize sentiment lexicons for contemporary Chinese because there is a partial overlap between these lexicons and sentiment expressions in classical poetry. We also evaluate lexical items in our sentiment lexicon appearing only in classical poetry. In the extrinsic evaluation, we test whether our sentiment lexicon can be used to predict sentiment orientation of classical Chinese poetry.

4.1 Intrinsic Evaluation

Test Datasets. To evaluate our approach, we compile two test datasets. The first dataset (SentiLexicon) contains 933 sentiment words taken from three Chinese sentiment lexicons: HowNet[3], NTUSD (Ku et al., 2006), and Tsinghua sentiment lexicon[4]. Although these lexicons are for contemporary Chinese, some words keep the same meaning and polarity as in classical Chinese poetry. We merge these three lexicons by removing duplicate or contradictory entries. This yields a big sentiment lexicon containing 12,945 positive words[5] and 17,114 negative words. We then create SentiLexicon by choosing single-character words and two-character words from the big sentiment lexicon if they do not appear in the set of sentiment seeds (Table 1) and occur at least 50 times[6] in the Complete Anthology of Tang Poetry. This leads to a dataset containing 532 positive lexical items and 401 negative lexical items.

However, SentiLexicon does not reflect an important aspect of classical Chinese poetry, i.e., emotions are expressed implicitly through imagery. Skilled poets often apply concrete imagery to evoke emotions and sensations. Certain imageries have fixed emotional connotations. For example, the falling autumn leaf ("落叶") often refers to personal or dynastic decline. We call such words imagery words. We collect 55 typical imagery words (ImageryLexicon) from literature of imagery analysis for Tang poetry. Every word in ImageryLexicon does not appear in SentiLexicon. Table 2 shows some examples of ImageryLexicon.

[3] http://www.keenage.com/html/e_index.html

[4] http://nlp.csai.tsinghua.edu.cn/~lj/

[5] A word can contain one character or several characters.

[6] We carried out preliminary experiments with the thresholds ranging from ten to 50. We found that the accuracy of our method varies in a small range, and our approach outperforms the baseline at all threshold levels.

	Characters
positive	鸳鸯 (mandarin duck) 芙蓉 (hibiscus) 凤凰 (phoenix) 兰 (orchid) 竹 (bamboo)
negative	梧桐 (sycamore) 鸦 (crow) 柳 (willow) 鹧鸪 (partridge) 夕阳 (sunset) 子规 (cuckoo)

Table 2: Examples of ImageryLexicon.

	SentiLexicon	ImageryLexicon
	Accuracy	Accuracy
PMI	60.8	70.2
WPPR	**64.4**$\star$	**74.5**

Table 3: Accuracy of WPPR compared to PMI (baseline) for two test datasets. $\star$ indicates significant improvement relative to the baseline (McNemar's test at $p < 0.05$ level).

Baseline. We reimplement a previous PMI-based approach (Turney and Littman, 2003) as the baseline. We use the same sentiment seeds and the same co-occurrence window of five characters as our method. The sentiment orientation of a lexical item (single or two-character) is calculated as follows:

$$\mathrm{SO}\,(w) = \sum_{s \in pSeeds} \mathrm{PMI}\,(w,s) - \sum_{s \in nSeeds} \mathrm{PMI}\,(w,s) \quad (4)$$

Results on test datasets. Table 3 shows the results of our method described in Section 3 (*WPPR*) and the baseline (*PMI*) against two test datasets. Our graph-based approach outperforms the baseline in both cases. Our method is more robust than the baseline because it measures the similarity between the candidate lexical item and the whole positive (negative) sentiment seeds together.

Evaluation on sample data. Our test datasets (SentiLexicon and ImageryLexicon) only cover about 11.5% of lexical items of our sentiment lexicon. To evaluate the lexical items that are not in the test sets, we randomly choose 100 items (50 single and 50 two-character lexical items, both with the equal positive/negative sentiment distribution). They were manually checked by the first author. We obtain an accuracy of 53% in this hard evaluation setting.

4.2 Extrinsic Evaluation

We also carry out an extrinsic evaluation to judge whether our sentiment lexicon can be utilized to analyze sentiment orientation of classical Chinese poetry. We choose 160 poems from the Tang poetry analysis dictionary (Xiao, 1999), which contains around 1,000 Tang poems paired with professional reviews. We manually annotate the sentiment of each poem as positive or negative according to the reviewers' analysis. This leads to a dataset (sentiPoetry) containing 83 negative poems and 77 positive poems. For each poem, we predict its sentiment based on the accumulated sentiment orientations of all lexical items (single and two-character) in the poem. Specifically, a poem is predicted as positive if its accumulated sentiment orientation is bigger than a threshold t, and negative otherwise. A subset of sentiPoetry containing 30 positive poems and 30 negative poems is used to tune the threshold t, the remaining 100 poems are reserved as test data. Table 4 shows the accuracy of predicting poetry sentiment on the test dataset using the sentiment lexicon for contemporary Chinese described in Section 4.1, as well as the two lexicons based on the baseline (*PMI*) and our method (*WPPR*) respectively. Using our lexicon achieves an accuracy of 71% on predicting poetry sentiment, which is 14% better than using *PMI Lexicon*. It is obvious that the Out-of-Domain lexicon (*contemporarySenti Lexicon*) performs the worst because of its low coverage of lexical items used in classical Chinese poetry. A closer look at the results indicates that positive poems are hard to predict because happy/joyful emotions are often expressed in a very subtle, implicit way.

	Accuracy
contemporarySenti Lexicon	51.0
PMI Lexicon	57.0
WPPR Lexicon	**71.0**

Table 4: Results for poetry sentiment prediction.

5 Analyzing Sentiment in Tang Poetry

Poems are saturated with emotions that correlate to positive or negative sentiment. But how are sentiments expressed in different topics? How does sentiment differ between individual poets? We aim to answer these questions in this section.

5.1 Sentiment-based Topic Distribution

Position-aware sentiment-topic model. Traditional topic models like latent Dirichlet allocation (LDA) (Blei et al., 2003) have been explored extensively to discover topics from text. Recently,

LDA has been extended to capture correlations between sentiment and topic from textual data (Mei et al., 2007; Titov and McDonald, 2008; Lin and He, 2009; He et al., 2011; Lazaridou et al., 2013; Li et al., 2013).

Here we modify a joint sentiment-topic model (JST) (Lin and He, 2009) to extract topics associated with positive/negative sentiment. Lin and He (2009) assume that topics are generated dependent on sentiment distributions and words are generated conditioned on the sentiment-topic pairs. JST can detect sentiment and topics simultaneously by encoding word prior sentiment information. However, words in the JST model are position-unaware, i.e., words from the same sentence/clause thus can have different topics or sentiments. We modify the JST model by assuming that lexical items from the same couplet are generated conditioned on the same sentiment-topic pairs. In Chinese poetry, a couplet is a pair of lines which have the same length and express a complete meaning. Lexical items within the same couplet usually relate to the same topic and keep the same polarity. Our position-aware JST model is depicted in Figure 1.

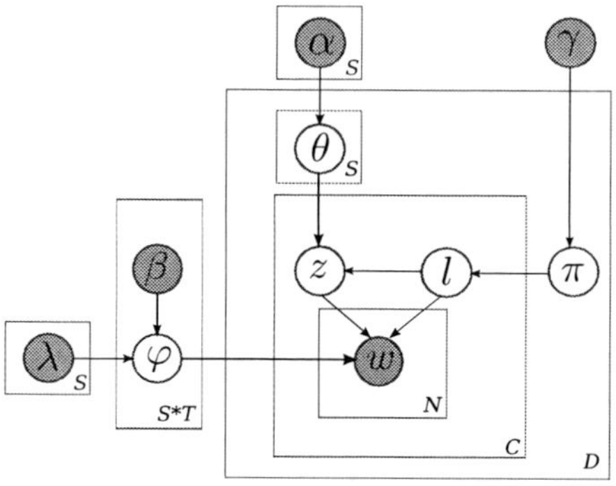

Figure 1: Position-aware JST model.

Assume we have a corpus consisting of D documents; each document is a sequence of C couplets and each word (lexical item) in the couplet is an item from a vocabulary index with V distinct terms; let S be the number of distinct sentiment labels and T the total number of topics. The process of generating a word w in document d under our position-aware JST model is as follows:

- For each sentiment label $l \in S$ and each topic $j \in T$, draw $\varphi_{lj} \sim Dirichlet(\lambda_l \times \beta_{lj}^T)$
- For each document d,
  - Draw the document's sentiment distribution $\pi_d \sim Dirichlet(\gamma)$
  - For each sentiment label l, draw a topic distribution $\theta_{d,l} \sim Dirichlet(\alpha)$
  - For each couplet,
    1. choose a sentiment label $l_i \sim Multinomial(\pi_d)$
    2. choose a topic $z_i \sim Multinomial(\theta_{d,l_i})$
    3. generate words $w \sim \varphi_{l_i,z_i}$

Model Priors and hyperparameter settings. We incorporate our sentiment lexicon (described in Section 3) containing 4153 positive lexical items and 4503 negative lexical items as prior knowledge into the position-aware JST model. Specifically, if w is found in the sentiment lexicon, then the element $\lambda_{lw} = 1$, and zero otherwise. Following Lin and He (2009), we set the symmetric $\beta = 0.01, \gamma = (0.05 \times L)/S$, where L is the average document length, S is the total number of sentiment labels[7]. The asymmetric prior α is learned from data.

Topics under different sentiment polarities. We apply the position-aware sentiment-topic model to the Complete Anthology of Tang Poetry. The corpus contains 42,862 poems written by 2630 authors, with an average of 60 single characters in each poem. We represent each poem as couplets containing single and two-character lexical items[8]. We conduct experiments on $T = 15, 25, 50$ respectively. Table 5 shows the topic examples extracted by the position-aware sentiment-topic model with $T = 25$ under positive and negative sentiment labels respectively. The topics are labeled manually according to the lexical items found in them. Each topic is represented by the top 15 lexical items. These topics reflect common themes associated with positive/negative sentiment in Tang poetry. Moreover, the sentiment-topic distribution provides us with more insight on different aspects of social life in that historical period of China (AD 618 – 907).

For instance, poets wrote poems to praise the beauty of women and flowers (topic PT0 and

[7] In our experiments, the value of γ is around 1.00. This means that we do not assume any prior knowledge of the sentiment distribution of a poem and all possible sentiment distributions are equal.

[8] Similar to lexical network construction (Section 3.3), the two-character lexical items should appear at least 50 times in the whole corpus.

Positive Sentiment	
Topics	**Lexical items**
PT0: beautiful women	玉 (jade) 金 (gold) 红 (red) 罗 (silk) 香 (perfume) 女 (women) 翠 (green jade) 歌 (song) 舞 (dance) 楼 (building) 画 (painting) 珠 (pearl) 眉 (eyebrow) 双 (pair) 锦 (brocade)
PT1: feast_drinking	酒 (wine) 醉 (drunk) 歌 (song) 杯 (cup) 欢 (happy) 殷勤 (attentive) 客 (guest) 对 (face to face) 饮 (drink) 弦 (chord) 乐 (happy) 劝 (advise) 酌 (drink) 酣 (intoxicated) 筵 (feast)
PT2: war_victory	军 (military) 旌 (banner) 旗 (banner) 马 (horse) 将军 (general) 天 (god) 剑 (sword) 骑 (ride) 弓 (bow) 戎 (army) 功 (achievement) 旌旗 (banner) 箭 (arrow) 战 (battle) 射 (shoot)
PT3: literary	诗 (poetry) 文 (article) 书 (letter) 名 (reputation) 题 (inscribe) 句 (sentence) 君 (gentleman) 字 (character) 章 (chapter) 才 (gift) 篇 (article) 咏 (sing) 赋 (compose) 笔 (pen) 高 (high)
PT4: royal graciousness	德 (moral) 神 (god) 礼 (ritual) 乐 (music) 圣 (holy) 灵 (spirit) 明 (bright) 万 (great number) 惟 (only) 肃 (pay respect) 皇 (emperor) 帝 (emperor) 国 (country) 功 (achievement) 天 (god)
PT5: supernature	仙 (god) 玉 (jade) 丹 (vermilion) 天 (god) 神 (god) 霞 (rosy clouds) 紫 (violet) 灵 (spirit) 龙 (dragon) 烟 (mist) 神仙 (god) 瑶 (fairy) 清 (clean) 蓬 (fairyland)
PT6: Buddhism	香 (perfume) 禅 (meditation) 师 (master) 心 (heart) 世 (world) 法 (dharma) 清 (clean) 真 (truth) 莲 (lotus) 道 (Taoism) 净 (clean) 钟 (bell) 界 (world) 士 (scholar) 佛 (buddhism)
PT7: traveling	楼 (building) 高 (high) 上 (go up) 登 (climb) 陵 (hill) 游 (travel) 州 (province) 台 (terrace) 南 (south) 长安 (place name) 下 (go down) 临 (overlook) 佳 (beautiful) 浮云 (clouds) 武陵 (place name)
PT8: flowers	香 (perfume) 花 (flower) 枝 (twig) 露 (dew) 芙蓉 (hibiscus) 桃 (peach) 光 (light) 芳 (fragrant) 轻 (gentle) 袅 (delicate) 艳 (charming) 团 (round) 新 (fresh) 翠 (green jade) 兰 (orchid)

Negative Sentiment	
Topics	**Lexical items**
NT0: lovesickness	别 (farewell) 离 (leave) 惆怅 (melancholy) 相思 (lovesick) 忆 (memorize) 望 (hope) 相逢 (meet) 恨 (hate) 送 (farewell) 年 (year) 君 (gentleman) 梦 (dream) 远 (remote) 归 (return) 泪 (tears)
NT1: hardness of life	老 (old) 病 (sickness) 多 (many) 无 (no) 白 (gray) 鬓 (temple hair) 不 (no) 吟 (sing) 愁 (anxious) 衰 (feeble) 贫(poor) 白头 (old age) 卧 (lie down) 更 (more) 难 (hard)
NT2: hardness of war	塞 (fortress) 边 (border) 城 (city) 河 (river) 胡 (barbarian) 关 (barrier) 征 (attack) 风 (wind) 月 (moon) 北 (north) 战(battle) 雪 (snow) 虏 (captive) 戍 (garrison) 鼓 (drum)
NT3: traveling by boat	江 (river) 水 (water) 舟 (boat) 湖 (lake) 波 (wave) 岸 (bank) 浪 (wave) 风 (wind) 沙 (sand) 帆 (sail) 孤(lonely) 海 (sea) 船 (boat) 浦 (riverside) 月 (moon)
NT4: homesickness	堪 (bear) 断 (break) 故 (home) 落 (fall) 乡 (home) 凄 (sorrow) 愁 (anxious) 归 (return) 泪 (tears) 路 (road) 肠(intestine, often used to describe heartbroken) 伤 (sad) 悲 (sad) 涯 (shore) 音 (news)
NT5: visiting monks	山 (mountain) 僧 (monk) 松 (pine) 寺 (temple) 石 (rock) 林 (forest) 深 (deep) 泉 (fountain) 夜 (night) 寒 (cold) 寻(search) 客 (guest) 峰 (peak) 云 (cloud) 溪 (stream)
NT6: sad scenery	秋 (autumn) 风 (wind) 叶 (leaf) 寒 (cold) 雨 (rain) 夕阳 (sunset) 晚 (evening) 水 (water) 暮 (twilight) 霜 (frost) 菊(chrysanthemum) 蝉 (cicada) 山 (mountain) 落 (fall) 凉 (cold)
NT7: sad scenery	雨 (rain) 猿 (ape) 峡 (gorge) 啼 (cry) 江 (river) 云 (clouds) 湘 (river name) 楚 (place name) 山 (mountain) 暮 (twilight) 蹉跎(waste time) 巫峡 (gorge name) 云雨 (clouds and rain) 梦 (dream) 巫山 (mountain name)
NT8: death and destruction	死 (death) 生 (birth) 苦 (miserable) 骨 (bone) 悴 (sad) 饥 (hungry) 血 (blood) 泥 (mud) 杀 (kill) 枯 (withered) 憔悴(thin and pallid) 鬼 (ghost) 恶 (evil) 祸 (disaster) 土 (dust)

Table 5: Examples of topics extracted by the position-aware sentiment-topic model.

PT8). They eulogized the Tang empire and were proud of the country's victory in war (topic PT4 and PT2). They enjoyed drinking at banquet (topic PT1), admire others' literary achievements (topic PT3) and praised beautiful landscapes while traveling (topic PT7). In addition, it seems that Buddhism and supernatural beings are the favored topics of poetry in the Tang Dynasty (topic PT6 and PT5). This might reflect that Buddhism was at its peak in the Tang Dynasty and many poets were devout Buddhists.

On the other hand, poets felt sad for women who separated with their loved ones (topic NT0). They were angry for death and destruction caused by tyranny and turmoil (topic NT8). Poets were tired of war (topic NT2) and they were homesick while traveling alone (topic NT3 and NT4).

It is worth noticing that some topics are associated with both positive and negative sentiment. For instance, poets were happy about the victory of war (topic PT2). At the same time, they were sad about the destruction/pain caused by war (topic NT2), i.e., soldiers were forced to leave their homelands and loved ones. Also, traveling could involve both sentiments: poets praised the beauty of nature (PT7); but they also felt lonely while traveling alone (NT3, NT4). Specifically, some scenes during traveling become common imageries/symbols which imply sad emotions, such as things related to water (i.e., 江 (river), 舟 (boat), 湖 (lake), 波 (wave), 岸 (bank), 帆 (sail), 浪 (wave), 浦 (riverside) in topic NT3), or 猿 (ape) in topic NT7. This also reflects that poets liked traveling and that traveling by boat was popular in the Tang Dynasty.

5.2 Sentiment of Different Poets

In order to analyze how sentiment differs among poets, we choose four famous poets from the Tang dynasty: 李白 (Li Bai), 杜甫 (Du Fu), 王维 (Wang Wei), and 白居易 (Bai Juyi).

Li Bai enjoys the title of the "Supernatural Being of Poem". His works are full of passion, imagination and elegance. Du Fu, known as the "Poet Sage", is known for his anti-war stance and concerns for the poor. Wang Wei, the poet of landscape, has written lots of elegant and exquisite poems. Bai Juyi has been known for his plain and easily comprehensible style of poem, and for his social and political criticism. Table 6 lists the poets' lifetimes and the number of their poems collected in the Complete Anthology of Tang Poetry.

Poet	Lifetime	Number of Poems
李白 (Li Bai)	701 – 762	891
杜甫 (Du Fu)	712 – 770	1,151
王维 (Wang Wei)	701 – 761	350
白居易 (Bai Juyi)	772 – 846	2,640

Table 6: Number of poems by chosen poets.

On the basis of our sentiment lexicon, we predict the sentiment orientation of each poem using the method described in Section 4.2 with threshold $t = 0$[9]. We then compare the percentage of poems with different sentiment for each poet.

Figure 2 shows that the percentage of positive poems written by Li Bai is the highest among our four poets, whereas the percentage of negative poems written by Du Fu is the highest[10]. It

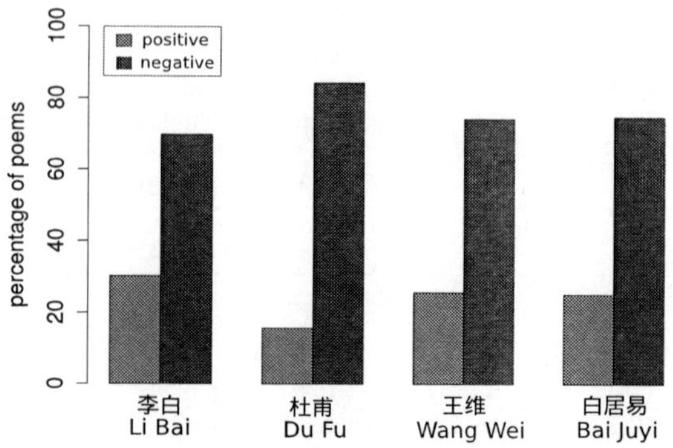

Figure 2: Sentiment of different poets.

seems that Du Fu expressed sad emotions more frequently in his poems. This may relate to his frustrating experiences. He aspired a career as a civil servant, but his failure in the examination put an end to his chances to have an official career. During the period of political turmoil, Du Fu fled to the capital. But he was captured and then wandered as a refugee. Most of Du Fu's life was spent in poverty. One of his sons even died from starvation because of the family's poverty. Du Fu wrote several poems to express his deep sadness for his son's death. It is worth noting that although Bai Juyi has been known for his critical political poems, he also wrote a great amount of poems expressing leisurely and comfortable mood, especially in his late years.

6 Conclusions

We propose a novel graph-based method to build a sentiment lexicon for classical Chinese poetry. Our approach is weakly supervised and outperforms a previous PMI-based approach (Turney and Littman, 2003) in different evaluation settings. On the basis of our sentiment lexicon, we analyze sentiment in Tang poetry from different perspectives: which topics are associated with positive and negative sentiment, and how sentiment is distributed among different poets. Our analysis results are in line with the main findings established in classical Chinese literary studies.

The work presented in this paper provides a quantitative means to study sentiment in classical Chinese poetry. We hope it can benefit other research topics, such as poetry generation (He et al., 2012; Zhang and Lapata, 2014) and poetry imagery/style analysis (Fang et al., 2009).

[9]We could also use our position-aware sentiment-topic model to predict the sentiment orientation of each poem. However, for the task of predicting sentiment orientation of poems, we found that the position-aware JST model does not perform as well as our simple method described in Section 4.2 on the same test dataset.

[10]We find that the comparison under different value of t keeps the same pattern as shown in Figure 2.

References

Eneko Agirre and Aitor Soroa. 2009. Personalizing PageRank for word sense disambiguation. In *Proceedings of the 12th Conference of the European Chapter of the Association for Computational Linguistics,* Athens, Greece, 30 March – 3 April 2009, pages 33–41.

Stefano Baccianella, Andrea Esuli, and Fabrizio Sebastiani. 2010. SentWordNet 3.0: An enhanced lexical resource for sentiment analysis and opinion mining. In *Proceedings of the 7th International Conference on Language Resources and Evaluation,* La Valetta, Malta, 17–23 May 2010, pages 2200–2204.

David M. Blei, Andrew Y. Ng, and Michael I. Jordan. 2003. Latent dirichlet allocation. *J. Mach. Learn. Res.*, 3(1):993–1022.

Sergey Brin and Lawrence Page. 1998. The anatomy of a large-scale hypertextual web search engine. *Computer Networks and ISDN Systems*, 30(1–7):107–117.

Andrea Esuli and Fabrizio Sebastiani. 2005. Determining the semantic orientation of terms through gloss analysis. In *Proceedings of the ACM SIGIR Conference on Information and Knowledge Management (CIKM).*

Alex Chengyu Fang, Fengju Lo, and Cheuk Kit Chinn. 2009. Adapting NLP and corpus analysis techniques to structured imagery analysis in classical Chinese poetry. In *Proceedings of the RANLP 2009 Workshop on Adaptation of Language Resources and Technology to New Domains,* Borovets, Bulgaria, 14 June 2013, pages 27–34.

Ahmed Hassan, Amjad Abu-Jbara, Rahul Jha, and Dragomir Radev. 2011. Identifying the semantic orientation of foreign words. In *Proceedings of the ACL 2011 Conference Short Papers,* Portland, Oreg., 19–24 June 2011, pages 592–597.

Taher H. Haveliwala. 2002. Topic-sensitive PageRank. In *Proceedings of the 1th World Wide Web Conference,* Honolulu, Hawaii, USA, 7–11 May 2002, pages 517–526.

Yulan He, Harith Alani, and Deyu Zhou. 2010. Exploring English lexicon knowledge for chinese sentiment analysis. In *CIPS-SIGHAN Joint Conference on Chinese Language Processing.* Beijing, China, 28-29 August 2010, pages 121–128.

Yulan He, Chengua Lin, and Harith Alani. 2011. Automatically extracting polarity-bearing topics for cross-domain sentiment analysis. In *Proceedings of the 49th Annual Meeting of the Association for Computational Linguistics,* Portland, Oreg., 19–24 June 2011, pages 123–131.

Jing He, Ming Zhou, and Long Jiang. 2012. Generating chinese classical poems with statistical machine translation models. In *Proceedings of the 26th Conference on the Advancement of Artificial Intelligence,* Toronto, Canada, 22–26 July 2012, page 1650–1656.

Junfeng Hu. 2001. *The Lexicon Meaning Analysis-based Computer Aided Research Work of Chinese Ancient Poems.* Ph.D. thesis, Peking University. Published by Graduate Linguistics Student Organisation.

Nobuhiro Kaji and Masaru Kitsuregawa. 2007. Building lexicon for sentiment analysis from massive collection of HTML documents. In *Proceedings of the 2007 Joint Conference on Empirical Methods in Natural Language Processing and Computational Language Learning,* Prague, Czech Republic, 28–30 June 2007, pages 1075–1083.

Jaap Kamps, Maarten Marx, Robert J. Mokken, and Maarten de Rijke. 2004. Using WordNet to measure semantic orientation of adjectives. In *Proceedings of the 4th International Conference on Language Resources and Evaluation,* Lisbon, Portugal, 26–28 May 2004, pages 1115–1118.

Hiroshi Kanayama and Tetsuya Nasukawa. 2006. Fully automatic lexicon expansion for domain-oriented sentiment analysis. In *Proceedings of the 2006 Conference on Empirical Methods in Natural Language Processing,* Sydney, Australia, 22–23 July 2006, pages 355–363.

Yu-kung Kao and Tsu-lin Mei. 1971. Syntax, diction, and imagery in T'ang poetry. *Harvard Journal of Asiatic Studies*, 31(2):49–136.

Yu-kung Kao and Tsu-lin Mei. 1978. Meaning, metaphor, and allusion in T'ang poetry. *Harvard Journal of Asiatic Studies*, 38(2):281–355.

Svetlana Kiritchenko, Xiaodan Zhu, and Sarif Mohammad. 2014. Sentiment analysis of short informal texts. *Journal of Artificial Intelligence Research*, 50(1):723–762.

Lun-Wei Ku, Yu-Ting Liang, and Hsin-Hsi Chen. 2006. Tagging heterogeneous evaluation corpora for opinionated tasks. In *Proceedings of the 5th International Conference on Language Resources and Evaluation,* Genoa, Italy, 22–28 May 2006, pages 667–670.

Angeliki Lazaridou, Ivan Titov, and Caroline Sporleder. 2013. A Bayesian model for joint unsupervised induction of sentiment, aspect and discourse representations. In *Proceedings of the 51st Annual Meeting of the Association for Computational Linguistics,* Sofia, Bulgaria, 4–9 August 2013, pages 1630–1639.

John Lee and Yin Hei Kong. 2012. A dependency treebank of classical chinese poems. In *Proceedings of the 2012 Conference of the North American Chapter of the Association for Computational Linguistics: Human Language Technologies,* Montréal, Québec, Canada, 3–8 June 2012, pages 191–199.

John Lee and WONG Tak-sum. 2012. Glimpses of ancient china from classical chinese poems. In *Proceedings of the 24th International Conference on Computational Linguistics,* Mumbai, India, 8–15 December 2012, pages 621–632.

Chiwei Li, Myle Ott, and Claire Cardie. 2013. Identifying manipulated offerings on review portals. In *Proceedings of the 2013 Conference on Empirical Methods in Natural Language Processing,* Seattle, Wash., 18–21 October 2013, pages 1933–1942.

Chenghua Lin and Yulan He. 2009. Joint sentiment/topic model for sentiment analysis. In *Proceedings of the ACM 18th Conference on Information and Knowledge Management (CIKM 2009),* Hong Kong, 2–6 November 2009, pages 375–387.

Fengzhu Luo. 2009. The application of affective and semantics computing in literature and history research. *Literature Heritage,* 1(1):138–141.

Qiaozhu Mei, Xu Ling, Matthew Wondra, Hang Su, and ChengXiang Zhai. 2007. Topic sentiment mixture: Modeling facets and opinions in weblogs. In *Proceedings of the 16th World Wide Web Conference,* Banff, Canada, 8–12 May, 2007, pages 171–180.

Saif Mohammad, Cody Dunne, and Bonnie Dorr. 2009. Generating high-coverage semantic orientation lexicons from overtly marked words and a thesaurus. In *Proceedings of the 2009 Conference on Empirical Methods in Natural Language Processing,* Singapore, 6–7 August 2009, pages 599–608.

Delip Rao and Deepa avichandran. 2009. Semi-supervised polarity lexicon induction. In *Proceedings of the 12th Conference of the European Chapter of the Association for Computational Linguistics,* Athens, Greece, 30 March – 3 April 2009, pages 675–682.

Hiroya Takamura, Takashi Inui, and Manabu Okumura. 2005. Extracting semantic orientation of words using spin model. In *Proceedings of the 43rd Annual Meeting of the Association for Computational Linguistics,* Ann Arbor, Mich., 25–30 June 2005, pages 133–140.

Ivan Titov and Ryan McDonald. 2008. A joint model of text and aspect ratings for sentiment summarization. In *Proceedings of the 46th Annual Meeting of the Association for Computational Linguistics: Human Language Technologies,* Columbus, Ohio, 15–20 June 2008, pages 308–316.

Peter D. Turney and Michael L. Littman. 2003. Measuring praise and criticism: Inference of semantic orientation from association. *ACM Transactions on Information Systems (TOIS),* 21(4):315–346.

Rob Voigt and Dan Jurafsky. 2013. Tradition and modernity in 20th century Chinese poetry. In *Proceedings of the NAACL-HLT 2013 Workshop on Computational Linguistics for Literature,* Atlanta, USA, 14 June 2013, pages 1–6.

Xiaojun Wan. 2008. Using bilingual knowledge and ensemble techniques for unsupervised Chinese sentiment analysis. In *Proceedings of the 2008 Conference on Empirical Methods in Natural Language Processing,* Waikiki, Honolulu, Hawaii, 25–27 October 2008, pages 553–561.

Xiaojun Wan. 2009. Co-training for cross-lingual sentiment classification. In *Proceedings of the Joint Conference of the 47th Annual Meeting of the Association for Computational Linguistics and the 4th International Joint Conference on Natural Language Processing,* Singapore, 2–7 August 2009, pages 235–243.

Burton Watson. 1971. *Chinese Lyricism: Shih Poetry from the Second to the Twelfth Century.* New York: Columbia University Press.

Scott White and Padhraic Smyth. 2003. Algorithms for estimating relative importance in networks. In *Proceedings of the 9th ACM SIGKDD Conference on Knowledge Discovery and Data Mining,* Washington DC, USA, 24–27 August 2004, pages 266–275.

Difei Xiao, editor. 1999. *Tang Poetry analysis dictionary.* Shanghai Lexicographical Publishing House, Shanghai, China.

Wenpu Xing and Ali Ghorbani. 2004. Weighted PageRank algorithm. In *Proceedings of the Second Annual Conference on Communication Networks and Services Research,* Fredericton, N.B., Canada, 19-21 May 2004, pages 305–314.

Taras Zagibalov and John Carroll. 2008. Automatic seed word selection for unsupervised sentiment classification of Chinese text. In *Proceedings of the 22nd International Conference on Computational Linguistics,* Manchester, U.K., 18–22 August 2008, pages 1073–1080.

Xingxing Zhang and Mirella Lapata. 2014. Chinese poetry generation with recurrent neural networks. In *Proceedings of the 2014 Conference on Empirical Methods in Natural Language Processing,* Doha, Qatar, 25–29 October 2014, pages 670–680.

Chang-Le Zhou, Wei You, and Xiao-Jun Ding. 2010. Genetic algorithm and its implementation of automatic generation of Chinese SONGCI. *Journal of Software,* 21(3):427–437.

Measuring the Structural and Conceptual Similarity of Folktales using Plot Graphs

Victoria Anugrah Lestari and Ruli Manurung
Faculty of Computer Science, Universitas Indonesia
Depok 16424, West Java, Indonesia
victoria.anugrah@ui.ac.id, maruli@cs.ui.ac.id

Abstract

This paper presents an approach to organizing folktales based on a data structure called a *plot graph*, which captures the narrative flow of events in a folktale. The similarity between two folktales can be computed as the structural similarity between their corresponding plot graphs. This is performed using the well-known Needleman-Wunsch algorithm. To test the efficacy of this approach, experiments are carried out using a small collection of 24 folktales grouped into 5 categories based on the Aarne-Thompson index. The best result is obtained by combining the proposed structural-based similarity measure with a more conventional bag of words vector space model, where 19 out of the 24 folktales (79.16%) yield higher average similarity with folktales within their respective categories as opposed to across categories.

1 Introduction

Folktales are prevalent in almost all cultures, and are a rich and valuable part of our cultural heritage. They serve as a valuable resource for many studies into our history, sociology, and language. Analysis and classification has typically been done by folklorists, with one of the most well-known methods being the Aarne-Thompson index (Uther, 2004), which organizes folktales around the concept of motifs and themes. Folktales that are deemed to be similar based on such concepts are grouped together.

Recently, a significant amount of research has been conducted on the application of natural language processing and computational linguistics to automatically organize folktale data (Karsdorp and van den Bosch, 2013; Lobo and de Matos, 2010; Nguyen et al., 2012; Nguyen et al., 2013). Most of these approaches use the bag of words model, which measures similarity based on the number of shared features, namely words. This paper proposes a method that also takes into account the structural similarity between the sequences of events found in folktales.

The goal of our work is to develop a data structure that can be utilized to capture the structure of events, relations, and entities of a folktale. For that purpose, we propose a data structure known as a *plot graph* based on the work of McIntyre and Lapata (2010). The purpose of the plot graph is to record the plot movers and preserve the sequence of events in folktales. The similarity between two plot graphs can be compared by first measuring the similarity between words in corresponding vertices. The similarity between words is measured using the Wu-Palmer method of WordNet-based lexical semantic similarity (Wu and Palmer, 1994). The vertices in the plot graphs are aligned using the Needleman-Wunsch algorithm (Needleman and Wunsch, 1970).

The outline of the paper is as follows. An overview of related work is presented in Section 2, followed by discussion of the proposed plot graph data structure in Section 3 and how to measure the similarity of plot graphs in Section 4. Finally, Section 5 provides details of experimental results and Section 6 offers our conclusion and suggestions for future work.

2 Related Work

The Aarne-Thompson index or classification system (Uther, 2004) is a widely adopted and standardized index used by many folklorists. It was first developed by Antti Aarne in 1910, revised by Stith Thompson in 1928 and 1961, and by Hans-Jörg Uther in 2004. The system identifies a folktale through its motifs and structural patterns rather than the particular details of its characters

Proceedings of the 9th SIGHUM Workshop on Language Technology for Cultural Heritage, Social Sciences, and Humanities, pages 25–33, Beijing, China, July 30, 2015.

actions.

In recent years, there has been a significant amount of research in trying to automatically organize folktale data using standardized indices such as the Aarne-Thompson index. In the work of Karsdorp and van den Bosch (2013), motifs in a folktale are identified using the Labeled-LDA (Latent Dirichlet Allocation), which represents motifs as distribution over words. A training model is built utilizing TF-IDF (term frequency × inverse document frequency) weights as the attributes of each folktale. In the work of Lobo and de Matos (2010), a fairy tale corpus is partitioned into semantically related clusters using Latent Semantic Mapping. The model is built by first constructing a term-document matrix and then applying the singular value decomposition (SVD) matrix factorization followed by dimensionality reduction (achieved by rank reduction) to obtain a lower dimensional space that maps documents in a conceptual space. Finally, the works of (Nguyen et al., 2012; Nguyen et al., 2013) employ a supervised classification approach using a labeled corpus and various linguistic features. The former uses the SVM classifier whereas the latter employs learning-to-rank strategies.

One thing to note is that all of these existing approaches measure the similarity between folktales based on the degree of overlapping features that are typically derived from the co-occurrence of specific words or phrases. In other words, most of these approaches tend to view folktales using an approach that is known as the bag of words model. However, this approach fails to recognize the complex structure of a narrative found within a folktale, which involves plot movers and sequences of events. Since folktales are narratives, which necessarily convey a sequence of events, we argue that this narrative flow of events can possibly represent the underlying characteristic of a folktale better than bag of words methods. Furthermore, this may coincide well with the Aarne-Thompson index, as it is known that Antti Aarne focused on the morphology, or structure, of the folktale. We provide an illustrative example in Section 3.

In terms of cognitive models of similarity, we can say that the existing approaches adopt a more feature-based similarity model (Tversky, 1977), whereas we argue in favor of an approach that also takes into account structural similarity (Gentner, 1983).

In trying to formulate a model that takes into account the structural nature of narratives, one work that is of special interest is McIntyre and Lapata (2010), which develops a plot graph for the purpose of story generation. The graph captures the plot of a story by storing each entity in a vertex and each action in another vertex. Through genetic algorithm techniques, the plot graph experiences mutation and crossover with another plot graph, resulting in a new, randomized graph to generate a new story. Although the end task is significantly different, i.e. the generation of new stories, the approach to modelling plot structure is one that we adopt.

Our approach, which we will now describe in Sections 3 and 4, differs from the aforementioned works of Lobo and de Matos (2010; Nguyen et al. (2012; Nguyen et al. (2013; Karsdorp and van den Bosch (2013) in that it does not adopt a bag of words approach to capture the motif of a folktale. Rather, we build the plot graph based on the work of McIntyre and Lapata (2010), although with some modifications.

3 Structural similarity and plot graphs

Based on work in the area of cognitive science (Love, 2000), we propose two factors that must be considered when modelling human perception of similarity: *structural similarity* and *conceptual similarity*. Structural similarity measures the degree of isomorphism between complex objects. Conceptual similarity is a measure of relatedness between two corresponding concepts, assuming that the entities in the complex objects have been appropriately mapped.

This model can be applied to a system that has the ability to detect plot similarity the way humans do. Humans can determine whether two folktales are similar not by counting how many of the same words are shared in the folktales, but by recognizing the plot similarities of the folktales. For example, the folktales "Aladdin and the Wonderful Lamp" and "The Magic Ring" can be judged as similar. Both folktales contain magic objects (the lamp in "Aladdin and the Wonderful Lamp" and the ring in "The Magic Ring") and rag-to-riches protagonists, who meet magical helpers and marry the princess. Details such as the protagonists' names (Aladdin or Martin), the helpers' forms (a genie, a dog, or a cat), and the magic objects (a lamp or a ring) are overlooked when humans judge the similarities of the folktales.

3.1 Definition of a plot graph

We define the plot of a folktale as a sequence of events consisting of the following parts:

Action – The main word, usually a verb, that drives the course of events in a sentence. A sentence may have more than one action.

Child – A word related to an action based on its dependency relation. An action may have zero to many children.

Entity – An actor or object contained in the event. A sentence may have more than one entity.

The plot graph represents the sequence of events and the entities involved in a folktale. Thus, two plot graphs can be compared to yield a similarity score. In our experiments, we use the dependency parser (de Marneffe and Manning, 2008) and coreference resolution tool (Lee et al., 2013) found in Stanford CoreNLP library[1]. Our algorithm processes one sentence at a time. A sentence is parsed, and its coreferences are resolved. The actions, children, and entities are identified to be stored in the plot graph.

More formally, a plot graph is a directed acyclic graph representing a folktale that has been decomposed into actions, children, and entities. A plot graph is more predictable than a regular graph because it has a pattern, a start, and an end. Formally, a plot graph ***G*** is defined as an ordered six-tuple $(V_1, V_2, V_3, E_1, E_2, E_3)$ with the following specification:

- V_1 is a set of vertices that represent actions in the folktale. V_1 may have n elements, with $n \geq 1$. An element of V_1 is called *action vertex*.

- V_2 is a set of vertices that represent children (words related to actions) in the folktale. V_2 may have k elements, with $k \geq 1$. An element of V_2 is called *child vertex*.

- V_3 is a set of vertices that represent entities in the folktale. V_3 may have m elements, with $m \geq 1$. An element of V_3 is called *entity vertex*.

- E_1 is a set of edges that links exactly two elements of V_1. E_1 may have $n-1$ elements. An element of E_1 is called *action–action edge*.

- E_2 is a set of edges that links an element of V_1 and an element of V_2. E_2 may have up to $n \times k$ elements. An element of E_2 is called *action-child edge*.

- E_3 is a set of edges that links an element of V_2 and an element of V_3. E_3 may have up to $m \times k$ elements. An element of E_3 is called *entity–child vertex*.

Figure 1 provides an illustration of the schema of a plot graph.

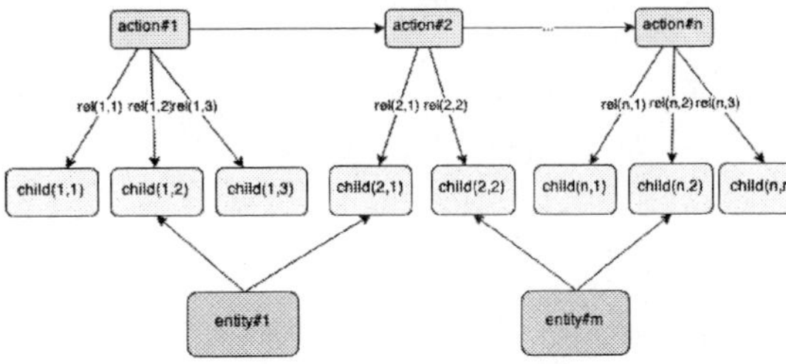

Figure 1: Schema of a plot graph

Note that there are some differences between our plot graphs as defined above with the plot graphs of McIntyre and Lapata (2010), where our plot graph is not an entity-based graph and that a vertex only contains a single event or entity.

3.2 Construction process

The construction of a plot graph is shown in the following example. Consider the first paragraph of the short folktale "A Friend in Need Is a Friend Indeed":

> Once upon a time there lived a lion in a forest. One day after a heavy meal, it was sleeping under a tree. After a while, there came a mouse and it started to play on the lion.

With the dependency parser, we extract the dependency relations between the words in the folktale and identify the verbs, if there are any, as the actions. A dependency relation takes the form of relation(word1, word2), where word1 is the *governor* and word2 is the *dependent*. The above paragraph yields the following relations:

> advmod(lived-6, Once-1)
> nsubj(**lived-6**, there-5)
> dobj(lived-6, lion-8)

[1]http://nlp.stanford.edu/software/corenlp.shtml

prep_in(lived-6, forest-11)

npadvmod(sleeping-10, day-2)
prep_after(sleeping-10, meal-6)
nsubj(**sleeping-10**, it-8)
aux(sleeping-10, was-9)
prep_under(sleeping-10, tree-13)

prep_after(came-6, while-3)
expl(**came-6**, there-5)
dobj(came-6, mouse-8)
conj_and(came-6, started-11)

nsubj(**started-11**, it-10)
xcomp(started-11, play-13)

aux(**play-13**, to-12)
prep_on(play-13, lion-16)

First, observing that the governors of the relations nsubj (nominal subject), expl (expletive "there"), and aux (auxiliary) are best identified as the actions of the folktale, the action words "lived", "sleeping", "came", "start", and "play" are obtained, and are used to form the action vertices.

Next, the words that are related to the actions (namely, the *dependent* of the relation) are obtained and identified as the children. These are used to form the child vertices, after first removing words such as "once", "there", and "was". Finally, coreference resolution is used to detect anaphoric references between the entities. Entity vertices are formed and linked to the child vertices. Entities that only occur once in the sentence are not included in the entity vertices. Thus, there are only two entities that are identified in this example, namely "the lion" in sentence 1, and "the mouse" in sentence 3. The resulting plot graph can be seen in Figure 2.

4 Similarity Measurement

The similarity between two plot graphs is represented by a score in the interval [0,1]. A score of 0 denotes that the plot graphs are completely dissimilar, while a score of 1 denotes that the plot graphs are identical. To measure the similarity between plot graphs, first we align the action vertex sequences of the respective plot graphs.

		live	sleep	disturb
	0 (done)	-1 (←)	-2 (←)	-3 (←)
eat	-1 (↑)	0.29 (↖)	0 (↖)	-1 (←)
live	-2 (↑)	-0.71 (↑)	0.54 (↖)	1 (↖)
rest	-3 (↑)	-1.71 (↖)	-0.38 (↖)	**0.79** (↖)

Table 1: The final state of alignment matrix

Strictly speaking, computing a structural similarity mapping between two such complex expressions is an instance of the NP-hard graph isomorphism problem. However, if we observe the definition of the plot graph, we can see that it is mostly linear in structure: the sequence of event vertices forms the spine of the graph, and it is this sequence that most determines the plot. Thus, we can reduce the problem of mapping two plot graphs to a linear case of sequence matching, for which much more efficient algorithms are known.

We use the Needleman-Wunsch algorithm to obtain the maximum score of the optimal alignment. As a variation of the edit distance measurement, the Needleman-Wunsch algorithm uses a dynamic programming approach to fill two matrices: the alignment matrix and the trace-back matrix (Needleman and Wunsch, 1970).

In this work, we use the Wu-Palmer similarity measurement for the scoring matrix (Wu and Palmer, 1994). If a vertex is aligned with a gap instead of another vertex, we give a gap penalty. Then we compute the word similarity between two corresponding action vertices of the respective plot graphs. We also compute the word similarity between two corresponding child vertices.

The following example shows how the Needleman-Wunsch algorithm is used to align folktales. Suppose we have two plot graphs. The first has the action vertices containing the words "live", "sleep", and "disturb". The second has the action vertices containing the words "eat", "live", and "rest". We build the scoring matrix using the Wu-Palmer similarity measurement and determine the gap penalty to be -1. After filling the alignment matrix and the trace-back matrix according to the algorithm, we obtain the final conditions of both matrices as shown in Tables 1.

The similarity score between two plot graphs p_1 and p_2 is the sum of total action vertex similarity multiplied by a coefficient, total child vertex similarity multiplied by a coefficient, and the sum of gap penalty, as seen in Equation (1).

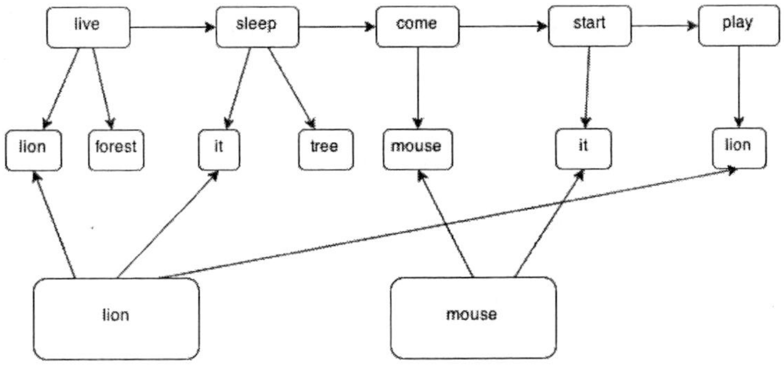

Figure 2: Plot graph representation of "A Friend in Need is a Friend Indeed"

$$sim(p_1, p_2) = \alpha \times \sum_{i=1}^{n} sim(a_{1i}, a_{2i}) + \sum g + \beta \times \sum_{i=1}^{n} sim(c_{1i}, c_{2i}) \quad (1)$$

with:
p_1 = the first plot graph
p_2 = the second plot graph
α = coefficient for action vertex similarity
β = coefficient for child vertex similarity
(a_{1i}, a_{2i}) = ordered pair of action vertices from the alignment of p_1 and p_2
g = gap penalty
(c_{1i}, c_{2i}) = ordered pair of child vertices from the alignment of p_1 and p_2
n = alignment length of p_1 and p_2

To obtain a similarity score between 0 and 1, we normalize the score from Equation (1) with a feature scaling equation, as seen in Equation (2).

$$x' = \frac{x - min(x)}{max(x) - min(x)}$$
$$max(x) = max(length(s_1), length(s_2)) \quad (2)$$
$$min(x) = max(x) \times g$$

with:
x' = transformed score
x = the previous score
s_1 = the first sequence
s_2 = the second sequence
g = gap penalty

Given two plot graphs, p_1 and p_2, each having length n, the maximum similarity score is n. For each alignment of action vertices, the score is 1, leading to the maximum score, $n \times 1 = n$. On the other hand, the minimum score is obtained when a plot graph with length n is compared to an empty plot graph (without vertices), where each action vertex is aligned with a gap. Therefore, the minimum score is $n \times g$.

5 Experiments

5.1 Parameter tuning

The coefficients α and β determine the relative importance to be placed on the similarity of the actions as opposed to the corresponding entities involved in the actions, whereas g determines how much the similarity measure is willing to tolerate skips or swaps in the action sequences. To empirically determine the best values for these three values, a small experiment using 6 short folktales from an online collection of simple short stories[2] is conducted. Each folktale is manually modified into 5 different paraphrases through word substitution, sentence structure changes, and insertion or deletion of words or sentences. We experiment with 3 different α and β values and 3 gap penalty values for a total of 9 combinations, as can be seen in Table 2. With this scheme, we expect to see the behavior of the system when we put more weight on action vertex similarity, equal weight on both action similarity and child similarity, and more weight on child vertex similarity.

After extracting plot graphs from each folktale and their 5 paraphrases, we do a complete pairwise comparison between all plot graphs. We then average the similarity between each folktale and its 5 paraphrases, and separately we average the

[2] http://www.english-for-students.com/Simple-Short-Stories.html

Experiment	α	β	g
1	0.7	0.3	0
2	0.7	0.3	-0.5
3	0.7	0.3	-1
4	0.5	0.5	0
5	0.5	0.5	-0.5
6	0.5	0.5	-1
7	0.3	0.7	0
8	0.3	0.7	-0.5
9	0.3	0.7	-1

Table 2: Parameter variation for fine-tuning experiment

similarity between different folktales. We seek the parameter combination that maximizes the former value, because the paraphrases are essentially different ways of retelling the same folktale, whilst minimizing the latter value, because the similarity between genuinely different folktales should be low. In other words, we seek to find the parameter combination that maximizes the difference between these two values, as it leads to the strongest discriminatory power.

Table 3 shows the lowest similarity scores of comparison between paraphrases, the highest similarity scores of comparison between folktales, and the average scores of both comparisons.

Based on this empirical study, the values $\alpha = 0.3$, $\beta = 0.7$, and $g = 0$ are determined as the best parameters. It is interesting to note that the parameters that maximize perceived similarity are those that place more weight on the similarity of corresponding child nodes, i.e. the entities that are associated with the actions. We believe this may be a reflection of how humans are sensitive to higher order matches, i.e. when not only elements from one analog map to elements in the other analog, but also when their respective parents and/or children are also in correspondence (Love, 2000). In other words, analogs are perceived as similar when they have a common relational structure (Gentner, 1983).

5.2 Comparison to bag of words

Having concluded the parameter tuning experiment, we move on to our main experiment that seeks to observe the efficacy of plot graphs as a representation of folktales. We compare it to a representative bag of words method, and also a combination where the average between both similarities is used. For this experiment, we use 24 folktales from the Fairy Books of Andrew Lang, available under Project Gutenberg[3]. We classify the folktales into 5 groups according to the Aarne-Thompson index. The groups are as follows:

- **Supernatural Adversaries** — Bluebeard; Hansel and Gretel; Jack and the Beanstalk; Rapunzel; The Twelve Dancing Princesses.
- **Supernatural or Enchanted Relatives** — Beauty and the Beast; Brother and Sister; East of the Sun, West of the Moon; Snow White and Rose Red; The Bushy Bride; The Six Swans; The Sleeping Beauty.
- **Supernatural Helpers** — Cinderella; Donkey Skin; Puss in Boots; Rumpelstiltskin; The Goose Girl; The Story of Sigurd.
- **Magic Objects** — Aladdin and the Wonderful Lamp; Fortunatus and His Purse; The Golden Goose; The Magic Ring.
- **Other Stories of the Supernatural** — Little Thumb; The Princess and the Pea.

Note that it does not matter if the groups are unequal in size, since we are only analyzing the similarity scores of folktales between groups and within groups.

As before, the 24 folktales are automatically converted into plot graphs, and a pairwise comparison between all the plot graphs is conducted using the similarity measure described in Section 4. The longest of these folktales, Beauty and the Beast, yields 1,208 action vertices, 2,229 child vertices, and 694 entity vertices, whereas the shortest folktale, Jack and the Beanstalk, yields 633 action vertices, 1,260 child vertices, and 497 entity vertices.

For the bag of words comparison, the folktales are first converted into vectors of words. Each component of the vector is the term frequency (TF) of the word in the folktale. We compare the vectors with each other using the cosine similarity measure:

[3]`http://www.gutenberg.org/ebooks/30580`

		α = 0.7, β = 0.3			α = 0.5, β = 0.5			α = 0.3, β = 0.7		
		g = -1	g = -0.5	g = 0	g = -1	g = -0.5	g = 0	g = -1	g = -0.5	g = 0
Comparison	**Avg.**	0.83	0.80	0.74	0.83	0.80	0.73	0.83	0.79	0.71
between paraphrases	**Min.**	0.69	0.61	0.53	0.69	0.60	0.49	0.68	0.58	0.45
Comparison	**Avg.**	0.37	0.30	0.15	0.41	0.32	0.12	0.45	0.33	0.09
between folktales	**Max.**	0.55	0.45	0.25	0.55	0.43	0.20	0.55	0.42	0.16
Min. - Max.		0.14	0.16	0.28	0.14	0.17	0.29	0.13	0.16	0.29
Diff. between averages		0.46	0.50	0.59	0.42	0.48	0.61	0.38	0.46	0.62

Table 3: Results of parameter tuning

$$\cos(\angle \vec{A}\vec{B}) = \frac{\vec{A} \cdot \vec{B}}{||\vec{A}||||\vec{B}||} \quad (3)$$

with $\vec{A}$ and $\vec{B}$ denoting vectors of words.

The experiment is done under the expectation that the average similarity scores between folktales within a group are higher than the average similarity scores between folktales across the different groups. In other words, "Aladdin and the Wonderful Lamp" should have a higher similarity score to "The Magic Ring", since both of them belong to the **Magic Objects** group, than to "Beauty and the Beast", which belongs to the **Supernatural or Enchanted Relatives**.

When using the plot graph-based similarity scores, out of the 24 folktales, only 10 folktales (41.67%) yield higher average scores within their respective groups than when compared to folktales across groups. When using the bag of words comparison method, 14 folktales (58.33%) yield higher scores in the "within group" comparison. However, the combination experiment yields the best result, with 19 folktales (79.16%) yielding higher scores in the "within group" comparison. The details of the experiment result can be seen in Table 4. The shaded cells show instances of folktales that yield a higher score for the "within group" comparison as opposed to the "across group" comparison. Note that no such instances are found in the last group, which can probably be explained due to it being the catch-all "Other stories" group.

The proposed plot graph similarity does not perform as well as the bag of words approach. Upon further inspection of the data, we note that most instances that do not fit our expectation occurs due to limitations in the automatic plot graph construction method that we have implemented rather than the theoretical model itself. We note several problems. The way the plot graph is constructed based on the Stanford dependency parser can cause the system to judge two semantically identical sentences with different syntactic structures as different. For example, the sentence "If I am hungry, I will eat" will generate a plot graph consisting of action vertices **hungry** followed by **eat**, whereas the sentence "I will eat if I am hungry" will generate a plot graph **eat** followed by **hungry**[4]. Similarly, two semantically similar but structurally different sentences can generate significantly different plot graphs and, therefore, produce a lower similarity score. For example, the sentence "The lion is very hungry" will generate a plot graph with an action vertex **hungry** and a child vertex **lion**, whereas the sentence "The lion has an extreme hunger" will generate a plot graph with an action vertex **have** and child vertices **lion** and **hunger**. When the plot graphs are compared, the action vertices **hungry** and **have** will be compared, yielding a low similarity score.

Nevertheless, the best scenario is obtained when the similarity score of two folktales is the average of their plot graph similarity and bag of words cosine similarity. This suggests that the information in the two representations is complementary, and that both structural and feature-based similarity models may play a role in organizing folktales.

6 Summary

In this paper we have proposed a data structure called a plot graph to represent folktales. This plot graph maintains the sequence of events in the folktale by preserving the words and their relations to each other. The aim is to facilitate a similarity measure that takes into account both structural and conceptual similarity, as humans are sensitive to higher order relational matching.

From our experiments, the best scenario is obtained when the similarity score of two folktales is the average of their plot graph similarity and bag of words cosine similarity. This suggests that the

[4]The Stanford dependency parser identifies the word "hungry" as the governor of the dependent word "I".

Group	Title	Plot Graph		Bag of words		Combination	
		Within	Across	Within	Across	Within	Across
Supernatural Adversaries	Bluebeard	0.1000	0.1037	0.8629	0.8618	0.4814	0.4586
	Hansel and Gretel	0.1075	0.1157	0.8492	0.8630	0.4783	0.4894
	Jack and the Beanstalk	0.1050	0.1110	0.9050	0.8891	0.5050	0.5001
	Rapunzel	0.1000	0.1047	0.8790	0.8575	0.4895	0.4571
	The Twelve Dancing Princesses	0.1125	0.1073	0.8808	0.8631	0.4966	0.4610
Supernatural or Enchanted Relatives	Beauty and the Beast	0.0767	0.0705	0.8803	0.8605	0.4785	0.4397
	Brother and Sister	0.1233	0.1135	0.8881	0.8722	0.5057	0.4654
	East of the Sun, West of the Moon	0.1117	0.1012	0.8914	0.8571	0.5015	0.4525
	Snow White and Rose Red	0.1200	0.1165	0.8650	0.8566	0.4925	0.4865
	The Bushy Bride	0.1200	0.1182	0.8862	0.8739	0.5031	0.4960
	The Six Swans	0.0925	0.1100	0.9006	0.8662	0.5020	0.4881
	The Sleeping Beauty	0.1125	0.1194	0.8990	0.8918	0.5087	0.5056
Supernatural Helpers	Cinderella	0.1180	0.1144	0.8150	0.8306	0.4665	0.4725
	Donkey Skin	0.1040	0.1122	0.8873	0.9025	0.4956	0.5074
	Puss in Boots	0.1175	0.1095	0.8170	0.8486	0.4672	0.4551
	Rumpelstiltskin	0.0750	0.0858	0.8467	0.8569	0.4609	0.4478
	The Goose Girl	0.1240	0.1178	0.8617	0.8624	0.4928	0.4643
	The Story of Sigurd	0.1080	0.1178	0.8516	0.8670	0.4800	0.4664
Magic Objects	Aladdin and the Wonderful Lamp	0.0975	0.091	0.8958	0.8664	0.4946	0.4559
	Fortunatus and His Purse	0.1133	0.1185	0.8945	0.8306	0.5039	0.4519
	The Golden Goose	0.1033	0.1155	0.9006	0.8529	0.50123	0.4611
	The Magic Ring	0.1033	0.1040	0.9120	0.8960	0.5077	0.4762
Other Stories	Little Thumb	0.0300	0.1214	0.7444	0.8562	0.3872	0.4675
	The Princess and the Pea	0.0300	0.0405	0.7444	0.7844	0.3872	0.3945

Table 4: Experimental Results

information in the two representations is complementary, and that both structural and feature-based similarity models play a role in organizing folktales.

An analysis of the experimental results reveal that the parsed dependency relations are still too sensitive towards syntactic variations, thus more work must be carried out to reliably produce plot graphs that are able to abstract away from these variations and to represent the structural properties of the narrative in a more consistent fashion. For future work, one approach that can be explored is the use of frame vertices using Semantic Role Labeling techniques (Gildea and Jurafsky, 2002), as this can further abstract away from syntactic variations.

Finally, it would also be interesting to see how to incorporate manually richly-annotated narratives, e.g. (Elson and McKeown, 2010).

References

Marie-Catherine de Marneffe and Christopher D. Manning. 2008. The stanford typed dependencies representation. In *Proceedings of the workshop on Cross-Framework and Cross-Domain Parser Evaluation*, pages 1–8, Manchester, UK.

David K. Elson and Kathleen R. McKeown. 2010. Building a bank of semantically encoded narratives. In Nicoletta Calzolari (Conference Chair), Khalid Choukri, Bente Maegaard, Joseph Mariani, Jan Odijk, Stelios Piperidis, Mike Rosner, and Daniel Tapias, editors, *Proceedings of the Seventh International Conference on Language Resources and Evaluation (LREC'10)*, Valletta, Malta. European Language Resources Association (ELRA).

Dedre Gentner. 1983. Structure-mapping: A theoretical framework for analogy. *Cognitive Science*, 7(2):155–170.

Daniel Gildea and Daniel Jurafsky. 2002. Automatic labeling of semantic roles. *Computational Linguistics*, 28(3):245–288.

Folgert Karsdorp and Antal van den Bosch. 2013. Identifying motifs in folktales using topic models. In *Proceedings of the 22nd Annual Belgian-Dutch Conference on Machine Learning*, pages 41–49, Nijmegen, Netherlands.

Heeyoung Lee, Angel Chang, Yves Peirsman, Nathanael Chambers, Mihai Surdeanu, and Dan Jurafsky. 2013. Deterministic coreference resolution based on entity-centric, precision-ranked rules. *Computational Linguistics*, 39(4):885–916.

Paula Cristina Vaz Lobo and David Martins de Matos. 2010. Fairy tale corpus organization using latent semantic mapping and an item-to-item top-n recommendation algorithm. In *Proceedings of the 2010 Language Resources and Evaluation Conference (LREC 2010)*, Valletta, Malta.

Bradley C. Love. 2000. A computational level theory of similarity. In *Proceedings of the 22nd Annual Meeting of the Cognitive Science Society*, pages 316–321, Philadelphia, USA.

Neil McIntyre and Mirella Lapata. 2010. Plot induction and evolutionary search for story generation. In *Proceedings of the 48th Annual Meeting of the Association for Computational Linguistics*, pages 1562–1572, Uppsala, Sweden. Association for Computational Linguistics.

Saul B. Needleman and Christian D. Wunsch. 1970. A general method applicable to the search for similarities in the amino acid sequence of two proteins. *Journal of Molecular Biology*, 48:443–453.

Dong Nguyen, Dolf Trieschnigg, Theo Meder, and Mariët Theune. 2012. Automatic classification of folk narrative genres. In *Proceedings of KONVENS 2012 (LThist 2012 workshop)*, pages 378–382, Vienna, Austria.

Dong Nguyen, Dolf Trieschnigg, and Mariët Theune. 2013. Folktale classification using learning to rank. In *Proceedings of the 35th European Conference on IR Research (ECIR 2013)*, pages 195–206, Moscow, Russia.

Amos Tversky. 1977. Features of similarity. *Psychological Review*, 84(4):327–352.

Hans-Jörg Uther. 2004. *The Types of International Folktales: A Classification and Bibliography*. Academia Scientiarum Fennica, Helsinki, Finland.

Zhibiao Wu and Martha Palmer. 1994. Verb semantics and lexical selection. In *Proceedings of the 32nd Annual Meeting on Association for Computational Linguistics*, pages 133–138, Stroudsburg, USA.

Towards Annotating Narrative Segments

Nils Reiter
Institute of Natural Language Processing,
Stuttgart University
nils.reiter@ims.uni-stuttgart.de

Abstract

We report on first annotation experiments on narrative segments. Narrative segments are a pragmatic intermediate layer that allows studying more complex narratological phenomena. Our experiments show that segmenting on limited context information alone is difficult. High inter-annotator agreement on this task can be achieved by coupling the segmentation with summarization and aligning parts of the summaries to segments of the text.

1 Introduction

In this paper, we present ongoing work and first insights into the manual annotation of narrative segments. We introduce the notion of narrative segments as a pragmatic intermediate layer, that is a first step towards annotation of more complex narratological phenomena and has the prospects of being identifiable automatically. Furthermore, narrative segments can serve as an abstraction layer for applications such as social network extraction. If narratives describe connected events (Mani, 2012), we define a narrative segment as a coherent and separable sub-sequence of the events in a full narrative. A narrative segment ends, e.g., when place or time of the events change.

(1) [...] With a whirl of skirts and with the brilliant sparkle still in her eyes, she cluttered out of the door and down the stairs to the street.

Where she stopped the sign read: "[...]"

In (1), (O. Henry: *The Gift of the Magi*), an undefined amount of time passes between the character running down the stairs and stopping at the sign. Since the time and place of the events change, this would be the beginning of a new segment. Coincidentally, there is also a paragraph boundary at this position.

Working quantitatively with a specific theory requires annotations of text(s). Unfortunately, instantiating a theory such that it is annotatable is challenging (Hovy and Lavid, 2010), especially within Digital Humanities. The annotation process, however, can also be a productive way of validating and objectifying a theory. In this paper, we showcase how to systematically explore different ways of formalizing and annotating narrative segments, a category that is implicitly present in narratological theory, but not spelled out in detail.

2 Related Work

Related work to this paper falls in three areas: Segmentation of narrative texts (and the corresponding annotation efforts), narratology-driven annotation and discourse annotation. In the project Heurecléa[1], a corpus of German and English literary texts is being annotated (Gius and Jacke, 2014), following closely the narratological theories (Genette, 1980; Lahn and Meister, 2008). To our knowledge, annotations are still work in progress and not yet released.

There are publications about topical segmentation of narratives, for which annotated data has been created. Kazantseva and Szpakowicz (2014) have used a novel that has been annotated with topical segments by 3-6 people (differing by chapters). The authors report a mean pairwise segmentation similarity of 0.79. The evaluation data set used by Kauchak and Chen (2005) consists of two novels and is based on the chapter segmentation done by the authors of the novels. To our knowledge, there are no previous works on segmenting narrative texts into plot parts, which does not presume a topical shift.

There are annotated news corpora in the area of discourse, (Carlson et al., 2002; Prasad et al., 2008) that feature fine-grained discourse relations

[1] http://heureclea.de

Proceedings of the 9th SIGHUM Workshop on Language Technology for Cultural Heritage, Social Sciences, and Humanities, pages 34–38, Beijing, China, July 30, 2015.

between relatively small text spans. Although larger structures have been discussed in the literature (J. Grosz and L. Sidner, 1986) but not (yet) annotated. Move analysis (Biber et al., 2007) provides a framework for corpus-based study of discourse structures, but assumes discourse moves to be defined functionally and not by plot content.

3 Annotating Narratological Theory

3.1 Narratological Theory

Three time-related phenomena can be discerned: Order, duration and frequency (Genette, 1980). Narratives often deviate from the chronological *order* and include anachronies, e.g., flash-forwards (prolepsis). The emphasized sentence in (2), from *Chris Farrington: Able Seaman* (Jack London) shows a flash-back.

(2) The boats could not be back before midnight. *Since noon the barometer had been falling* [...], [and signs were ripe for a storm.]

Many narratives contain slow and fast parts since the *duration* of different parts of the narrative varies. This is formalized as the relation between story time (ST, the time that passes within the story) and narrating time (NT, the time "consuming" the story takes). The phenomena *pause* ($ST = 0$), *slow down* ($ST < NT$), *scene* ($ST = NT$), *summary* ($ST > NT$) and *ellipsis* ($NT = 0$) are straightforwardly distinguished. The emphasized sentence in (2) is also a summary, because the falling of the barometer (ST) has been taking a lot longer than to read the sentence (NT).

The term *Frequency* is used to describe the relation between the number of times an event happens (n) within the story and the number of times it is narrated (m). Schematically, one can distinguish five cases: (i) $n = 1 = m$, (ii) $n = 1, m > 1$, (iii) $n > 1, m = 1$, (iv) $n = m > 1$ and (v) $n > 1, m > 1, m \neq n$.

These categories – anachrony, pause, ...– are not categories of the entire text, but of specific "narrative segments" (Genette, p. 35). These implicitly assumed narrative segments are not defined in any way by Genette. However, the detection of such segments is a prerequisite in order to investigate these phenomena.

3.2 Annotation Setup

To formalize the notion of narrative segments, there are a number of aspects to consider. Our aim

Exp.	Context	Autom. Task	Annotators
1	10 sent.	classification	non-experts
2	full text	segmentation	students
3	full text	summ. align.	students

Table 1: Experiment Overview

is developing a formalization that is both theoretically motivated and can be annotated reliably.

Context Knowledge In contrast to most linguistic concepts, which are done with a limited amount of context, full text knowledge is an underlying assumption in literary studies. Requiring annotators to have full text knowledge makes the annotation process slower. In crowd sourcing, it is hard to control whether annotators will have read the entire (possibly long) text.

Annotation Unit and Task The annotation unit is the text portion that is annotated, i.e., assigned to a given category. In NLP, these are usually defined in linguistic terms, e.g., sentences, phrases, or tokens. The theoretical literature in narratology does not presume a fixation on a linguistic unit, but instead allows freedom on the selection of the actual unit. The examples shown by Genette (1980) range from noun phrases ("the prospect of a war", prolepsis) to multiple sentences. The decision on the annotation unit also influences the task this problem can be cast as for automatization: Annotating full sentences would allow casting as a classification task in the future, while allowing free spans to be annotated would lead to a segmentation task.

Annotator Selection Crowd sourcing experiments allow asking non-experts for their intuitions. This requires to break down the annotation task such that knowledge of theory or terminology are no longer required. Also, the amount of time that workers spend can not be fully controlled. Expert annotations are harder to organize, but ideally allow annotating higher level concepts and use of domain terms.

4 Annotation Experiments

We conducted three experiments to explore different ways of setting up the task regarding the aspects discussed above. In all experiments we ask annotators to detect narrative segments and calculate inter-annotator agreement as a measure of

Does the yellow sentence start a new narr. unit?
A narrative unit starts, whenever

- the speed of narration changes (e.g., more time passing than before as in "Ten days later, ..."),
- time and place change (e.g., flashbacks as in "Ten years ago, I was a successful businessman in ..."), or
- the narrator changes (e.g., longer segments of direct or indirect speech, attributed to a character in the narration; internal monologue).

Figure 1: Worker instructions in Exp. 1

the "annotatability". Table 1 shows a schematic overview of the experiments.

4.1 Experiment 1: Crowd Sourcing

The first experiment was conducted as a crowd sourcing classification task using CrowdFlower[2]. The workers were presented a sentence (in yellow) within a context of ten sentences before and after. They were given a yes/no question, but with an additional "I can't tell" option. The workers annotated all sentences from two narrative texts, *Chris Farrington: Able Seaman* (J. London) and *The Winepress* (J. Essberger), in random order. The exact definitions are shown in Fig. 1. Due to difficulties in automatic parsing, we opted for annotating full sentences in this experiment.

Results and Discussion In total, we collected 1,763 ratings from 315 different workers, for $ 64. Of these ratings, 1,406 (79.8%) are of the non-new class, 339 (19.2%) of the new class. Our data set included eleven test questions and the following results are based on the five ratings for each item from the most trust-worthy workers (measured against the test questions).

We evaluate the workers' performance using inter-annotator agreement Fleiss' κ (Fleiss, 1971) and show the fraction of different kinds of majority cases. The results can be seen in Table 2. The workers achieve a κ-agreement of 0.27 and 0.21. In part, the low score can be explained by skewedness of the task – most sentences are of the same category (not starting a new segment), which makes the chance-agreement very high (0.67 and 0.73). There is a large portion (57.8% and 44.7%) of sentences where all workers are in agreement.

[2]https://www.crowdflower.com

Text	*Seaman*	*Winepress*
Fleiss' κ	0.27	0.21
$\frac{5}{5}$-agreement	57.8%	44.7%
$\frac{4}{5}$-agreement	28.3%	34.9%
$\frac{3}{5}$-agreement	13.9%	20.3%

Table 2: Quantitative analysis results of Exp. 1

Manual inspection revealed that most disagreement cases are sentences involving direct speech and thoughts representation or giving background information (3). These cases were not covered by the guidelines.

(3) The *Sophie Sutherland* was a seal-hunter, registered out of San Francisco, [...].

4.2 Experiment 2: Student Annotators

In this experiment, we collected two annotations for each of 19 short stories from (paid) students of German literature. As a general design change, we asked the annotators to first read the entire text and only make boundary annotations in a second step. We also made several definitions for cases that were difficult in previous experiments: a) Dramatic scenes (dialogues) typically belong to a narrative segment, b) encyclopedic parts (e.g., landscape descriptions) and c) events that are not "really" happening in the narrative (e.g., thoughts, possibilities) can constitute segments on their own.

Additionally, we allowed the annotators to mark segment boundaries on different levels. This allows finer distinction between segment boundaries of different granularities. We asked the annotators to first mark the most clear, top-level segmentations and in a second (and third) step subdivide the segments into smaller pieces. A boundary of level n is also a boundary of level $n + 1$.

Corpus The stories have been selected randomly out of the TextGrid[3] corpus, the only restrictions being on the genre (narratives) and length ($2k$ – $12k$ tokens). In total, the corpus contains 4.692 sentences (avg. length: 21.9 tokens).

Agreement We calculated κ agreement using boundary similarity (Fournier, 2013) as a measure for observed agreement [4]. Boundary similarity is

[3]http://www.textgridrep.de

[4]Since chance agreement is very low (< 0.1) the numbers in the table are almost identical to boundary similarity.

	κ-Agreement per level		
Text	1	2	3
1009	0.409	0.517	0.478
14	0.393	0.375	0.28
weighted avg.	0.263	0.384	0.347

Table 3: Annotator agreement in Experiment 2

based on an edit distance measure and penalizes near misses less than full misses. We used a near miss window of two avgerage sentences (44).

Results and Discussion The κ agreement scores for two individual and all texts can be seen in Table 3, separated by level. In general, we take these results as an indicator that narrative segments are something that annotators can agree upon, but that there is some room for improvement of our guidelines and definitions. Regarding the different levels of segmentation, we have to note that the annotators did have different understandings of these levels and used them very differently. This can be seen in the fact that the agreement on level 3 is higher than on level 1.

Interestingly, the total number of boundaries annotated by the annotators do not differ that much: A1 added 3.825 boundaries, while A2 added 4.293. Although it was not required or suggested, the majority of boundaries fall on sentence boundaries (A1: 67.4%, A2: 80.2%). Most of the remaining boundaries are annotated on clause boundaries.

4.3 Experiment 3: Summary Annotations

In the third experiment, we asked the annotators from the second experiment to summarize the text and then align parts of the summary with specific text segments. The idea behind this experiment was to couple the segmentation task with a "real" task that makes sense outside of the annotation task and guides decisions on granularity. We evaluated only the (now implicit) segmentation of the texts, using the same measures as before. An advantage of this setup is that the summaries allow insight into the annotators' intentions.

Results and Discussion Figure 2 shows the resulting segmentations of the two annotators and the corresponding agreement scores on the right side. In terms of the scores, the agreement is much higher than in Exp. 2. All annotated segment boundaries fall on sentence boundaries. Since the annotators have participated in Exp. 2, they are

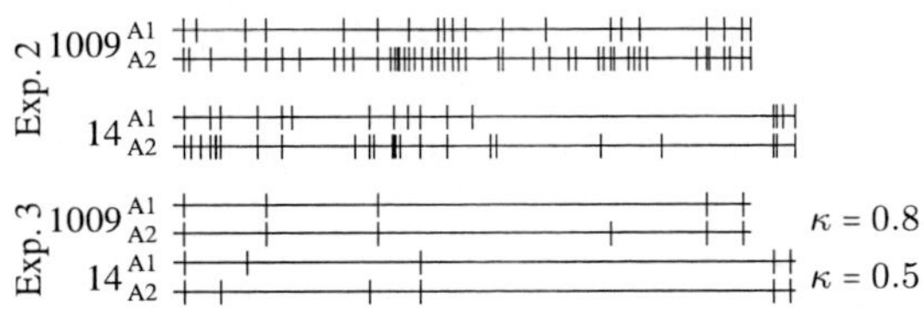

Figure 2: Segmentation Annotations

more trained than before. As the two stories were not discussed in group meetings, they should not be biased towards specific segmentations.

In the figure, we can also compare the segmentations of the same texts in Exp. 2 for each annotator. As can be seen, the annotators produced much larger segments in the third experiment, while annotator A2 still created a finer segmentation. The only remaining difference among the segmentations on text 1009 can be explained with the help of the summaries: An event that is deemed important by one annotator is not even mentioned by the other and therefore, not summarized separately. In this way, the two segmentations reflect also on different literary interpretations of the texts.

5 Conclusions and Future Work

We presented first annotation experiments on narrative segmentation. We see it as i) a prerequisite step towards quantitative analyses of complex phenomena from narratological theory and ii) useful for applications (e.g., social network extraction). Furthermore, systematically exploring different possibilities in formalizing concepts from humanities theories in this way can help bridge the gap between theoretical concepts and annotatable categories. Although events play a major role in narratives, we are aiming for pragmatic annotations that tap into intuitive understanding of narratives without presuming event annotations.

Our annotation experiments indicate that annotating segment boundaries in isolation is difficult. However, when coupled with a more involved task (like summarizing a narrative), higher agreement can be achieved and also allows insight into the intention of annotators. In the future, we will extend these experiments on annotation and use these annotations as test and training data for automatic segmentation of narrative texts.

Acknowledgements

We thank our annotators Hannah Franz and Dominik Wabersich and our collaboration partner Marcus Willand.

References

Douglas Biber, Ulla Connor, and Thomas A. Upton. 2007. *Discourse on the Move*. Number 28 in Studies in Corpus Linguistics. John Benjamins Publishing Company, Amsterdam.

Lynn Carlson, Daniel Marcu, and Mary Ellen Okurowski. 2002. Rst discourse treebank, ldc2002t07. Technical report, Philadelphia: Linguistic Data Consortium.

J.L. Fleiss. 1971. Measuring nominal scale agreement among many raters. *Psychological Bulletin*, 76(5):420–428.

Chris Fournier. 2013. Evaluating text segmentation using boundary edit distance. In *Proceedings of the 51st Annual Meeting of the Association for Computational Linguistics (Volume 1: Long Papers)*, pages 1702–1712. Association for Computational Linguistics.

Gérard Genette. 1980. *Narrative Discourse*. Cornell University Press, Ithaca, New York. Translated by Jane E. Lewin.

Evelyn Gius and Janina Jacke. 2014. Zur annotation narratologischer kategorien der zeit. Annotation Manual 1.0, Hamburg University, January.

Eduard Hovy and Julia Lavid. 2010. Towards a 'science' of corpus annotation: A new methodological challenge for corpus linguistics. *International Journal of Translation Studies*, 22(1), January.

Barbara J. Grosz and Candace L. Sidner. 1986. Attention, Intentions, and the Structure of Discourse. *Computational Linguistics*, 12(3):175–204, July.

David Kauchak and Francine Chen. 2005. Feature-based segmentation of narrative documents. In *Proceedings of the ACL Workshop on Feature Engineering for Machine Learning in Natural Language Processing*, pages 32–39, Ann Arbor, Michigan, June. Association for Computational Linguistics.

Anna Kazantseva and Stan Szpakowicz. 2014. Hierarchical topical segmentation with affinity propagation. In *Proceedings of COLING 2014, the 25th International Conference on Computational Linguistics: Technical Papers*, pages 37–47, Dublin, Ireland, August. Dublin City University and Association for Computational Linguistics.

Silke Lahn and Jan Christoph Meister. 2008. *Einführung in die Erzähltextanalyse*. Metzler, Stuttgart, Germany.

Inderjeet Mani. 2012. *Computational Modeling of Narrative*, volume 5 of *Synthesis Lectures on Human Language Technologies*. Morgan & Claypool Publishers, December.

Rashmi Prasad, Alan Lee, Nikhil Dinesh, Eleni Miltsakaki, Geraud Campion, Aravind Joshi, and Bonnie Webber. 2008. Penn Discourse Treebank Version 2.0 LDC2008T05. Web download, Linguistic Data Consortium, Philadelphia.

Ranking Relevant Verb Phrases Extracted from Historical Text

Eva Pettersson, Beáta Megyesi and Joakim Nivre
Department of Linguistics and Philology
Uppsala University
firstname.lastname@lingfil.uu.se

Abstract

In this paper, we present three approaches to automatic ranking of relevant verb phrases extracted from historical text. These approaches are based on conditional probability, log likelihood ratio, and bag-of-words classification respectively. The aim of the ranking in our study is to present verb phrases that have a high probability of describing work at the top of the results list, but the methods are likely to be applicable to other information needs as well. The results are evaluated by use of three different evaluation metrics: precision at k, R-precision, and average precision. In the best setting, 91 out of the top-100 instances in the list are true positives.

1 Introduction

Automatic analysis of historical text is of great interest not only to the language engineering community, but also to historians and other researchers in humanities, for which historical texts contain information relevant to their research. This information is however not easily accessed. Even in cases where the text has been digitized, contemporary tools for linguistic analysis and information extraction are often not sufficient, since historical text differs in many aspects from modern text, with longer sentences, a different vocabulary, varying word order, and inconsistencies in both spelling and syntax.

In this paper we address the problem of information extraction from historical text, more specifically automatic extraction and ranking of verb phrases describing work. This particular information need has arisen within the *Gender and Work* project, where historians are storing information in a database on what men and women did for a living in the Early Modern Swedish society (i.e. approximately 1550–1800). During this work they have found that working activities in their source material are most often expressed in the form of verb phrases, such as *to fish herring* or *to sell clothes* (Ågren et al., 2011). Our approach to information extraction from historical text, and ranking of the extracted results, is however likely to be applicable to other information needs as well. Furthermore, the methods presented in this paper are not dependent on semantically annotated data, since the only information required is a goldstandard containing positive and negative phrases.

In the ideal case, we would like to extract all verb phrases from a historical text, correctly classify each instance as either describing work or not, and finally present all phrases denoting work, and no other phrases, to the end user. In reality, this is however a tricky task. Even though we have access to a database of phrases previously extracted by the historians as describing work, this does not guarantee that we know how to categorise similar phrases occurring in other texts. For example, the verb *köpa* ('to buy') is sometimes a working activity related to trade, whereas in other contexts, people buy things for non-commercial reasons. In previously unseen texts, there will also most certainly be previously unseen word forms present, which a classifier would not know how to handle. This problem is further aggravated by the high degree of spelling variation in historical text, and inconsistently extracted phrases in the goldstandard (see further Section 3).

Instead of doing a binary classification into phrases denoting work versus phrases not denoting work, we therefore try a ranking approach aiming

Proceedings of the 9th SIGHUM Workshop on Language Technology for Cultural Heritage, Social Sciences, and Humanities, pages 39–47,
Beijing, China, July 30, 2015.

to present those verb phrases that most probably describe work at the top of the results list, whereas phrases that are less likely to describe work will be presented further down in the list. In this paper we present three different approaches to verb phrase ranking, based on 1) conditional probability, 2) log likelihood ratio, and 3) bag-of-words classification.

The outline of the paper is as follows. Related work is given in Section 2. In Section 3 we describe the corpus data used in our study. The verb phrase extraction method is presented in Section 4, whereas the ranking methods are described in detail in Section 5. In Section 6, the metrics used for evaluating the ranking approaches are introduced. Finally, the results are presented in Section 7, and conclusions are drawn in Section 8.

2 Related Work

Previous work on information extraction and retrieval from historical text has mainly focused on the problem of searching for certain word forms in historical documents, where spelling variation is challenging.

Baron et al. (2009) addressed the issue of text mining from historical text by developing the VARD 2 tool for automatic translation of historical word forms to a modern spelling as a preprocessing step to text mining. The tool is dictionary-based, and specifically aimed at the Early Modern English language. However, the tool comes with a graphical user interface for interactive semi-automatic adaptation of the tool for handling other language variants as well. They evaluated the adaptability of the tool on Shakespeare's First Folio by first training the tool in the interactive mode on a small sample of the text (5 000 words) corresponding to approximately 6% of the document. Then the proportion of replaced spelling variants was evaluated on the rest of the document, showing an increase from 70.33% for VARD 2 in its original setting to 73.75% after semi-automatic training.

Hauser and Schultz (2007) tried an approach based on weighted edit distance comparisons to match search strings written in Modern German against word forms occurring in documents from the Early New High German period. Pairs of historical word forms and their corresponding modern spelling, retrieved from several lexical sources, were used as training data when learning edit distance weights for commonly occurring differences in spelling between the historical language and the modern language. They showed an increase in information retrieval f-scores for historical tokens from 0.201 without edit distance matching to 0.603 in the best setting.

Pettersson et al. (2013) presented an approach to automatic verb phrase extraction from Early Modern Swedish text. Similar to the methods presented above, the verb phrase extraction process involves a spelling normalisation step, where the historical word forms are translated to a modern spelling, before the extraction of verb phrases is performed. This way, modern taggers and parsers can be used for the linguistic analysis. In their study, the spelling normalisation step is performed by use of character-based statistical machine translation techniques. The verb phrase extraction results showed an increase in the amount of correctly identified verbs from 70.4% for the text in its original spelling to 88.7% in its automatically modernised spelling. Accordingly, the amount of correctly identified complements (including partial matches) increased from 32.9% to 46.2%.

Outside the context of historical data, there is of course a lot of research done on information extraction and data mining, which will not be presented here. Nevertheless, our ranking approaches and the metrics used for evaluating them are inspired by research within this area.

3 Data

In our experiments, we make use of a subset of the Gender and Work (GaW) corpus of Swedish court records and church documents from the Early Modern period. This subset consists of text snippets, referred to as *cases* by the historians. Each case typically contains 4–5 sentences, and comprises at least one phrase describing a working activity. The corpus has been manually analysed by the historians, and those phrases that were judged as denoting work are stored in the GaW database, with information on which case the phrase has been extracted from. This means that we have access both to the source text, and to the phrases within this text that actually describe work. By automatically extracting all the verb phrases from the corpus (see further Section 4 for details on the verb phrase extraction process), it is also possible to infer what verb phrases in the corpus that have **not** been stored in the database, and thus have been judged **not** do describe work.

This binary classification of verb phrases is of crucial importance to the verb phrase ranking approaches presented in this paper. It is however not a trivial task to decide which of the automatically extracted verb phrases that should be classified as denoting work, when comparing them to the gold-standard of phrases extracted by the historians. Requiring the automatically extracted phrase to be identical to the manually extracted phrase would not be suitable, since the phrases extracted by the historians are not always phrases in the linguistic sense, but may include constituents that would normally be regarded as not belonging to the verb phrase, such as clause adverbials, prepositional phrases, and relative pronouns. Likewise, the manually extracted segments sometimes exclude constituents that would normally be regarded as belonging to the verb phrase, such as indirect objects and adverbial complements. There are also inconsistencies in the spans of the manually extracted phrases, probably partly due to different excerptors.

Similarly, the automatic extraction of verb phrases also results in incomplete verb phrases and phrases containing superfluous constituents. Still, since the overall aim of the verb phrase extraction process is to present elements in the text that may be of interest to the historians, partial phrases and phrases containing extra constituents would still point the user to the right text passage in the source material. Thus, both for training and evaluation we judge an automatically extracted verb phrase as describing work, if there is at least one verb in common between the automatically extracted phrase and the manual excerpt. This means that we run the risk of extracting the wrong instance and still judge it as correct, if there are several instances of the same verb form in the same case. This is especially true for frequent homonyms such as *ha* ('have'), which may be either a temporal auxiliary or a main verb and thus occur several times within the same case or even within the same sentence. In most cases, though, if the automatic excerpt has a verb in common with the manual excerpt, both phrases refer to the same instance. One authentic example from the GaW database is the phrase *sålt een gårdh till hr Leijon Crona* ('sold a farm to Mr Leijon Crona'), which in the automatic excerpt is given as the shorter phrase *sålt een gårdh* ('sold a farm'), but will still be regarded as a true positive (i.e. a phrase describing work).

Even though it has been stated that working activities in the GaW corpus are most often expressed in the form of verb phrases, the phrases stored in the GaW database do not always contain a verb. Common non-verb phrases in the GaW database are noun phrases (*träägårdz dräng på gården*, 'garden servant at the farm'), present participles (*lius säljning*, 'selling of candles'), and past participles or adjectival phrases (*avlönad vid Gripsholm 1572*, 'paid at Gripsholm 1572'). Since our verb-oriented approach explicitly aims at extraction of verb phrases, only phrases in which the tagger is able to identify a verb has been included in our datasets, both for training and for evaluation.

The datasets used in our experiments are presented in Table 3, where *sents* refers to the number of sentences in the corpus, *VPs* are the total amount of verb phrases in the corpus, and *Work VPs* are the amount of these verb phrases that have been judged by the historians as denoting work.

	sents	**VPs**	**Work VPs**
Training	10,623	37,606	10,241
Evaluation	1,358	4,770	1,254

Table 1: Datasets used in our experiments.

As seen from the table, approximately 27% of the verb phrases in the corpus are phrases describing work. It should however be noted that this subset of the corpus is biased towards phrases describing work, since the corpus does not comprise the whole source documents, but only those sections within the documents that actually contain some element describing work.

4 Verb Phrase Extraction

For the task of verb phrase extraction from historical text, we adopt the method introduced by Pettersson et al. (2013), as illustrated in Figure 1.

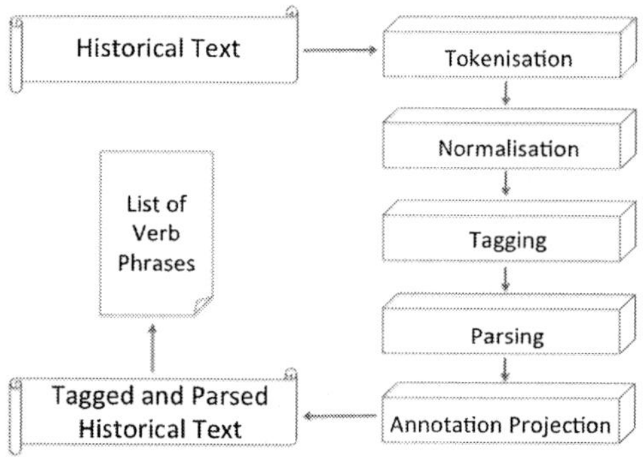

Figure 1: Verb phrase extraction overview.

First, the historical text is tokenised using standard tokenisation methods. The tokenised text is then automatically normalised to a modern spelling, using character-based statistical machine translation methods trained on the same data as described in Pettersson et al. (2013). After spelling normalisation, the modernised text is tagged and parsed using state-of-the-art tools trained for the contemporary language, in this case the HunPOS tagger (Halácsy et al., 2007) with a Swedish model based on the Stockholm-Umeå corpus, SUC (Ejerhed and Källgren, 1997), and the dependency parser MaltParser version 1.7.2 (Nivre et al., 2006a) with a pre-trained model based on the Talbanken section of the Swedish Treebank (Nivre et al., 2006b). Finally, the resulting annotation is projected back to the text in its original, historical spelling. This yields a tagged and parsed version of the historical text in its original spelling, from which the verb phrases are extracted based on the annotation labels.

Using this method, Pettersson et al. (2013) reported an f-score of 88.7% for verb identification, with 46.2% correctly identified complements. In the following, we will focus on the succeeding verb phrase ranking problem, disregarding potential verb phrases that were not found in the extraction process.

5 Verb Phrase Ranking

In the ranking phase, the extracted verb phrases are to be ordered so that those phrases that most probably describe work are presented at the top of the list, and those that most probably do **not** describe work are presented at the bottom of the list. Even though we are focusing on ranking, the training data available is not ranked, but rather classified into phrases describing work and phrases not describing work. This poses special challenges in training the ranking system. We try three different approaches to verb phrase ranking, based on conditional probability, log likelihood calculations, and bag-of-words classification respectively. As a preprocessing step, automatic lemmatisation of the extracted verb phrases (in their automatically modernised spelling) is performed, based on the Saldo dictionary of present-day Swedish word forms (Borin et al., 2008), and the manually lemmatised SUC corpus (Ejerhed and Källgren, 1997).

5.1 Conditional Probability

In the *conditional probability* approach, the probability that a verb phrase describes work, given the verbs present in the phrase, is estimated. For every verb in the phrase to be ranked, the probability that this verb describes a working activity is here estimated using the following formula:

A = number of times the specific verb is part of a verb phrase judged as describing work in the training corpus

B = total frequency of the verb in the training corpus

$$\mathbf{P(A|B)} = \frac{P(A \cap B)}{B}$$

As the final ranking score for the phrase we use either the maximum (i.e. the conditional probability for the verb with the highest conditional probability score), or the average (i.e. the average conditional probability score over all the verbs in the phrase). Furthermore, the conditional probability approach is applied both to purely tokenised data (after spelling normalisation) and to lemmatised data, yielding a total of four different settings for this approach.

5.2 Log Likelihood Ratio

Similar to the conditional probability approach, the *log likelihood* approach also compares the number of times a certain kind of verb phrase has been judged as denoting work to the number of times it has occurred in the corpus without being extracted. One advantage of the log likelihood ratio is however that it also takes into account the number of times a specific token occurs in the corpus, relative to other tokens, rendering a more fair score for low-frequency tokens as compared to high-frequency tokens. We calculate the log likelihood ratio (llr) in accordance with the formula presented by Dunning (1993), defined as below:

	Event A	Everything but A
Event B	k_11: A + B	k_12: B only
Everything but B	k_21: A only	K_22: Neither A nor B

H = Shannon's entropy, computed as the sum of
(k_ij / sum(k)) log (k_ij / sum(k))
llr = 2 sum(k) (H(k) - H(rowSums(k)) - H(colSums(k)))

Applied to the verb phrase ranking problem, the following values are used for the log likelihood variables in order to retrieve a ratio for the likelihood that a certain verb denotes work:

- **k_11**
  The number of times a specific verb occurred in the training corpus and was part of a phrase that the historians extracted as a phrase describing work.
- **k_12**
  The number of times the same verb occurred in the training corpus without being extracted.
- **k_21**
  The number of times any other verb occurred in the training corpus and was part of a phrase that the historians extracted as a phrase describing work.
- **k_22**
  The number of times any other verb occurred in the training corpus without being extracted.

The log likelihood ratio is always given as a positive number. Thus a high number could either mean a high probability that the phrase describes work, or a high probability that the phrase does **not** describe work. For the actual ranking, we have therefore taken into account the relative frequency with which the verb has been judged as describing work in the training corpus, compared to the frequency with which the verb occurred in the training corpus without being extracted. If the verb in question occurs most frequently without being extracted, the log likelihood ratio is prefixed with a minus sign, and treated as representing the probability that the phrase at hand does not describe a working activity. In other cases, the probability score is left as a positive number, thus representing the probability that the phrase at hand actually describes a working activity.

We have tried the following log likelihood settings applied to the ranking problem, where each setting has been tested based on normalised word forms as well as lemmatised data, yielding a total of twelve different settings:

words/lemmas The log likelihood ratio is calculated on the basis of all the tokens (or lemmas) in the phrase. The log likelihood score for the token/lemma with the highest log likelihood ratio is chosen as the ranking score for the whole phrase.

vb The log likelihood ratio is calculated solely on the basis of the verbs in the phrase. The likelihood score for the verb with the highest log likelihood ratio is chosen as the ranking score for the whole phrase.

vbcomp The log likelihood ratio is calculated separately for the verbs and for the non-verb tokens (or lemmas) in the verb phrase. The sum of the maximum verbal log likelihood and the maximum non-verbal log likelihood is chosen as the ranking score for the whole phrase. The hypothesis is that the verbal complements are of importance to distinguish in what contexts a certain verb describes a working activity. For intransitive verbs, only the maximum verbal log likelihood ratio is used for scoring.

vbcomp nn The log likelihood ratio is calculated as in the vbcomp setting, but for the non-verbal calculations, only the nouns are taken into account.

cooc The log likelihood ratio is calculated for the co-occurrence of the verb and each token (or lemma) in the complements. The maximum co-occurrence log likelihood is chosen as the ranking score for the whole phrase. For intransitive verbs, the maximum verbal log likelihood ratio is used for scoring.

cooc nn The log likelihood ratio is calculated as in the cooc setting, but only the nouns in the complements are accounted for.

5.3 Bag-of-Words Classification

In the bag-of-words classification approach, we run a support vector machine (SVM) classifier with the sequential minimal optimization (SMO) algorithm as defined by Platt (1998). All experiments presented here are run with the default linear kernel SVM/SMO settings in the Weka data mining software package version 3.6.10 (Hall et al., 2009). As training data we use the verb phrases in the training part of the GaW corpus, classified into those that do describe working activities (i.e. have been extracted by the historians) and those that do not describe working activities (consequently those that were not extracted by the historians). We try three different feature selection models for the verb phrase ranking problem, where each model has been applied both to normalised word forms and to lemmatised data, yielding a total of six different settings:

bag of words/lemmas Each word type (or lemma) occurring in the verb phrases in the training corpus is stored as a feature in the model. For every verb phrase to be ranked, each feature is then assigned a value of 1 or 0, depending on weather the specific word form (or lemma) represented by the feature is present in the phrase to be ranked or not.

bag of verbs In the bag-of-verbs setting, only those word forms (or lemmas) that the tagger has analysed as verbs are stored as features. Likewise, only word forms (or lemmas) in the phrase to be ranked that have been analysed as verbs will be compared towards the list of features.

bag of verbs and nouns The bag-of-verbs-and-nouns setting is similar to the bag-of-verbs setting, with the exception that both verbs and nouns are accounted for in this setting. The hypothesis is that the verbal complements, and in particular the nouns occurring in the complements, are of importance to distinguish in what contexts a certain verb describes a working activity.

6 Evaluation

Three different evaluation metrics are applied to the verb phrase ranking results: *precision at k*, *R-precision*, and *average precision*. In accordance with the arguments given in Section 3, an extracted verb phrase is here judged as describing work as long as there is at least one verb in common between the automatically extracted phrase and a manual excerpt from the same case.

6.1 Precision at k

Precision at k is defined as the precision at certain positions in the list of ranked instances (Manning et al., 2008). For example, precision at 10 is the precision achieved for the top-10 instances in the list. For our evaluation, we include precision at 10, 50, and 100 respectively.

6.2 R-precision

R-precision is similar to precision at k, but requires a goldstandard defining the total number of relevant instances. R-precision is then calculated by retrieving the precision score at the position in the list where the number of extracted verb phrases is equal to the number of relevant verb phrases in the goldstandard. At this point, precision and recall are the same, which is why this measure is sometimes also referred to as the *break-even point* (Craswell, 2009). R-precision can be summarised in the following formula:

R = number of relevant phrases in goldstandard
r = extracted relevant phrases at position R
R-precision = $\frac{r}{R}$

In our case we know that the total number of verb phrases denoting work in the evaluation part of the corpus is 1,254. Hence, R-precision is defined as precision at 1,254.

6.3 Average Precision

Average Precision (AVP) is calculated on the basis of the top n results in the extracted list, where n includes all positions in the list until all relevant instances have been retrieved (Zhang and Zhang, 2009). The average precision can be expressed by the following formula:

r = rank for each relevant instance
P@r = precision at rank r
R = number of relevant phrases in goldstandard
Average precision = $\frac{\sum_r P@r}{R}$

7 Results

7.1 Conditional Probability

Ranking based on conditional probability leads to a substantial improvement in the coverage of verbs denoting work among the top-listed instances, as compared to the baseline case, where the verb phrases are not ranked at all, but simply displayed in the order in which they appear in the source text.

As shown in Table 2, not a single verb phrase describing work is among the top-10 instances

	p10	p50	p100	R-pre	AVP
baseline	0.00	0.10	0.14	0.23	0.24
vb tok avg	0.50	0.66	0.63	0.46	0.44
vb lem avg	0.30	0.64	0.64	0.44	0.43
vb tok max	**0.80**	0.66	0.70	**0.48**	**0.49**
vb lem max	0.60	**0.68**	**0.72**	0.47	**0.49**

Table 2: Results for verb phrase ranking based on conditional probability. p10 = precision at 10, p50 = precision at 50, p100 = precision at 100, R-pre = R-precision, AVP = average precision, baseline = results for the unranked list, tok = token-based model, lem = lemma-based model, avg = probability score based on average value, max = probability score based on maximum value.

without ranking, and only 10% of the top-50 instances are phrases describing work. This could be compared to the token-based model using the maximum value for ranking, where eight out of the top-10 instances are true positives, and 66% of the top-50 instances denote work. At the break-even point (R-precision), nearly half of the positive instances are covered in this setting, as compared to only 23% without ranking. The average precision value follows the R-precision value closely for all settings.

The results also show that ranking based on the highest ranked verb for each phrase, rather than averaging over all the verbs, works the best. Furthermore, we had expected a positive effect of lemmatisation, but interestingly lemmatisation does not help much in the ranking process, and sometimes even lead to lower scores, especially for the models based on average. One reason could be that the kind of documents we are working with (court records and church documents) are almost exclusively written in the past tense, limiting the amount of different verb forms occurring for each lemma. There are also large groups of verbs denoting work, such as *köpa* ('to buy'), *sälja* ('to sell'), *arbeta* ('to work'), *tjäna* ('to serve') etc, that are so commonly occurring in the GaW database that lemmatisation is of little help in the ranking process.

Despite the promising results, there is still room for improvement. The main problem with the conditional probability approach is that no consideration is taken to the number of times a specific verb occurs in the training corpus. Hence, if a certain verb occurs only once in the training corpus, and has been extracted by the historians, it will get the probability 1 of denoting work, and end up at the top of the list. This will be disadvantageous to verbs like *sell* or *buy* that occur many times in the corpus and are often, but not always, extracted by the historians. Likewise, verbs occurring only once without being extracted will always end up at the bottom of the list, together with previously unseen verbs. As discussed in Section 5.2, this skewness is addressed by the log likelihood approach.

7.2 Log Likelihood Ratio

The log likelihood approach, being more sophisticated in balancing the probabilities for low frequency versus high frequency word forms, shows an improvement in the ranking results as compared to the conditional probability approach, as shown in Table 3.

	p10	p50	p100	R-pre	AVP
baseline	0.00	0.10	0.14	0.23	0.24
words	0.80	0.80	0.72	0.52	**0.52**
lemmas	0.60	0.70	0.74	0.45	0.47
vb tok	0.80	0.80	0.72	**0.53**	**0.52**
vb lem	0.50	0.68	0.77	0.51	0.49
vbcomp tok	0.80	**0.84**	**0.83**	0.46	0.49
vbcomp lem	0.80	0.80	0.79	0.45	0.49
vbcomp nn tok	**0.90**	0.82	0.78	**0.53**	**0.52**
vbcomp nn lem	**0.90**	0.82	0.80	0.46	0.49
cooc tok	**0.90**	0.76	0.81	0.36	0.42
cooc lem	0.70	0.74	0.78	0.35	0.40
cooc nn tok	0.50	0.76	0.77	0.31	0.35
cooc nn lem	0.50	0.74	0.77	0.31	0.35

Table 3: Results for verb phrase ranking based on the log likelihood ratio. p10 = precision at 10, p50 = precision at 50, p100 = precision at 100, R-pre = R-precision, AVP = average precision, baseline = results for the unranked list, tok = token-based model, lem = lemma-based model. See Section 5.2 for a description of the other abbreviations used in the table.

It is hard to tell which log likelihood setting is the best, since it depends on what evaluation metric we consider. One option would be to look closer at the results for precision at 100, since it would be a possible scenario to only display the top-100 instances to the user. From these results, we see that the models where the complements are taken into account (*vbcomp* and *cooc* in the table) yield better results than the plain verb-based models. It is also clear that it is more successful to calculate the log likelihood for the verb and the complement separately, and return the sum of these values (*vbcomp*), than to compute a log likelihood score for the co-occurrence of the verb and any of the word forms in the complement (*cooc*).

Furthermore, we get higher precision at k results when we compute the log likelihood for all the word forms in the complement, than when we only consider the nouns in the complement (even though R-precision and average precision are slightly higher for the noun-restricted settings). A closer look at the top-ranked phrases reveal that they all include the indefinite article, as in *sålt en* ('sold a'), *köpt en* ('bought a'), *skjutit en* ('shot a'), *stulit en* ('stolen a'), etc. This is logical in a way, since it indicates that it is of greater importance to the log likelihood ratio that **something** is sold or bought or worked with etc, than exactly **what** is sold or bought or worked with, where the latter would be better expressed by the nouns in the complement than by the indefinite article.

7.3 Bag-of-Words Classification

The ranking results for the bag-of-words classification approach are presented in Table 4.

	p10	p50	p100	R-pre	AVP
baseline	0.00	0.10	0.14	0.23	0.24
words	0.60	0.88	0.84	0.49	0.53
lemmas	0.50	0.82	0.81	0.49	0.52
vb tok	**1.00**	0.92	0.87	**0.52**	**0.55**
vb lem	**1.00**	**0.94**	0.85	0.50	0.53
vbnn tok	0.80	0.92	**0.91**	0.50	0.54
vbnn lem	0.70	0.92	0.88	0.50	0.54

Table 4: Results for verb phrase ranking based on machine learning. p10 = precision at 10, p50 = precision at 50, p100 = precision at 100, R-pre = R-precision, AVP = average precision, baseline = results for the unranked list, words = bag of words, lemmas = bag of lemmas, vb = bag of verbs, vbnn = bag of verbs and nouns, tok = token-based model, lem = lemma-based model.

The results are generally higher than for both the conditional probability method and the log likelihood calculations. For the best precision at 100 results, 91% of the instances are verb phrases describing work. Similar to the results for conditional probability and log likelihood ratio, lemmatisation generally has no positive effect on the results. Unlike the results for the log likelihood approach though, it seems beneficial to exclude non-nouns from the complements in the machine learning approach. This is however only true for the precision at 100 metric, whereas the other metrics indicate the opposite.

7.4 Summary of the Results

Table 5 summarises the results for the methods with the highest precision at 100 score within the three different approaches. As seen from the table, the bag-of-words classification approach yields the highest score for every evaluation metric used when comparing these results.

	p10	p50	p100	R-pre	AVP
baseline	0.00	0.10	0.14	0.23	0.24
cond prob	0.60	0.68	0.72	0.47	0.49
llr	**0.80**	0.84	0.83	0.46	0.49
bow	**0.80**	**0.92**	**0.91**	**0.50**	**0.54**

Table 5: Summary of the results for verb phrase ranking. p10 = precision at 10, p50 = precision at 50, p100 = precision at 100, R-pre = R-precision, AVP = average precision, baseline = results for the unranked list, cond prob = conditional probability, llr = log likelihood, bow = bag-of-words classification.

8 Conclusion

In this paper we have presented three approaches to ranking of relevant verb phrases extracted from historical text, based on 1) conditional probability, 2) log likelihood ratio, and 3) bag-of-words classification. Neither of the methods are dependent on semantically annotated data, since they all rely on binary classified training data of verb phrases containing the desired information versus other verb phrases.

Even though the ranking systems were trained on binary data rather than ranked data, all three methods yield very promising results. The bag-of-words classification approach reaches the highest scores according to all three evaluation metrics used (precision at k, R-precision, and average precision). The best bag-of-words setting is token-based (as opposed to lemma-based), taking both the verbs and the nouns in the verb phrases into account in the ranking process. In this setting, 91% of the top-100 instances in the results list are true positives.

Although the experiments were conducted for the specific task of extracting and ranking verb phrases describing work in historical Swedish text, the methods developed are language-independent and could easily be applied to other languages and information needs by simply altering the training data. It would therefore be interesting to evaluate the presented ranking methods on other information needs, document types, source languages, and time periods etc. Future work also includes a user-based evaluation together with the historians. The outcome of such an evaluation would not only show to what degree the system is useful in the extraction process, but also whether the phrases stored in the database will be different in any way when using our tool for extraction as compared to a fully manual extraction process, for instance regarding consistency.

References

Maria Ågren, Rosemarie Fiebranz, Erik Lindberg, and Jonas Lindström. 2011. Making verbs count. The research project 'Gender and Work' and its methodology. *Scandinavian Economic History Review*, 59(3):273–293.

Alistair Baron, Paul Rayson, and Dan Archer. 2009. Automatic standardization of spelling for historical text mining. In *Proceedings of Digital Humanities*.

Lars Borin, Markus Forsberg, and Lennart Lönngren. 2008. Saldo 1.0 (svenskt associationslexikon version 2). Språkbanken, University of Gothenburg.

Nick Craswell. 2009. R-precision. In Ling Liu and M. Tamer Özsu, editors, *Encyclopedia of Database Systems*, pages 2453–2453. Springer US.

Ted Dunning. 1993. Accurate methods for the statistics of surprise and coincidence. *Computational Linguistics*, 19(1):61–74.

Eva Ejerhed and Gunnel Källgren. 1997. Stockholm Umeå Corpus. Version 1.0. Produced by Department of Linguistics, Umeå University and Department of Linguistics, Stockholm University. ISBN 91-7191-348-3.

Péter Halácsy, András Kornai, and Csaba Oravecz. 2007. HunPos - an open source trigram tagger. In *Proceedings of the 45th Annual Meeting of the Association for Computational Linguistics*, pages 209–212, Prague, Czech Republic.

Mark Hall, Eibe Frank, Geoffrey Holmes, Bernhard Pfahringer, Peter Reutemann, and Ian H. Witten. 2009. The weka data mining software: An update. *SIGKDD Explorations*, 11:1.

Andreas Hauser and Klaus Schultz. 2007. Unsupervised learning of edit distance weights for retrieving historical spelling variations. In *Proceedings of FSTAS 2007*, pages 1–7.

Christopher Manning, Prabhakar Raghavan, and Hinrich Schütze. 2008. *Introduction to Information Retrieval.* Cambridge University Press.

Joakim Nivre, Johan Hall, and Jens Nilsson. 2006a. MaltParser: A data-driven parser-generator for dependency parsing. In *Proceedings of the 5th international conference on Language Resources and Evaluation (LREC)*, pages 2216–2219, Genoa, Italy, May.

Joakim Nivre, Jens Nilsson, and Johan Hall. 2006b. Talbanken05: A Swedish treebank with phrase structure and dependency annotation. In *Proceedings of the 5th international conference on Language Resources and Evaluation (LREC)*, pages 24–26, Genoa, Italy, May.

Eva Pettersson, Beáta Megyesi, and Joakim Nivre. 2013. An SMT approach to automatic annotation of historical text. In *Proceedings of the Workshop on Computational Historical Linguistics at NODALIDA. NEALT Proceedings Series 18; LinkÃűping Electronic Conference Proceedings.*, volume 87, pages 54–69.

John C. Platt. 1998. Sequential minimal optimization: A fast algorithm for training support vector machines. Technical report, Advances in Kernel Methods - Support Vector Learning.

Ethan Zhang and Yi Zhang. 2009. Average precision. In Ling Liu and M. Tamer Özsu, editors, *Encyclopedia of Database Systems*, pages 192–193. Springer US.

Ranking election issues through the lens of social media

Stephen Wan and Cécile Paris
CSIRO
Sydney, Australia
firstname.lastname@csiro.au

Abstract

Public events are often accompanied by a social media commentary that documents the public opinion and topics of importance related to these events. In this work, we describe work in collaboration with the State Library of New South Wales (NSW) to archive the social media commentary for the Australian state election in NSW, in March 2015, as a record for social scientists and historians to study in the years to come. Here, we provide an example of how one might utilise this data set, with an analysis of the data focusing on election issues. Specifically, we describe a method to produce rankings of election issues, which we find to correlate moderately to those of official commentators. Furthermore, using our time-series data, we show how the importance of key issues stabilises approximately a month before the actual election.

1 Introduction

The archival of online content for historians and social scientists of the future to study is a challenging problem that has been tackled from various perspectives. For example, in Australia, a conglomerate of state and federal archival institutions have been archiving web content about Australia for many years through the Pandora project[1]. However, projects like Pandora, conceived before the popularisation of social media channels, have only a limited coverage of social data.

We describe work with the State Library of New South Wales (NSW) to address this problem. Specifically, we tackle the collection of social media content for the NSW state election, held in March 2015. Collecting social media content pertinent to major NSW events is part of the libary's operations, complementing data archived through projects like Pandora. As part of this mandate, the library collected physical and ephemeral materials associated with the election, such as electronic version of election campaign materials as well as public discussions on social media.[2] To collect the latter, the library employed our social media monitoring tool, Vizie (Wan and Paris, 2014), to archive public discussions on Twitter[3], a predominant social media platform, that were authored by either the community or the election candidates.

In this paper, we explore the utility of such a data resource, which is intended to support the scholarly investigations of future researchers, such as social scientists and journalists. One could ask, how accurate would a picture of the election based on this data be? To address this, we present an analysis focusing on one aspect of the election, that of election issues.

We hypothesise that social media data can shed light on which issues were the most prevalent in the lead up to the elections. Specifically, for some given election issues, we explore the use of the data to produce a ranking of the issues. Our preliminary investigation focuses on obtaining these rankings based on news content shared as embedded links on Twitter. Our results show that our data-derived rankings have a moderate correlation to those eventually published in official election commentaries. In addition, utilising the time-series nature of our data, we highlight how the rankings of these issues stabilises in time, indeed weeks before the official commentary is released.

In the remainder of the paper, in Section 2, we outline related work. We describe the data collection process in 3. Section 4 describes our col-

[1] http://pandora.nla.gov.au

[2] This effort is described in: http://www.abc.net.au/news/2015-03-12/election-tweets-added-to-nsw-library-election-collection/6306490.

[3] www.twitter.com

Proceedings of the 9th SIGHUM Workshop on Language Technology for Cultural Heritage, Social Sciences, and Humanities, pages 48–52,
Beijing, China, July 30, 2015.

lection of ground truth data. We describe our approach for ranking election issues in Section 5. In Section 6, we present our analyses on election issues, which we then discuss in Section 7. Finally, we summarise our findings in Section 8.

2 Related Work

There has been much work in using Twitter to predict the outcome of an election e.g., (O'Connor et al., 2010), as well as critiques of such approaches (Gayo-Avello et al., 2011) and explorations of sentiment for prediction (Tumasjan et al., 2010).

Our work focuses on different types of media, specifically news and Twitter data. There are several investigations of media which take into account the diversity of platforms and data types. For example, some have examined the effect of different information sources on public discussion, e.g., (Scharl and Weichselbraun, 2006) and (Ahmad et al., 2011). (Declerck, 2013) mentions that it would be interesting to characterise the public discussion topics for an election. In this work, we assume that these topics are provided a priori and show how a ranking of election topics is possible.

Further afield from election-focused research, (Liu et al., 2011) also utilise embedded links in Twitter but for the purposes of generating summaries of events (see also (Nichols et al., 2012) and (van Oorschot et al., 2012)). Here, we examine how our ranking of issues based on embedded links compares with that of an official commentary, rather than generating event summaries.

3 Data Collection

Data is collected using our Vizie tool which provides an interface for configuring queries to be used with a number of social media platforms including Twitter and Facebook[4], amongst others (Wan and Paris, 2014). In this paper, we focus on Twitter content, which we collect via the free Twitter API[5]. Adherence to rate limits are observed, but for most queries we do not lose any data as a result of quota limitations.

The queries about candidates and parties were prepared by the library staff in advance of the election, using a query curation framework. (For an example of their social media collection framework for all public events in 2014, see (Barwick et al., 2014).) Some candidates, such as incumbents running for election again, were known ahead of time. Other candidates were added to the query list when the official candidate list was released by the Australian Electoral Commission, approximately two weeks before the election. This was the last date to register as an election candidate.

The full set of queries included candidate names specified as multi-word phrases, along with contextual query terms such as the party name or electorate. For example, for the candidate "Luke Foley", a "Labor" party candidate running for the seat of "Auburn", we had three queries, consisting of the different possible pairings of these three elements. Each query was sent to the Twitter API. Query terms also included known election issues, electorate names and party names. Library staff were able to use the tool to set up geographical filters based on time zones to exclude non-Australian content if the query was general enough to collect content from other parts of the world. Finally, Twitter accounts for candidates and parties were subscribed to, where these existed.

For all Twitter content collected, each tweet was automatically checked for an embedded URL. If one was found, the destination web content was retrieved and archived, along with a link to the tweet that referenced it.

4 Ground Truth Data

To obtain election issues, we use a number of different online commentaries about the election. These sources were: (1) news articles from prominent news companies[6] [7]; (2) issues extracted from a Vote Compass[8] questionnaire by the Vox Populi company; and (3) Wikipedia[9].

For our ground truth on a ranking of these issues, we used a ranking published in a news article which reported the results of the Vote Compass questionnaire.[10] This ranking is reproduced in Table 1. Interestingly, not all sources had the same set of issues. We used the Vote Compass issues as the canonical set as this was the largest set with a considerable overlap with commentaries by other news agencies.

[4] www.facebook.com

[5] dev.twitter.com

[6] http://www.abc.net.au/news/2015-03-07/seven-key-things-to-watch-during-the-nsw-election-campaign/6283582

[7] http://www.smh.com.au/nsw/nsw-state-election-2015

[8] http://www.abc.net.au/votecompass/

[9] page: New_South_Wales_state_election,_2015

[10] http://www.abc.net.au/news/2015-03-05/nsw-election-2015-vote-compass-issues-economy-asset-sales/6280030

#	Issue	#	Issue
1	Economy	13	Poverty
2	Asset sales	14	Housing
3	Cost of living	15	Taxation
4	Education	16	Defence
5	Environment	17	Population
6	Healthcare	18	Racism
7	Corruption	19	Petrol pr ices
8	Public transport	20	Drug abuse
9	Unemployment	21	Indigenous issues
10	Roads	22	Personal debt
11	Immigration	23	Drought relief
12	Crime		

Table 1: Ranked issues from Vote Compass.

Rank	Issue	#articles
1	Environment	137
2	Corruption	69
3	Leadership	60
4	Asset sales	56
5	Healthcare	42
6	Roads	34
7	Social Services, Education, Domestic violence	30
8	Prime Minister	22
9	Public transport	20
10	Crime	19
11	Balance of Power	8
12	Swing back	5
13	Indigenous issues	4
14	Defence, Drought relief, Personal debt, Poverty, Unemployment	1

Table 2: Ranked issues. Ranking is based on the number of news articles associated with that issue.

5 Generating a ranking of election issues

Our aim was to see what news articles shared on social media can reveal about the relative importance of different election issues. As such, we associated each article with an issue, using the simplifying assumption of one issue per article. This then allowed us to generate a ranking of election issues based on the number of shared news articles tagged with that issue.

To begin with, we retrieved the shared news articles from our database with publication dates falling between 12 Dec. 2014 to 27 Mar. 2015, a day before the election date. Due to limited computing resources, we limited our analysis to the top 1000 articles, ranked by the number of times it was shared in a tweet using an embedded URL.

Each of the 1000 articles was associated with an election issue using standard vector space methods —for an overview, see (Salton and McGill, 1983). Each issue was represented as a vector of word frequencies, and the closest matching issue to an article was determined using cosine similarity.

To derive our issue vectors, we used text describing each issue from our the sources listed in Section 4. Although each source used slightly different names for elections issues, these were trivially reconciled with the issues provided by Vote Compass. As an example, the gloss for the issue *"asset sales"* included text such as, *"Asset sales. New South Wales should lease its electricity transmission network to the private sector. To cover infrastructure costs the government should privatise public assets rather than raise taxes."*[11] Glosses from different sources were then merged to form a single gloss for each issue.

To avoid spurious associations between articles and issues, we processed the glosses to ensure that they represented the core elements of an issue. This was done by removing words from one of three categories of words lists: i) stopwords, ii) words belonging to multiple issues, and iii) words refering to elections in general.

For (ii), we removed words occurring in more than one gloss. For example, *"taxes"* in the gloss for "asset sales" also occurs in the gloss for "taxation" and is thus not deemed to be indicative of any one particular issue.

For (iii), we determined words to do with the general topic of elections in Australia by mining specific Wikipedia pages. Words were obtained from the first paragraph of the "NSW 2015 election" Wikipedia page, and from the first two sections ("Federal Parliament" and "Voting") of the Wikipedia page on "Elections in Australia". The intuition is that by removing words about elections in general, the inferred link between an article and an issue will be more acccurate.

We use the remaining words in the glosses to produce the vector space representations of each election issue. We normalised words to be in lowercase, and all non-alphabetic characters, aside from whitespace, were removed. The vector was weighted using term frequency.

Each of these news articles was then compared to each ground truth issue based on a comparison between a vector for the news article and a vector for the election issue. For this, words in the article's title were processed in a similar manner to the glosses. We then counted the number of articles associated with each issue and then ranked issues by this count. Table 2 shows the resulting ranked issues. We note that not all ground truth

[11]Text from http://www.abc.net.au/votecompass/

election issues are represented in our data set.

6 From Social Data to Election Insights

6.1 Comparing rankings of election issues

We compare the common elements of the ranked list in Table 2 with that of Table 1 using Kendall tau Rank Correlation (Kendall, 1938).[12] We find a tau value of 0.55 (2-sided $p = 0.047$), which is statistically significant at $\alpha = 0.05$. For this test, we omitted the items at rank 14 as these were found only once in the data and may be spurious matches. Including them would inflate tau and make the result significant at $\alpha = 0.01$.

We find this moderate correlation encouraging. However, we note that the simplicity of our method for labelling election issues may be one reason that we do not find a stronger correlation. In future work, we will explore whether supervised machine learning methods for assigning labels can help improve our correlation.

6.2 Ranking stabilisation across time

A key feature of our data set is that it is time-series data and, in some future application, one could conceivably show rankings of issues before any official commentary emerges. For such a system, we would assume that it has a generic election issue detector (perhaps based on a text classification method such as labelled LDA methods (Ramage et al., 2010)). To explore this further, we repeat the study in Section 6.1 so that the end date is set at weekly intervals starting in January 2015, using our ground truth election issues.

Figure 1 shows the probability of the null hypothesis; that there is no correlation when comparing the ground truth Vote Compass ranking to the data-derived rankings each interval (Kendall's tau$=0$). For each probability, the tau value is shown in the upper curve. We see that the p-value drops below $\alpha = 0.05$ around Feb. 23rd. This accords with our intuition: there is more uncertainty about the election issues early in the election period, and so the data-driven rankings fluctuate more. We note that our gold standard article with the ranked issues was published on Mar. 5th.

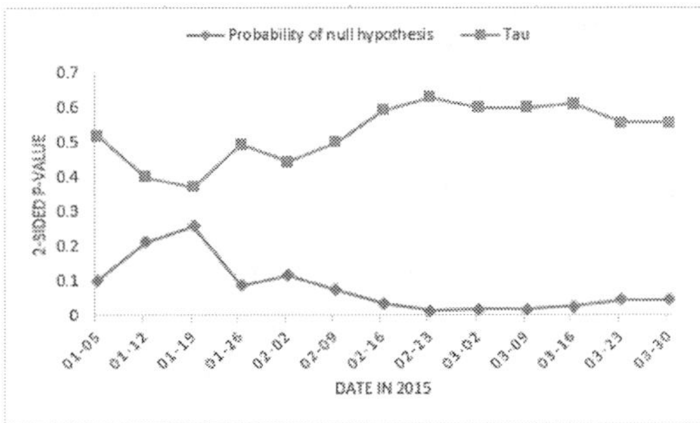

Figure 1: Kendall's tau (and the associated 2-sided p-value for significance testing) for ranked issues at weekly intervals.

7 Discussion

With statistically significant correlation between the rankings, we conclude that Twitter shared news content about an election can provide insights on the importance of election issues. As an added advantage, our approach can also rank issues that were not mentioned by Vote Compass but which were described in our other sources.[13] These issues concern politics and government, whereas the Vote Compass issues are societal.

We note that the analysis described here is susceptible to campaigning and lobbying activity. We are unable to tell from this analysis whether the prevalence of an issue is due to intensive lobbying or a reflection of widespread concern.

8 Conclusion

In this work, we presented an analysis which provided a ranking of election issues based on shared news articles found in Twitter content about the 2015 NSW state election. With respect to the issues that found a voice on Twitter, we observed a moderate correlation with official commentaries. Furthermore, utilising the time-series nature of our data set, we show when the ranking of the election issues seems to stabilise during the election period, suggesting the potential for this analysis to provide some monitoring functionality.

Acknowledgments

We thank Brendan Somes and Kathryn Barwick, who curated queries and oversaw the data collection process at the State Library of NSW; Brian Jin and James McHugh from the CSIRO for their software engineering expertise; and the anonymous reviewers for their insights on improving the readability of this paper.

[12]Kendall's tau was calculated with the online tool: http://www.wessa.net/rwasp_kendall.wasp (Wessa, 2012)

[13]These issues were Leadership, Prime Minister, Swing back, and Balance of Power issues.

References

Khurshid Ahmad, Nicholas Daly, and Vanessa Liston. 2011. What is new? news media, general elections, sentiment, and named entities. In *Proceedings of the Workshop on Sentiment Analysis where AI meets Psychology (SAAIP 2011)*, pages 80–88, Chiang Mai, Thailand, November. Asian Federation of Natural Language Processing.

Kathryn Barwick, Mylee Joseph, Cécile Paris, and Stephen Wan. 2014. Hunters and collectors: seeking social media content for cultural heritage collections. In *VALA 2014: Streaming With Possibilities*.

Thierry Declerck. 2013. Integration of the thesaurus for the social sciences (thesoz) in an information extraction system. In *Proceedings of the 7th Workshop on Language Technology for Cultural Heritage, Social Sciences, and Humanities*, pages 90–95, Sofia, Bulgaria, August. Association for Computational Linguistics.

Daniel Gayo-Avello, Panagiotis Takis Metaxas, and Eni Mustafaraj. 2011. Limits of electoral predictions using twitter. In Lada A. Adamic, Ricardo A. Baeza-Yates, and Scott Counts, editors, *ICWSM*. The AAAI Press.

Maurice Kendall. 1938. A new measure of rank correlation. *Biometrika*.

Fei Liu, Yang Liu, and Fuliang Weng. 2011. Why is "sxsw" trending? exploring multiple text sources for twitter topic summarization. In *Proceedings of the Workshop on Language in Social Media (LSM 2011)*, pages 66–75, Portland, Oregon, June. Association for Computational Linguistics.

Jeffrey Nichols, Jalal Mahmud, and Clemens Drews. 2012. Summarizing sporting events using twitter. In *Proceedings of the 2012 ACM International Conference on Intelligent User Interfaces*, IUI '12, pages 189–198, New York, NY, USA. ACM.

Brendan O'Connor, Ramnath Balasubramanyan, Bryan R. Routledge, and Noah A. Smith. 2010. From tweets to polls: Linking text sentiment to public opinion time series. In William W. Cohen and Samuel Gosling, editors, *ICWSM*. The AAAI Press.

Daniel Ramage, Susan Dumais, and Dan Liebling. 2010. Characterizing microblogs with topic models. In *ICWSM*.

G. Salton and M. J. McGill. 1983. *Introduction to modern information retrieval*. McGraw-Hill, New York.

Arno Scharl and Albert Weichselbraun. 2006. Web coverage of the 2004 us presidential election. In *Proceedings of the 2Nd International Workshop on Web As Corpus*, WAC '06, pages 35–42, Stroudsburg, PA, USA. Association for Computational Linguistics.

A. Tumasjan, T.O. Sprenger, P.G. Sandner, and I.M. Welpe. 2010. Predicting elections with twitter: What 140 characters reveal about political sentiment. In *Proceedings of the Fourth International AAAI Conference on Weblogs and Social Media*, pages 178–185.

Guido van Oorschot, Marieke van Erp, and Chris Dijkshoorn. 2012. Automatic extraction of soccer game events from twitter. In Marieke van Erp, Laura Hollink, Willem Robert van Hage, Raphal Troncy, and David A. Shamma, editors, *Proceedings of the Workhop on Detection, Representation, and Exploitation of Events in the Semantic Web (DeRiVE 2012)*, volume 902, pages 21–30, Boston, USA, 11. CEUR.

Stephen Wan and Cécile Paris. 2014. Improving government services with social media feedback. In *IUI'14 19th International Conference on Intelligent User Interfaces, IUI'14, Haifa, Israel, February 24-27, 2014*, pages 27–36.

Wessa. 2012. Kendall tau rank correlation (v1.0.11) in free statistics software (v1.1.23-r7).

Word Embeddings Pointing the Way for Late Antiquity

Johannes Bjerva
University of Groningen
The Netherlands
j.bjerva@rug.nl

Raf Praet
University of Groningen
The Netherlands
r.g.l.praet@rug.nl

Abstract

Continuous space representations of words are currently at the core of many state-of-the-art approaches to problems in natural language processing. In spite of several advantages of using such methods, they have seen little usage within digital humanities. In this paper, we show a case study of how such models can be used to find interesting relationships within the field of late antiquity. We use a word2vec model trained on over one billion words of Latin to investigate the relationships between persons and concepts of interest from works of the 6th-century scholar Cassiodorus. The results show that the method has high potential to aid the humanities scholar, but that caution must be taken as the analysis requires the assessment by the traditional historian.

1 Introduction

Continuous space representations of words are currently the backbone of several state-of-the-art approaches to problems in natural language processing. The distributional hypothesis, summarised as: 'You shall know a word by the company it keeps' (Firth, 1957) is the basis of many approaches for obtaining such representations. Word embeddings are an example of such a model (e.g. Collobert and Weston (2008)), and have been found to encapsulate interesting semantic properties; in a model presented by Mikolov et al. (2013b), the result when calculating $\overrightarrow{\text{KING}} - \overrightarrow{\text{MAN}} + \overrightarrow{\text{WOMAN}}$, is close to $\overrightarrow{\text{QUEEN}}$.

In this work in progress within the Cassiodigitalis project, we investigate how such representations can be adapted to aid humanities researchers, using the case of late antiquity as an example. Using such a model has several advantages, such as speed and cost-effectiveness. An automated method such as presented here can save time by, e.g., finding potentially interesting interrelations between historical figures and concepts, or quantitatively corroborate results of an otherwise qualitative study. It is, of course, not expected that this can replace the manual perusal of a historian. The goal is, indeed, to use these models to point the way for late antiquity. We expect that the method outlined in this paper can also be used for other disciplines within the humanities.

The digital approach is easily applicable to historical research of periods which are highly documented, i.e., from the beginning of printing up to today. Yet in this paper we want to ascertain whether a digital approach could be relevant to periods which are less documented. As for classical studies, the field of late antique studies is relatively recent, following the seminal work of Brown (1971). This crucial period of transition from antiquity to the middle ages could prove a fertile ground for a digital approach; the late antique world abounds in dense networks of scholars and politicians who publish their letters in order to further their ambitions. We chose to focus on the person of Cassiodorus for several reasons; this 6th-century scholar was a pivotal figure in the transition of classical literature and knowledge through his Vivarium monastery (O'Donnell, 1979). Yet many aspects of his biography remain enigmatic. A digital analysis of his vast oeuvre could show us new ways to answer questions as why Cassiodorus abandoned his political ambitions to found his monastery.

In this paper, we demonstrate how word embeddings can be used to aid humanities scholars by showing that relations between concepts and historical characters can be found and corroborated. The embeddings used in this paper are released along with scripts to reproduce our plots.[1]

[1] github.com/bjerva/cassiodigitalis

Proceedings of the 9th SIGHUM Workshop on Language Technology for Cultural Heritage, Social Sciences, and Humanities, pages 53–57,
Beijing, China, July 30, 2015.

The rest of the paper is organised as follows. Related work is briefly covered in Section 2. The methodology is detailed in Section 3. Section 4 contains the experiment overview and results. We discuss the results in Section 5 and conclude in Section 6.

2 Related Work

Word embeddings have seen much recent use within computational linguistics, however usage within digital humanities appears to be limited. Recent work by Koopman et al. (2015) employs vector representations to calculate similarities between entities such as authors and journals in an article database. Usage of word embeddings in the humanities is further discussed by Tahmasebi et al. (2015), who suggest that they could be useful for comparing word vectors trained on different epochs of time, thus revealing changes in usage of words across time. The usage of digital methods within the late antiquities in particular largely focusses on approaches such as the use of geopositioning data to aid classicists and archaeologists, or linking data from, e.g., funerary monuments in order to facilitate research (cf. Bodard and Mahony (2012)). This field should therefore provide fertile grounds for this relatively new approach. Our contribution to previous work thus constitutes a first study showing concrete usages of word embeddings for the late antiquities in particular, and digital humanities in general.

3 Method

The core of the method used in this paper is based on the freely available *word2vec* tool, which can be used to quickly create high quality word embeddings based on a large corpus of text (Mikolov et al., 2013a).[2] We train word2vec using parameters similar to those used for the best performing English vectors in Baroni et al. (2014). We use the continuous bag-of-words model, a window size of 5, a vector dimensionality of 400, 10 negative samples and set subsampling to $1e^{-5}$. We further allow the model to train on the corpus over the course of 100 epochs.

3.1 Data

3.1.1 Large Corpus of Latin

Our word2vec model is trained on a large corpus of Latin texts, containing about 1.38 billion tokens, collected from 11,261 texts spanning two millennia of use of Latin (Bamman and Crane, 2011; Bamman and Smith, 2012). This corpus is freely available.[3] The texts have been manually confirmed as containing Latin text. Seeing as the texts have been OCR-scanned, the quality varies widely. Prior to training the word2vec model, we pre-process the corpus in order to reduce noise. We convert all text to lower case, remove all punctuation and non-alphanumeric characters.

3.1.2 Cassiodorus' Variae

Flavius Magnus Aurelius Cassiodorus Senator (c. 485 – c. 585) served under the Ostrogothic king Theodoric and his successors until the collapse of the kingdom under the Byzantine armies (535 – c. 540). After his stay (or detention) in Constantinople (c. 540 – 554), he fully concentrated on his own Christian didactical project within the confines of his Vivarium monastery in the south of Italy (O'Donnell, 1979). The main testimony to his political career were the Variae, a collection of state letters in twelve books (Fridh and Halporn, 1973; Zecchini et al., 2014). Cassiodorus wrote them on behalf of king Theodoric, his successors, or on his own account as praetorian prefect. The date of the compilation and composition of the Variae is posited between 540 and the mid-540's. In this paper, the Variae are used as a source of historical figures and concepts.

4 Mapping Person – Concept Relations

Our experiment deals with investigating relations between historical figures and central concepts in the period in question. We compile a list of six concepts with their related Latin words which were deemed relevant for the investigation in question. The selected concepts are shown in Table 1. We further compile a list of 14 persons of interest within Cassiodorus' Variae. These historical figures were selected based on their proximity to Cassiodorus and their significance in the presentation of Cassiodorus and his Ostrogothic masters in the Variae. We selected several historical characters who were Cassiodorus' peers and competitors in cultural networks (Boethius, Symmachus), political networks (Liberius) and ecclesiastical circles (Agapetus). Furthermore we added representatives of the political forces with whom the Ostrogothic kingdom in Italy in-

[2] code.google.com/p/word2vec/

[3] cs.cmu.edu/~dbamman/latin.html

teracted and competed: apart from the Ostrogothic kings themselves (Theodoric, Athalaric, Theodahad), we have their barbarian predecessors (Alaric and Odoacer), and the Roman emperors from the Byzantine east (Anastasius, Iustinianus, Theodora). This selection of persons, along with relevant details, is shown in Table 2.

Table 1: Relevant concepts used in the study, with related Latin words.

Concept	Words		
Modernity	Modernus	Novus	Novitas
Romanness	Romuleus	Quirites	Latialis
Greekness	Graecus	Graeculus	Atticus
Gothness	Gothus	Hamalus	Gothicus
Antiquity	Vetus	Antiquitas	Senex
Liberty	Libertas	Libertatus	Liber

Table 2: Persons of interest used in the study, along with personal details.

Name	Status	Lifetime
Cassiodorus	scholar, Ostrogothic official	c. 485 – c. 585
Theoderic	Ostrogothic king of Italy	454 – 526
Alaricus	Visigothic king	c. 370 – 410
Odovacer	barbarian general, king of Italy	433 – 494
Athalaricus	Ostrogothic king of Italy	516 – 534
Theodahadus	Ostrogothic king of Italy	c. 480 – 536
Anastasius	Byzantine emperor	c. 431 – 518
Iustinianus	Byzantine emperor	c. 482 – 565
Theodora	Byzantine empress	c. 500 – 548
Boethius	scholar, Ostrogothic official	c. 480 – 524
Symmachus	mecenas, Ostrogothic official	? – 526
Liberius	Ostrogothic/Roman official	c. 465 – c. 554
Agapetus	pope	? – 536

We calculate the relatedness between each person and concept as follows. For each concept, x, we amass a set of vectors $\mathbb{X}$ based on the related Latin words. For each person, y, we use the vector representation in our model based on the nominative form of the person's name. We then find the smallest cosine distance between each vector representation of a concept, $\vec{x_i} \in \mathbb{X}$, and each person's vector representation, $\vec{y}$. We take this distance to be a measure of the relationship between a person of interest and the concept in question.

Before visualizing the results, we split the persons of interest into two groups. Group 1 consists of the leading figures of the 6th-century political patchwork. Group 2 consists of Cassiodorus' colleagues and competitors. Heat maps of the relationships between each person and concept are shown in Figure 1 and Figure 2. Blue is used to indicate an absent or relatively small relationship, while red is used to indicate a relatively strong relationship.

5 Discussion

5.1 The Blurring of the Barbarian-Roman Boundary

Whereas the Visigoth king Alaric and the barbarian general Odoacer are intensively associated with words which denote the Goths, this association fades away with the rulers of the Ostrogoth kingdom in Italy: Theodoric and his successors Athalaric and Theodahad (see Figure 1). This could reflect the success of Theodoric's cultural and political profiling as being the true heir to the Roman legacy in Italy (Jones, 1962; Heather, 1992). This diminishing association with the Goths does not, however, correlate with an increasing association with the Romans; Theodoric and Theodahad's association with "Romanness" are rather meagre in comparison with Odoacer. This could be explained by Odoacer's exemplary role as the general who officially put an end to the Western Roman empire by deposing its last emperor, Romulus Augustulus (ca. 464 – ca. 507). This negative association with the legacy of Rome apparently endured in the reception of this historical character.

5.2 The Roman Empire is Dead, Long Live the Byzantine Empire!

The transition of the Roman empire into a medieval Byzantine empire was a gradual and evasive process, which cannot be exactly pinpointed in time. However, the rule of the emperor Justinian has been considered to be pivotal in this gradual process (Maas, 2005). The digital approach seems to corroborate Justinian's role; whereas there still is a high association between "Romanness" and Anastasius, the emperor of the Eastern Roman empire before Justinian's dynasty, this association dramatically diminishes in the case of Justinian (see Figure 1). This would mean that in the Latin sources, or, from a western perspective, Justinian is considered emperor of the Greeks instead of Roman emperor. However, caution has to be exhibited when comparing Justinian to Anastasius, as there are several historical characters extant with the name Anastasius and the word representations used only consider the surface forms of the names in question.

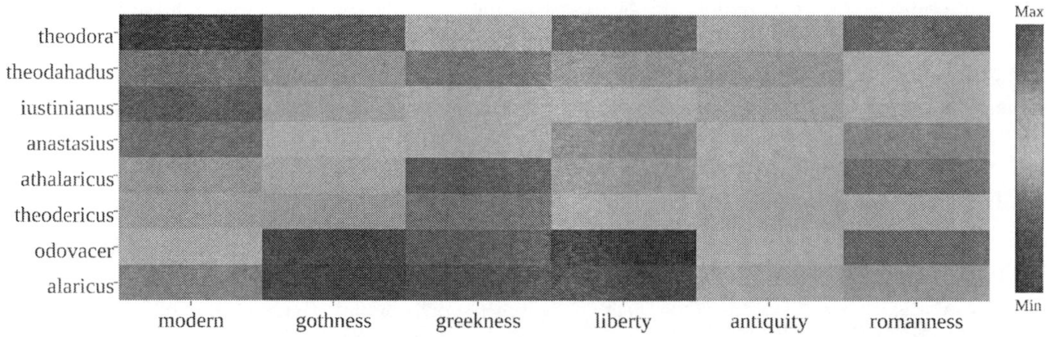

Figure 1: Heatmap showing relationships between persons and concepts in group 1.

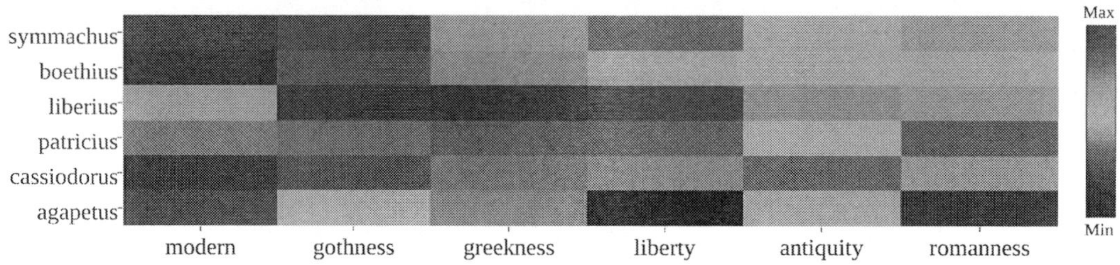

Figure 2: Heatmap showing relationships between persons and concepts in group 2.

5.3 Different Intellectual Profiles

When we compare the results of the contemporaries Cassiodorus, Liberius, Symmachus and Boethius, we can see some differences. Symmachus and Boethius have a distinct association with the Greek cultural sphere, whereas Cassiodorus and Liberius lack this link (see Figure 2). In this case the results shed a light on the social networks and cultural aspirations of both pairs. Symmachus and his son-in-law Boethius had, as members of the senatorial aristocracy, close ties with their counterpart in the Greek Eastern Roman empire, as they still cherished the cultural ideal of a bilingual Roman legacy. Boethius translated Greek philosophical treatises, and Symmachus was involved in the bilingual project of the grammarian Priscian of Caesarea (around 500) (Marenbon, 2003). Liberius and Cassiodorus foreshadow the gradual disintegration of the links between the east and the west. Liberius' long political career was mainly based in Gaul and Italy (O'Donnell, 1981), whereas Cassiodorus was active in the administration of the Ostrogothic realm in Italy. Cassiodorus' association with antiquity points to his success as central figure in the transmission of ancient works of literature and science through his Vivarium monastery (see Figure 2). Furthermore, this association can be traced to the meticulous self-presentation in his letter collection Variae as an ardent intellectual. The high association between Liberius and the concept of liberty should be disregarded because of linguistic reasons; naturally there is a high association between the concept of liberty and a name which can also be a form of the adjective liber, 'free'.

6 Conclusion

In this paper, we have shown an example of how word embeddings can be used to point the way for late antiquity, and in extension, humanities. Such a digital method has high potential to aid the humanities scholar in assessing different historiographical questions. Not only do the results corroborate or nuance the findings of qualitative research. Surprising results also generate new historiographical questions. Nevertheless, the example of Liberius and liberty urges to exhibit caution; the digital approach cannot be used without the guiding assessment of the traditional historian.

Acknowledgements

The authors would like to thank the anonymous reviewers for their helpful suggestions, and Vivian Bouwer for her input on earlier versions of this manuscript.

References

Bamman, D. and Crane, G. (2011). Measuring historical word sense variation. In *Proceedings of the 11th annual international ACM/IEEE joint conference on Digital libraries*, pages 1–10. ACM.

Bamman, D. and Smith, D. (2012). Extracting two thousand years of latin from a million book library. *Journal on Computing and Cultural Heritage (JOCCH)*, 5(1):2.

Baroni, M., Dinu, G., and Kruszewski, G. (2014). Don't count, predict! A systematic comparison of context-counting vs. context-predicting semantic vectors. In *Proceedings of the 52nd Annual Meeting of the Association for Computational Linguistics*, volume 1.

Bodard, G. and Mahony, M. S. (2012). *Digital research in the study of classical antiquity*. Ashgate Publishing, Ltd.

Brown, P. (1971). *The World of Late Antiquity: from Marcus Aurelius to Muhammad*. London.

Collobert, R. and Weston, J. (2008). A unified architecture for natural language processing: Deep neural networks with multitask learning. In *Proceedings of the 25th international conference on Machine learning*, pages 160–167. ACM.

Firth, J. R. (1957). A synopsis of linguistic theory. pages 1930–1955. 1952–1959:1–32.

Fridh, A. and Halporn, J. (1973). Magni aurelii cassiodori senatoris opera pars i: Variarum libri xii. *Corpus Christianorum, Series Latina, 96*.

Heather, P. J. (1992). The historical culture of Ostrogothic Italy. In *Teoderico il Grande e i Goti d'Italia*. Atti del XIII Congresso internazionale di studi sull'Alto Medioevo.

Jones, A. H. M. (1962). The constitutional position of Odoacer and Theoderic. *Journal of Roman Studies*, 52(1-2):126–130.

Koopman, R., Wang, S., Scharnhorst, A., and Englebienne, G. (2015). Ariadne's thread: Interactive navigation in a world of networked information. In *Proceedings of the 33rd Annual ACM Conference Extended Abstracts on Human Factors in Computing Systems*, pages 1833–1838. ACM.

Maas, M. (2005). Roman Questions, Byzantine Answers. *The Cambridge Companion to the Age of Justinian (Cambridge: Cambridge University Press)*, pages 3–27.

Marenbon, J. (2003). *Boethius*. Oxford University Press.

Mikolov, T., Chen, K., Corrado, G., and Dean, J. (2013a). Efficient estimation of word representations in vector space. *arXiv preprint arXiv:1301.3781*.

Mikolov, T., Yih, W.-t., and Zweig, G. (2013b). Linguistic regularities in continuous space word representations. In *Proceedings of NAACL-HLT*, pages 746–751.

O'Donnell, J. J. (1979). *Cassiodorus*. Los Angeles: University of California Press.

O'Donnell, J. J. (1981). Liberius the Patrician. *Traditio*, pages 31–72.

Tahmasebi, N., Borin, L., Capannini, G., Dubhashi, D., Exner, P., Forsberg, M., Gossen, G., Johansson, F. D., Johansson, R., Kågebäck, M., et al. (2015). Visions and open challenges for a knowledge-based culturomics. *International Journal on Digital Libraries*, 15(2-4):169–187.

Zecchini, G., Giardina, A., Cecconi, G., Tantillo, I., Oppedisano, F., Marcone, A., Lo Cascio, E., LA Rocca, A., La Rocca, C., Neri, V., et al. (2014). *Cassiodoro Varie. Volume 2: Libri III, IV, V*. Erma di Bretschneider.

Enriching Interlinear Text using Automatically Constructed Annotators

Ryan Georgi
University of Washington
Seattle, WA 98195, USA
rgeorgi@uw.edu

Fei Xia
University of Washington
Seattle, WA 98195, USA
fxia@uw.edu

William D. Lewis
Microsoft Research
Redmond, WA 98052, USA
wilewis@microsoft.com

Abstract

In this paper, we will demonstrate a system that shows great promise for creating Part-of-Speech taggers for languages with little to no curated resources available, and which needs no expert involvement. Interlinear Glossed Text (IGT) is a resource which is available for over 1,000 languages as part of the Online Database of INterlinear text (ODIN) (Lewis and Xia, 2010). Using nothing more than IGT from this database and a classification-based projection approach tailored for IGT, we will show that it is feasible to train reasonably performing annotators of interlinear text using projected annotations for potentially hundreds of world's languages. Doing so can facilitate automatic enrichment of interlinear resources to aid the field of linguistics.

1 Introduction

In this paper we discuss the process by which a highly multilingual linguistic resource (greater than 1,200 languages) can be built and then subsequently automatically enriched. Although we touch upon tools for building and maintaining such a resource, our focus in this paper is not so much on the process by which we curate the data, but the process by which automatically enrich the data with additional layers of linguistic analysis. Crucially, we show that the linguistic knowledge encapsulated in all of the data, irrespective of the language, can improve the accuracy of NLP tools that are developed for any specific language. This is particularly true for languages that are otherwise highly under-resourced, and where the development of automated NLP tools, such as taggers, are either not possible or very expensive to develop using traditional methods.

We will focus on the development of Part-of-Speech (POS) taggers. POS tagging is generally thought of as a solved task for many languages, with per-token accuracies reaching 97% (Brants, 2000; Toutanova et al., 2003). While these high accuracies can certainly be achieved for languages with substantial annotated resources, many low-resource languages have little to no annotated data available, making such traditional supervised approaches impossible. Given the cost in developing such resources, many languages with insufficient economic or strategic interest may never see dedicated tools. If annotated resources are not available, what methods can be used?

Several approaches have been proposed to solve the problems posed by the shortage of labeled training data. The first are purely unsupervised techniques. POS induction techniques, such as class-based n-grams (Brown et al., 1992) or feature-based HMM (Berg-Kirkpatrick et al., 2010) induce parts-of-speech without the need for labeled data by finding the ways in which words appear to pattern similarly in clusters. However, as Christodoulopoulos et al. (2010) noted, the way to map the induced clusters to meaningful tags is not straightforward.

Other work has looked at solving the issue of a lack of data by using two or more closely related languages where one of the languages is resource-rich. Hana et al. (2004) used Czech resources to tag Russian. This, however, requires the languages to be closely related, and not all resource-poor languages have closely-related resource-rich languages.

Another path of inquiry has been to use one unrelated resource-rich language and alignment tech-

Proceedings of the 9th SIGHUM Workshop on Language Technology for Cultural Heritage, Social Sciences, and Humanities, pages 58–67,
Beijing, China, July 30, 2015.

```
LANG   nnisaau daxalna makaatibahunna
GLOSS  the-women(3.PL.F.)-NOM entered-3.PL.F office(PL.)-ACC-their(F.)
TRANS  "The women have entered their offices."
```

Figure 1: An example of Interlinear Glossed Text (IGT) in Arabic from (Nasu, 2001), with an English translation.

niques to "project" information from the resource-rich language to the resource-poor one. Yarowsky and Ngai (2001); Das and Petrov (2011) both investigated training POS taggers by projecting labels from one language to another, while Hwa et al. (2004) looked at projecting dependency parsers.

In this paper, we focus on using a resource known as Interlinear Glossed Text (IGT) as a possible source of linguistic knowledge for the POS tagging task on resource-poor languages, and apply it to the enrichment of a linguistic resource composed of IGT data. An example of IGT is shown in Fig. 1. IGT is a format used by linguists for giving examples of linguistic phenomena, and since linguists study a large number of languages, IGT instances can be found for hundreds of languages. We will explain the precise structure of the data in depth later, but IGT as a resource is appealing not only for its broad coverage, but also the linguistic knowledge it contains. Although it does not typically contain POS tags explicitly, these examples often contain enough data to make inferences which can be used to enrich the data, whether with POS tags or with other syntactic information (Lewis and Xia, 2010).

We present a system which takes advantage of the structure of IGT instances in order to perform automatic part-of-speech tagging of the target language, regardless of the language. While the tagging performance is not necessarily competitive with state-of-the-art supervised systems, it shows great promise for languages with which such supervised systems are not currently possible, and can increase the value of the entire resource to the linguistic and computational linguistic communities.

POS taggers are intrinsically valuable to computational linguists, since they are building blocks for a number of other NLP tools. Theoretical and descriptive linguists might question their value to them; however, they only represent a class of possible annotators. The projection methodology, especially the fact that projection accuracy is boosted by relying on an entire corpus, can be applied to other forms of annotation, such as tags or analyses that may be of benefit for subsequent analyses. Although such taggers will not be as accurate as human annotators, they could reduce workload by doing first pass analyses automatically.

2 The IGT Data Type

As shown in Fig. 1, IGT instances typically contain one line in the target language, then a word-for-word gloss in the language of the paper from which the example is drawn (typically English) and finally a translation. The gloss line is of particular interest for our purposes because of tokens such as the `(3.PL.F)-NOM` often found in IGT, as shown in Fig. 1. This token is intended to signify that the Arabic token `nnisaau` is third person, plural, feminine, and in the nominative case. Each portion of the token, `3`, `PL`, `F`, and `NOM` are grammatical annotations, or **grams** for short[1]. While these grams by themselves do not guarantee that the token is necessarily a noun, they are a strong indicator. We will show how this information may be used in Section 4.

Also of note is that while the gloss line aligns one-to-one with the language line, with three words mapping to three gloss tokens, the translation line has six words. Aligning these tokens is made easy by the words in the gloss line matching words in the translation line. This allows for projection to be performed more precisely than might otherwise be possible using statistical alignment methods.

Previous work on projecting syntactic information between languages differs from our approach in two significant ways. First, projection in previous work has relied on bitexts, which do not benefit from the additional information the gloss line of IGT provides. Therefore, these past methods have relied upon statistical alignment between languages. Obtaining alignments of sufficient quality would likely not be possible for resource-poor languages, since statistical alignment methods require large amounts of parallel text. Using IGT, however, alignment can be obtained more precisely with smaller amounts of data.

[1]While the "gram" moniker is typically used to refer to grammatical function tags specifically, we will use it in this paper to refer generally to all segments of the gloss line that are not whitespace delineated.

Second, while many-to-one are a source of problems for past approaches, IGT offers a possible solution for disambiguating tag-word alignments by examining the grams directly. For instance, the gloss token `boys.ran.3.PRES` may align to both NOUN and VERB tags, but the `3` and `PRES` grams provide evidence that the token is most likely a verb showing agreement. In this paper, we will explore how both of these solutions may help us over traditional approaches to projection.

2.1 Previous Uses of IGT

A number of studies have shown the linguistic knowledge contained in IGT data to be useful. The Online Database of INterlinear text (ODIN) (Lewis and Xia, 2010) contains over 190,000 IGT instances for over 1,000 languages. While still short of the approximately 6,900 languages that exist in the world (Lewis, 2009), this covers an enormous range of languages for which few other resources exist. Using ODIN as a resource, Lewis and Xia (2008) demonstrated via projection using IGT alignments that basic word order of a language could be determined with 99% accuracy if the language contained at least 40 instances of IGT. Georgi et al. (2014) used IGT instances to produce sets of dependency trees which were then corrected and used to learn automatic correction rules.

2.2 INTENT: a Package for Creating Enriched IGT

In the previous sections, we described the forms of useful information that IGT contains. The next step is to programmatically harness that information in order to construct automatic annotators. This is what our system, the INterlinear Text ENrichment Toolkit (INTENT), was designed for. INTENT takes IGT instances as input and produce automatically enriched IGT instances as output. A more in-depth discussion of the system can be found in Xia et al. (2015).

Word alignment is the first crucial phase of INTENT's enrichment strategy. Due to IGT's structure providing a one-to-one gloss and language word alignment, and a gloss line containing many English-language words that co-occur in the translation line, the gloss line can be used as a pivot to align the English language with the target language. INTENT does this either by matching the words from the gloss and translation lines, on a string and morphological heuristics, or by using GIZA++ as a statistical alignment approach.

INTENT's second primary purpose in this paper is to provide part-of-speech tags, which are produced in one of two ways. Either INTENT uses one of the word alignment methods to project the English POS tags onto the gloss, and subsequently the target language word, or it takes advantage of the extra grammatical markers such as *-Nom* (nominative case) or *-Dec* (declarative marker) as features for a classifier to recognize the part-of-speech tag that a gloss word is most likely to be annotating in the target language, without ever needing to look at the target language directly. This means that INTENT can theoretically provide tags for any language for which interlinear text is available.

2.3 Use of INTENT for Linguists

In the Spring of 2015 at the University of Washington, our colleague Prof. Emily Bender used the INTENT system as part of a course, Computational Methods in Language Documentation[2]. The INTENT system was used to enrich IGT instances from the Language CoLLAGE project (Bender, 2014). The students then worked on methods by which typological phenomenon might be determined from the automatically enriched data, following Bender et al. (2013, 2014). This type of inquiry shows the large-scale enrichment of a wide variety of languages that INTENT is intended for, and how this can be used to answer interesting linguistic questions.

Other such uses might be enriching collected IGT instances automatically, to create an annotated corpus from IGT data while being able to greatly reduce the amount of human annotators needed for the task.

For these goals to be effective, INTENT must be able to generate sufficiently reliable POS tags on resource-poor languages. Whether or not that is the case is the question we seek to answer in this paper.

3 Projecting Annotation in IGT

Projection-based approaches work by finding an alignment between two lines, where one has annotation and one does not, and "projecting" the annotations from one to the other. Figure 2 shows

[2]Course website available at: `http://faculty.washington.edu/ebender/2015_575/`

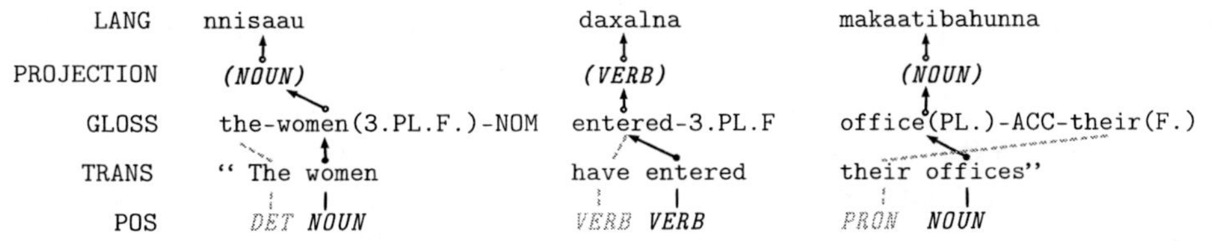

Figure 2: An illustration of how the gloss line from the IGT in Fig. 1 can be used for projection.

an illustration of how this projection occurs, using the sentence from Fig. 1.

Left unspecified is how the alignments between sentences are obtained. Previous papers generated alignments using statistical alignment. For instance, Yarowsky and Ngai (2001) showed 76% POS tag accuracy for projecting directly between English and French, using GIZA++ to automatically align the words and evaluating with a reduced tagset similar to the one used in this paper. Such an approach, however, required a set of parallel data consisting of roughly 2 million words per language, something which would not be available for resource-poor languages.

3.1 Using IGT to Bootstrap Alignment

While ODIN contains many IGT instances, it has nowhere approaching the 2 million sentences used in previous projection approaches, such as Yarowsky and Ngai (2001). Thankfully, IGT contains more information than simply the source and target language data—IGT also has gloss lines. The gloss line is a transliteration of the language line, containing many of the same words that are used in the translation, although in a different order. We can use the gloss line as a "pivot" to bootstrap our alignment, as shown in Fig. 2, and following Lewis and Xia (2008, 2010).

There are five steps to our process of projecting POS tags using the gloss line of IGT:

1. POS tag the translation line
2. Align the translation line with the gloss line
3. Disambiguate multiply-aligned gloss tokens
4. Attempt to resolve unaligned tokens in the gloss line
5. Project POS tags from gloss line to language line

1 – First, an English-language POS tagger is used to provide the POS tag sequence for the translation line. For our tests, we used the Stanford Tagger (Toutanova et al., 2003) trained on all sections of English Penn Treebank (Marcus et al., 1993) with the POS tags remapped from 45 down to the 12 tags in the universal tagset proposed by Petrov et al. (2011).

2 – Next, the words in the translation line and gloss line are aligned; this can be done by one of two ways: heuristically, or using statistical alignment. In the heuristic approach, words are aligned by exact string matches; then stemmed matches, and finally a series of gram mappings, such as `I` aligning to `1SG`. For this paper, we use the heuristic approach.

3 – After step 2, multiple translation words with differing POS tags may be aligned to the same gloss tokens. In Fig. 2, the translation tokens *The women* align to a single complex token `the-women(3.PL.F.)-NOM`. In an effort to use a language-independent way of resolving multiple tags on a single token, we specify an order of precedence by which a tag is selected, prioritizing content words over function words.[3]

4 – On gloss tokens that failed to receive an alignment, we attempt to retrieve a tag for the token based on a dictionary lookup of the individual subtokens. The dictionary is built using the part-of-speech tags from the English Penn Treebank (Marcus et al., 1993), and remapped to 12 universal POS tags following (Petrov et al., 2011). If one or more portions of the token are found in the dictionary, we use the most frequent tag for each of those words to label the token. Multiple tags are resolved the same as if the tags were projected.

5 – Finally, the tags projected to the gloss line are transferred to the language line assuming a one-to-one, monotonic alignment. Since the glosses of IGT are intended to be paired word-for-word with the target language, this is a reasonable assumption. Due to noise in the IGT text files[4],

[3]This order of precedence is: `VERB` > `NOUN` > `ADV` > `ADJ` > `PRON` > `DET` > `ADP` > `CONJ` > `PRT` > `NUM` > `PUNC` > `X`.

[4]Further discussion of the noise in these files is found in Xia et al. (2014).

however, there is not always a one-to-one alignment between the language line and gloss, and in these cases, we skip processing the IGT instance. In addition to alignment failures, noise is found in the form of a bias toward English, since all projections originate in English, as well as a bias toward unusual phenomena that the author of the paper from which the instance is extracted is focusing upon. These issues are discussed further in Lewis and Xia (2008), where they are referred to as the *English bias* and *IGT bias*, respectively.

3.2 Drawbacks of Projection

While Xia and Lewis (2007) show that the heuristic alignment approach can achieve 98% precision, and the recall is between 74% and 85% with fairly clean data. However, in our data, we found that upwards of 60% of tokens were unaligned (see Section 7.1). Tokens that are unaligned are left without a tag, and thus never labeled correctly. In order to address this issue, we next take a look at how the gloss line itself can be used as a means to obtain POS tags.

4 Building a Gloss-Line Classifier

There are three main areas in which the projection method discussed above shows weaknesses: gloss tokens with multiple POS tags aligned to them, gloss tokens that fail to be aligned or found in a dictionary, and the assumption that foreign-language words will share the same POS as the English words in the translation line[5]. For instance, a gloss token `run.NOM` might be labeled as **VERB**, due to aligning with the intransitive verb form of the word in the English line. However, the gram `NOM` is a strong indicator that the word is nominalized and should be tagged as `NOUN`.

It is not the case that the tokens in question lack information on which to base a decision, but rather that such information is perhaps not well-suited for a deterministic approach. Therefore, we propose building a gloss-line classifier that uses the individual subtokens of a gloss-line word as features to make a decision for the label of the token as a whole. Figure 3 illustrates how these subtoken level features might be used in this scenario. In addition to helping resolve the possible ambiguity of multiply-aligned tokens, our approach also avoids the indirection of finding the correct alignment for a gloss token and working on the gloss token directly.

By using the very precise, albeit low recall, heuristic alignment method, we can automatically generate training instances for the gloss-line tagger. Using these automatically-annotated gloss tokens, we then train a classifier using the MALLET package (McCallum, 2002) and its Maximum Entropy implementation. We experimented with different features, but the following set resulted in the highest performance on our development set for classifying a token i:

- Grams contained in token i
- Grams contained in token $i-1$, $i+1$
- Best dictionary tags for grams

Finally, this gloss line classifier can be used on IGT instances for the target language. After the gloss-line is labeled, the tags are transferred via one-to-one alignment with the language line.

4.1 Context-Sensitive Features

One of the things worth noting about this approach is that, while the IGT instances cover multiple different languages, we can opt to use the gloss lines from all the languages in our annotated data to train the classifier (as we do in Section 6.2). Although the gloss lines may annotate different languages, the tokens in the gloss line are all English words and grammatical markers. This results in a pseudo-language of sorts where the meaning of the tokens is largely consistent between languages.

Although it is convenient to think of the gloss-line as this pseudo-language for the purposes of POS tagging it, we also keep in mind that the word order of this pseudo-language is dependent upon

[5]This is an occurrence of the *English bias* noted by Lewis and Xia (2008)

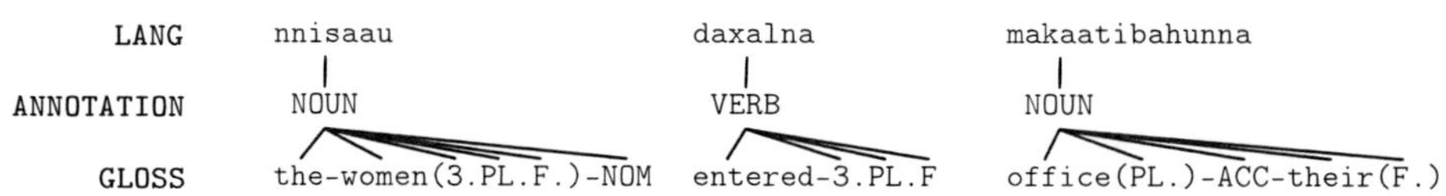

Figure 3: An IGT instance showing the classification-based approach, using the gram-level elements of the gloss line as features to choose a label for each token.

the language it is annotating, and thus context-sensitive features might not generalize well.

5 The Data

For our experiments, we used IGT instances from the Documentation of Endangered Languages (DOBES) project by Bickel et al. (2011) on the Chintang language of Nepal[6], an endangered language with intricate morphology. This corpus included not only thousands of instances, but also gold-standard POS tags for the language line. This high-quality enriched resource is one that allows us to evaluate our method on a truly low-resource language.

5.1 Splitting the Data

From the data above, we split the corpus 80-10-10 for training, development, and testing. Since this work is still in the early stages, only the results on the development set are given here. The breakdown of this data can be seen in Table 1.

5.2 Chintang Tagset

Although tags are manually provided, they are not the same tags as the universal tagset that INTENT uses, so we must map one or the other to evaluate correctly. Table 2 shows our mapping from tags used in the Chintang (CTN) tagset to those in the universal tagset.

Ideally, this mapping should be many-to-1; that is, each Chintang tag maps to a single tag in the universal tagset. However, some Chintang tags can map to multiple tags in the universal tagset.

For instance, for words with tag "*gm*" in Chintang, some are *grammatical markers* that do not have counterparts in English (e.g., a TOPIC marker) and therefore is mapped to *PRT* (for *particle*); others are listed as the English words *and*, *or*, or *but*, and should likely be labeled as conjunctions and mapped to *CONJ*. Other "*gm*" tagged words have variations of *DEM* (for *demonstrative*), and are likely pronoun-like, requiring the *PRON* tag. Table 3 shows the top 12 gloss tokens labeled "*gm*" in the data.

We experiment with two mappings: the first mapping, **Basic Mapping**, is many-to-1, and all *gm* words are mapped to *PRT*; in the second mapping, **Extended Mapping**, the *gm* tokens are split between *CONJ*, *PRT*, and *PRON*, with a simple, 14-token wordlist, consisting of the dozen tokens in Table 3, plus *or* and *DEM* and their associated tags. For the projection-only POS tagger, this extended mapping occurs as post-processing remapping step on the projected tags. For classification, the gloss words are added to the existing dictionary, creating an expanded dictionary with CTN-specific (gloss-token, tag) pairs. This dictionary is then used to provide the best-guess tag feature to the classifier at training and test time.

6 Experiments

For this work, we wanted to test three overall scenarios: using projection alone (§6.1), using the classifier trained on ODIN data (§6.2), and then using the classifier trained on Chintang data (§6.3). All three scenarios will be evaluated on the dev set of the Chintang corpus.

6.1 Projection Only

For the first scenario, since the projection method is deterministic and does not require training, only instances from the Chintang dev set are used. The

[6]http://dobes.mpi.nl/projects/chintang/

	Training Set	Dev Set
Instances	7,120	876
Tokens in lang/gloss lines	31,116	3,884
Tokens in trans lines	39,396	4,872

Table 1: Corpus statistics for Chintang IGT data (Bickel et al., 2011).

CTN Tag	Universal Tag	CTN Tag	Universal Tag
adj	ADJ	interj	PRT
adv	ADV	gm	PRT
sound	ADV	vt	VERB
n	NOUN	vi	VERB
predadj	NOUN	v	VERB
num	NUM	v2	VERB
pro	PRON	NoPOS	X

Table 2: Tagset mapping from CTN tags to Universal tagset tags.

Gloss Word	# Tokens	Tag	# Tokens
FOC	1049	CIT	360
TOP	1027	REP	243
SEQ	855	and	237
ADD	621	SURP	236
EMPH	504	SPEC.TOP	223
BUT	365	COND	207

Table 3: Top 12 gloss tokens labeled "*gm*," sorted by decreasing frequency.

projection method described in Section 3 is used, tagging the English translation line, finding alignments on the gloss line, and then using 1:1 alignment from gloss and language to assign tags to the language line. We then evaluate by comparing the projected tags with the manually assigned tags, while also keeping track of the unaligned tokens.

6.2 Classifier Trained with ODIN Data

For the first of the two classification-based settings, we follow the approach described in Section 4, by using our full set of ODIN instances to automatically label the gloss line via projection. We then again use the 1:1 alignments between gloss and language to project to the language and evaluate with those tags.

6.3 Classifier Trained with Unlabeled CTN Data

Finally, for the second classification based approach, we train the classifier with the training portion of the Chintang coprus, ignoring the gold-standard POS labels, to see what effect using instances specific to Chintang might have. In particular, since all the instances used to train the classifier were coming from the same language, we used this experimental setting to test whether adding context features to the classifier would help, in the case that there was enough single-language data.

7 Results

The results are presented in the order given in Section 6, with the projection-only approach first (§7.1), followed by the different classification approaches (§7.2).

7.1 Projection

The results of using projection alone on the Chintang dev set can be seen in Table 4, which shows the POS tagging accuracy in the first column, as well as the unaligned tokens (tokens assigned *UNALIGNED*) in the data.

With only the most basic mapping, we see that the projection-only approaches achieves a mere

Method	Accuracy	% Unaligned
Basic Mapping	12.6	83.8
Extended Mapping	39.6	57.1

Table 4: Results of projection-only approach.

```
hun-ko-i        tis-u-m              pache
DEM-NMLZ-LOC    put.into-3P-1/2nsA   SEQ
(pro)           (vt)                 (gm)
after putting dal or arum
```

Figure 4: An instance from the Chintang dev set, showing the lack of alignment between gloss line and translation line, as well as the gold standard POS tags.

12.6% accuracy, with an 83.8% of all tokens in the gloss line unaligned. Figure 4 shows a Chintang instance that illustrates part of the reason for this high amount of unaligned tokens. While many of the instances in the ODIN database frequently contain words that match (if only in their stemmed forms) between translation and gloss line, many of the instances in the Chintang corpus glossed the words only in terms of grammatical markers, such as "SEQ" or "DEM-NMLZ-LOC" as shown in this example.

The second row of Table 4 shows the result of adding Extended Mapping, which would correctly identify the gloss containing "DEM" as a *PRON* and the "SEQ" gloss as the mapped *PRT*.

7.2 Classification

Table 5 shows the results of the classification-based experiments outlined above, trained on either the ODIN instances or the Chintang (CTN) instances on their own, or combining the two. Shown for comparison also is the result of using the remapped gold standard tags from the Chintang training data to train the classifier, and evalu-

Training Data	Expanded Dictionary	Context Features	Accuracy
ODIN			43.1
	✓		53.0
CTN			75.0
	✓		74.9
		✓	74.8
	✓	✓	74.9
CTN+ODIN			61.6
	✓		70.7
	✓	✓	72.6
Supervised (with Labeled CTN)			89.6
	✓		90.6
	✓	✓	90.1

Table 5: Classification results showing different sets of training data and classifier features.

ating on the dev set.

7.2.1 ODIN-Only Training Data

As mentioned in Section 7.1, the IGT instances in the Chintang data look different from many of the instances in the ODIN data, and the accuracy results of 43.1% and 53.0% would seem to confirm the dissimilarities between the data sets. Though the expanded dictionary with CTN-specific gloss tokens seems to help somewhat, the ODIN data suffers because there are simply too many tags assigned by the classifier that do not occur in the CTN data, such as DET (for *determiner*) or ADP (for *adposition*). Even though the results are low, given that these are results for a system which has never been provided with a single instance of Chintang data, they are somewhat promising.

7.2.2 CTN Training Data

The classifier trained on CTN IGT instances fares much better, achieving 75% accuracy. It should be noted that when CTN instances were used to train the classifier, the automatically labeled training data is produced by the projection algorithm which uses the Extended Mapping described in Section 5.2, and thus the expanded dictionary is of little use above the training data that the classifier has already seen.

Finally, combining CTN training instances with ODIN IGT instances achieves only 61.6% without additional features, but when the expanded dictionary is added, as well as the CTN-specific contextual features, we see a result of 72.6%, getting closer to the result seen by the CTN data on its own.

While none of these methods come close to the 90% accuracies seen by the supervised system, our automated system shows promise given that it uses a far more impoverished set of information to train it. To compare these systems in a more real-world setting, we also looked at how the systems performed if the amount of data used to train each was scaled back from the approximately 32,000 tokens in the full training set.

7.2.3 Varying Amounts of Data

The graph in Fig. 5 shows the result of varying the amount of training data used for the different classification approaches. While all the classification-based approaches ultimately converge around 75% accuracy, we can see that when only 500 or fewer tokens are available, a setting which is much more realistic for low-resource languages, these approaches actually do not do poorly by comparison. We also see that the dictionaries help the most when the amount of training data is small.

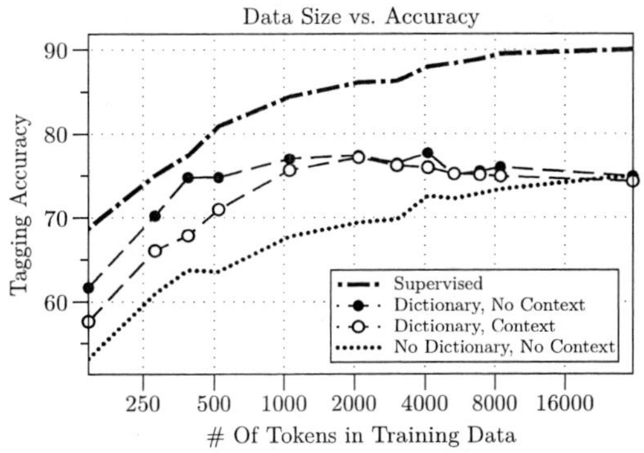

Figure 5: Graph showing how performance varies with respect to the number of training tokens available to the system.

8 Conclusion and Future Work

In this paper, we have demonstrated a proof-of-concept for a system that can potentially produce POS taggers for up to a thousand languages, many of which have little to no annotated linguistic resources available. While the performance is lower than state-of-the-art supervised systems for resource-rich languages, our approach demonstrates a method that can be applied to resource-poor languages, as shown by the Chintang results.

For subsequent work, our goal is to apply this technique to additional resource-poor languages, with different typological characteristics from Chintang, as well as take an additional step toward training monolingual parsers from the tagged language lines.

Acknowledgments

This work is supported by the National Science Foundation Grant BCS-0748919. We would also like to thank Balthasar Bickel and his team for allowing us to use the Chintang data set in our experiments, and our three anonymous reviewers for the helpful feedback.

References

Bender, E. M. (2014). Language CoLLAGE: Grammatical Description with the LinGO Grammar Matrix. In Calzolari, N., Choukri, K.,

Declerck, T., Loftsson, H., Maegaard, B., Mariani, J., Moreno, A., Odijk, J., and Piperidis, S., editors, *Proceedings of the Ninth International Conference on Language Resources and Evaluation (LREC'14)*, pages 2447–2451, Reykjavik, Iceland. European Language Resources Association (ELRA). ACL Anthology Identifier: L14-1508.

Bender, E. M., Crowgey, J., Goodman, M. W., and Xia, F. (2014). Learning Grammar Specifications from IGT: A Case Study of Chintang . In *Workshop on the Use of Computational Methods in the Study of Endangered Languages*, Baltimore, MD.

Bender, E. M., Goodman, M. W., Crowgey, J., and Xia, F. (2013). *Towards Creating Precision Grammars from Interlinear Glossed Text: Inferring Large-Scale Typological Propertie*. In *Proceedings of the ACL workshop on Language Technology for Cultural Heritage, Social Sciences and Humanities.*

Berg-Kirkpatrick, T., Bouchard-Côté, A., DeNero, J., and Klein, D. (2010). Painless unsupervised learning with features. Association for Computational Linguistics.

Bickel, B., Stoll, S., Gaenszle, M., Rai, N., Lieven, E., Banjade, G., Bhatta, T., Paudyal, N., Pettigrew, J., Rai, I., and Rai, M. (2011). *Audiovisual corpus of the Chintang language, including a longitudinal corpus of language acquisition by six children, paradigm sets, grammar sketches, ethnographic descriptions, and photographs.* DOBES Archive.

Brants, T. (2000). TnT — A Statistical Part-of-Speech Tagger. In *the sixth conference*, pages 224–231, Morristown, NJ, USA. Association for Computational Linguistics.

Brown, P. F., deSouza, P. V., Mercer, R. L., Pietra, V. J. D., and Lai, J. C. (1992). Class-based n -gram models of natural language. *Computational Linguistics*, 18(4):467–479.

Christodoulopoulos, C., Goldwater, S., and Steedman, M. (2010). Two decades of unsupervised POS induction: how far have we come? pages 575–584.

Das, D. and Petrov, S. (2011). Unsupervised part-of-speech tagging with bilingual graph-based projections. In *Proceedings of the 49th Annual Meeting of the Association for Computational Linguistics: Human Language Technologies (ACL HLT 2011)*, pages 600–609, Portland, OR, USA.

Georgi, R., Xia, F., and Lewis, W. D. (2014). Capturing divergence in dependency trees to improve syntactic projection. *Language Resources and Evaluation*, 48(4):709–739.

Hana, J., Feldman, A., and Brew, C. (2004). A Resource-Light Approach to Russian Morphology: Tagging Russian using Czech Resources. In *Proceedings of the Conference on Empirical Methods in Natural Language Processing*, pages 222–229. Rodopi Bv Editions.

Hwa, R., Resnik, P., Weinberg, A., Cabezas, C., and Kolak, O. (2004). Bootstrapping parsers via syntactic projection across parallel texts. *Natural Language Engineering*, 1(1):1–15.

Lewis, M. P., editor (2009). *Ethnologue: Languages of the World.* SIL International, Dallas, TX, USA, sixteenth edition.

Lewis, W. D. and Xia, F. (2008). Automatically identifying computationally relevant typological features. In *Proceedings of the Third International Joint Conference on Natural Language Processing*.

Lewis, W. D. and Xia, F. (2010). Developing ODIN: A Multilingual Repository of Annotated Language Data for Hundreds of the World's Languages.

Marcus, M. P., Santorini, B., and Marcinkiewicz, M. A. (1993). Building a large annotated corpus of english: The penn treebank. *COMPUTATIONAL LINGUISTICS*, 19(2):313–330.

McCallum, A. K. (2002). Mallet: A machine learning for language toolkit. http://mallet.cs.umass.edu.

Nasu, N. (2001). Towards a theory of non-cyclic A-movement. In *Essex Graduate Student Papers in Language and Linguistics*, volume 3, pages 133–160.

Petrov, S., Das, D., and McDonald, R. (2011). A universal part-of-speech tagset. *arXiv preprint arXiv:1104.2086*.

Toutanova, K., Klein, D., Manning, C. D., and Singer, Y. (2003). Feature-rich part-of-speech tagging with a cyclic dependency network. pages 173–180.

Xia, F., Goodman, M. W., Georgi, R., Slayden, G., and Lewis, W. D. (2015). Enriching, Editing, and Representing Interlinear Glossed Text. In *16th International Conference on Intelligent Text Processing and Computational Linguistics*, pages 1–16.

Xia, F., Lewis, W., Goodman, M. W., Crowgey, J., and Bender, E. M. (2014). Enriching odin. In Chair), N. C. C., Choukri, K., Declerck, T., Loftsson, H., Maegaard, B., Mariani, J., Moreno, A., Odijk, J., and Piperidis, S., editors, *Proceedings of the Ninth International Conference on Language Resources and Evaluation (LREC'14)*, Reykjavik, Iceland. European Language Resources Association (ELRA).

Xia, F. and Lewis, W. D. (2007). Multilingual Structural Projection across Interlinear Text. pages 452–459.

Yarowsky, D. and Ngai, G. (2001). Inducing multilingual POS taggers and NP bracketers via robust projection across aligned corpora. In *Second meeting of the North American Association for Computational Linguistics*, Stroudsburg, PA. Johns Hopkins University.

Automatic interlinear glossing as two-level sequence classification

Tanja Samardžić
Corpus Lab
URPP Language and Space
University of Zurich

Robert Schikowski
Department of
Comparative Linguistics
University of Zurich

Sabine Stoll
Department of
Comparative Lingistics
University of Zurich

tanja.samardzic | robert.schikowski | sabine.stoll@uzh.ch

Abstract

Interlinear glossing is a type of annotation of morphosyntactic categories and cross-linguistic lexical correspondences that allows linguists to analyse sentences in languages that they do not necessarily speak. Automatising this annotation is necessary in order to provide glossed corpora big enough to be used for quantitative studies. In this paper, we present experiments on the automatic glossing of Chintang. We decompose the task of glossing into steps suitable for statistical processing. We first perform grammatical glossing as standard supervised part-of-speech tagging. We then add lexical glosses from a stand-off dictionary applying context disambiguation in a similar way to word lemmatisation. We obtain the highest accuracy score of 96% for grammatical and 94% for lexical glossing.

1 Introduction

The annotation type known as interlinear glossing allows linguists to describe the morphosyntactic makeup of words concisely and language-independently. While glosses as a linguistic metalanguage have a long tradition, systematic standards for interlinear glossing have only developed relatively recently – cf. e.g. the Leipzig glossing rules.[1]

An example for an interlinear gloss is shown in (1), which is an Ewe serial verb construction taken from (Collins, 1997) with glosses in boldface. The combination of segmentation with English metalanguage labels for both lexical and grammatical segments allows linguists to observe how exactly the Ewe serial verb construction differs from the corresponding English construction.

(1) *Kofi tso ati-ɛ fo Yao (yi).*
Kofi take stick-DEF hit Yao P
Kofi took the stick and hit Yao with it.

With the development of annotated linguistic corpora of various languages, glosses are starting to be used in a new way. Traditionally, only individual sentences or small text collections were glossed to illustrate examples. Nowadays glosses are systematically added to large corpora in order to provide structural information necessary for quantitative cross-linguistic research.

Despite their great value for linguistic research, glossed corpora often remain rather small. The main reason for this is the fact that glossing requires a high level of linguistic expertise and is currently performed manually by trained experts. This practice makes the creation of glossed corpora extremely time-consuming and expensive. In order to obtain glossed corpora large enough for reliable quantitative analysis, the process of glossing needs to be automatised.

In this paper, we present a series of experiments performed with this precise aim.[2] We divide the traditional glossing procedure into several steps and define an automatic processing pipeline, which consists of some standard and some custom natural language processing tasks. The data we use for our experiments come from the Chintang Language Corpus (Bickel et al., 2004 2015), an exceptionally large glossed corpus, which has been developed since 2004 and is presently hosted at the Department of Comparative Linguistics at the University of Zurich.[3]

2 Related work

Data for comprehensive linguistic research need to be collected in a wide range of languages. Glosses

[1] Available at https://www.eva.mpg.de/lingua/resources/glossing-rules.php

[2] This work is partially supported by the S3IT computing facilities.

[3] http://www.clrp.uzh.ch

Proceedings of the 9th SIGHUM Workshop on Language Technology for Cultural Heritage, Social Sciences, and Humanities, pages 68–72, Beijing, China, July 30, 2015.

are especially important for research in under-resourced languages, the analysis of which requires more detailed information than it is the case with well documented and processed languages.

Approaches to under-resourced languages include developing tools to support manual rule crafting and deep rule-based analysis (Bender et al., 2014; Snoek et al., 2014), data collection by experts (Ulinski et al., 2014; Hanke and Bird, 2013) and through crowd-sourcing (Bird et al., 2014; Dunham et al., 2014), automatic translation and cross-linguistic projection using parallel corpora (Yarowsky et al., 2001; Scherrer, 2014; Scherrer and Sagot, 2014; Aepli et al., 2014), and part-of-speech tagging (Garrette and Baldridge, 2013).

These tasks target different representations, but the resources that they produce are not suitable for corpus-based quantitative linguistic research. Our approach to automatic linguistic glossing is intended to fill this gap. Like Garrette and Baldridge (2013), we learn our target representation from a relatively small sample of manually developed resources in the target language. However, we tackle a harder task and rely on more resources, which are becoming increasingly available through work on language documentation.

3 The structure of the Chintang corpus and glossing strategy

The corpus consists of about 290 hours (1,232,161 words) of video materials transcribed in broad IPA. 214 hours (955,025 words) have been translated to English and Nepali by native research assistants and glossed by trained non-native student assistants. The primary data are MPG-1 videos and WAV audio files. Morphological Transcriptions and translations were done in Transcriber and ELAN, glossing in Toolbox.

The basic unit of a Toolbox text is the record, which in oral corpora usually corresponds to one utterance. Records are separated from each other by double newlines. Each record may contain several tiers, each of which is coded as a line ended by a single newline. Within each tier, both words and morphemes are separated by whitespace. Free and bound morphemes are distinguished by adding a corresponding separator (prefixes end and suffixes begin with a "-"). Elements are implicitly aligned across tiers based on their position on a tier (e.g. the fifth element on the segment tier corresponds to the fifth element on the gloss tier).

record ID	rabbit.047			
transcription	mande		aba	katha
segmentation	mand	-e	abo	katha
glosses	be.over	-ind.pst	now	story
language	C	-C	C/N	N
lexicon ID	281	-1234	596	4505
PoS	vi	-gm	adv	n
English	Now the story is over.			

Table 1: Example for record structure in the Chintang Language Corpus

lexeme	mand
ID	281
variant	mai
PoS	vi
valency	S-NOM(1) V-s(S)
English gloss	be.finished; be.over; be.used.up
language	C

Table 2: Example for entry structure in the Chintang dictionary

Table 1 shows a simplified example of an analysed record. Beside segmentation and interlinear glosses, the analysis also includes POS tags, language labels, and lexical IDs for every morpheme.

The language labels are needed because mixing with other languages (Nepali and Bantawa) is frequent in Chintang (Stoll et al., 2015).

The lexical IDs provide a unique link to the entries of an electronic lexicon of Chintang, which contains rich information both on free and on dependent morphemes. A simplified example of a lexicon entry is given in Table 2.

Lexical IDs ensure good communication between the corpus and the lexicon, allowing for queries involving both resources at the same time (e.g. combining valency or etymology information from the lexicon with corpus counts) as well as systematic updates and synchronisation of both resources.

4 Automatic glossing pipeline

As shown in the previous section, linguistic annotation of the Chintang corpus consists of word segmentation and proper glossing.

Word segmentation can be seen as a preprocessing step that creates basic units of analysis to which glosses are assigned. Once the words are segmented into morphemes that encode either lexical content or grammatical categories, assigning glosses to the word segments reduces to a one-to-one mapping: each segment in a sentence is assigned exactly one gloss and vice versa.

We take manual segmentation as input and learn automatically the mappings between segments and glosses. This mapping includes referring to the corresponding lexicon and importing the information from lexical entries.

A simple way to learn this mapping would be to treat glossing as word-by-word translation from original text to an artificial language that consists of words and grammatical tags. Word order in the artificial language would be exactly the same as in the original text, so that the task would reduce to learning segment translation probabilities.

The main disadvantage of the translation-based approach is that it requires large corpora for training. This approach does not generalise beyond examples seen in the training set, which is why good coverage of a new text can be obtained only if the model is trained on a large corpus. In addition to this, the translation model would need to be complemented by a language model to account for context dependencies. However, large glossed corpora are almost never available for under-resourced languages, as discussed above.

Another possible approach is to treat glosses as a special kind of part-of-speech tags. The main obstacle for this approach is the fact that glosses contain lexical items (lexical glosses). Including lexical tags would result in a tag set too big to be learnt by standard part-of-speech tagging models.

We thus apply a two-level tagging approach where we first learn grammatical tags without lexical items in a standard supervised part-of-speech tagging setting. We then add lexical items from the lexicon using the sequences of grammatical tags for disambiguation. In the remainder of this section, we describe the two procedures in more detail and experiments performed to evaluate them.

4.1 Grammatical annotation as PoS tagging

To separate grammatical from lexical glossing, we merge two tiers of the original annotation. This is done by replacing lexical items in the gloss tier with their corresponding part-of-speech tags. In the case of grammatical items, we keep the original gloss. This results in a representation illustrated in (2), where the lexical glosses *be.over*, *now*, and *story* are replaced by their corresponding part-of-speech tags *vi*, *adv*, and *n*.

(2)	*mand*	*-e*	*abo*	*katha*
	vi	-ind.pst	adv	n

In this way, we obtain a corpus annotated with 233 distinct labels that describe relevant morphosyntactic categories in Chintang.

We then split the corpus into a train and a test set and apply a standard supervised part-of-speech tagging. We train and test a general-purpose state-of-the-art statistical tagger (Gesmundo, 2011; Gesmundo and Samardžić, 2012).

To assess how the quantity of training data influences the performance of the tagger, we run the experiment several times using increasing amounts of data for training. The results of the tagging experiments are presented in Figure 1.

4.2 Lexical annotation as lemmatisation

To recover the original glosses, we replace part-of-speech tags of words with lexical content by their corresponding English lemmas. English lemmas are associated to their corresponding Chintang segments in the lexicon, where each entry is identified with a unique numerical code (lexion ID). The task of inserting lexical glosses back is thus reduced to the task of finding the correct lexicon ID for each word segment in a sentence. We perform this in two steps.

In the first step, we search the lexicon to find all possible IDs for a given pair consisting of a segment and its grammatical tag assigned by the tagger. We select all entries where the given word appears as the main entry or as a variant, and the given grammatical tag appears either as the gloss or as the part-of-speech tag (see Table 2). Even though we look up word segments disambiguated for their grammatical category, approximately 15% of the pairs remain ambiguous in the sense that multiple possible lexicon IDs are assigned.

In the second step, we select a single ID through a disambiguation procedure that takes into account the previous context of the segment. This step is similar to the procedures used in the task of lemmatisation. We represent the previous context with a sequence of two grammatical tags assigned by the tagger to the preceding segments, t_{-2}, and t_{-1}. We estimate the probability of each of the possible lexicon IDs (id_0) given the previous two tags. We then select the most probable ID, as shown in (3).

$$\begin{aligned} id_0* &= arg\,max_{id_0} p(id_0|t_{-2}, t_{-1}) \\ &= arg\,max_{id_0} \frac{p(t_{-2}, t_{-1}, id_0)}{p(t_{-2}, t_{-1})} \end{aligned} \quad (3)$$

In the cases where the trigram-based estimation is not possible due to zero counts, we apply a three-step back-off strategy. If counts can be collected, we find the most probable ID given only one previous tag, as shown is (4). Otherwise, we select the most likely ID without the context information. Finally, if there are no corpus counts, we select one of the possible IDs randomly.

$$\begin{aligned} id_0* &= arg\,max_{id_0} p(id_0|t_{-1}) \\ &= arg\,max_{id_0} \frac{p(t_{-1}, id_0)}{p(t_{-1})} \end{aligned} \quad (4)$$

We evaluate lexical annotation in the same settings as in the case of part-of-speech tagging. The results are shown in Figure 1.

4.3 Results and discussion

Figure 1 shows the performance on the two tasks using different corpus sizes for training. In each run, we increase the length of the training set by approximately 50,000 tokens, keeping the test set constant (around 200,000 tokens).

The accuracy of part-of speech tagging obtained with the first set (50,000 tokens) is 90%. It increases by 1% with every increase till the size of 200,000. The increase after this point is much slower, reaching the best result of 96% accuracy using the full training set of around 800,000 tokens.

The performance curve is a little different for the task of lexical annotation. The accuracy is already 92% when the disambiguation model is trained on the smallest set. It reaches the maximal score of 94% with the training set of 200,000 tokens.

These results show that dividing glossing into two sequence classification tasks allows us to optimise manual work in developing new resources. A relatively small annotated corpus is used to model sequences of highly frequent items (grammatical words and their tags). Sparse but less ambiguous lexical items are glossed using a lexicon, ensuring good coverage. In this framework, new segments are addressed in two ways. Grammatical tags are assigned to new words based on the generalisations learnt by the tagger. Lexical tags are

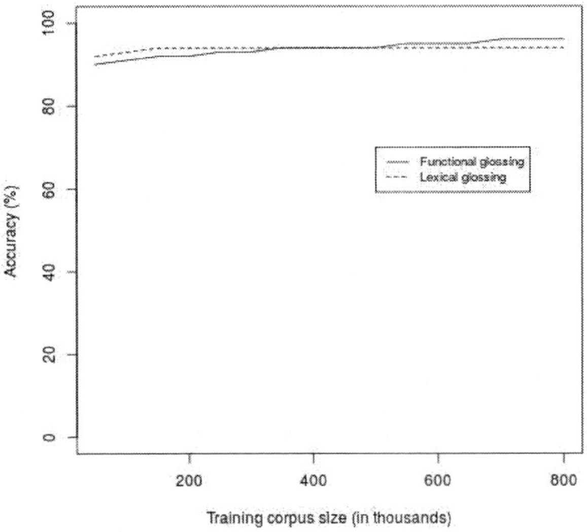

Figure 1: Performance on two glossing subtasks using increasing sizes of the train set.

expected to be covered by the lexicon. Items that are not covered need to be manually added to the lexicon, but they are then automatically applied in glossing.

A number of mismatches between predicted labels and the gold standard are caused by inconsistencies in the gold standard due to the changes in the label set over time. While we count all the mismatches as errors, an inspection of the output of automatic processing can be used to improve annotation consistency.

5 Conclusion and future work

We have shown in this paper how statistical natural language processing techniques can be adapted to the task of interlinear glossing, with the quality of the processing high enough to replace manual annotation. While an annotated sample corpus in the target language is needed to train the statistical models, we show that the initial training set can be relatively small, of the size of some existing glossed corpora.

A fully automatised glossing procedure would have to include an approach to word segmentation, which is not addressed here. We identify this task as the first step in our future work.

References

Noemi Aepli, Ruprecht von Waldenfels, and Tanja Samardžić. 2014. Part-of-speech tag disambiguation by cross-linguistic majority vote. In *First Workshop on Applying NLP Tools to Similar Languages, Varieties and Dialects (VarDial)*, Dublin, Ireland. Association for Computational Linguistics.

Emily M. Bender, Joshua Crowgey, Michael Wayne Goodman, and Fei Xia. 2014. Learning grammar specifications from igt: A case study of chintang. In *Proceedings of the 2014 Workshop on the Use of Computational Methods in the Study of Endangered Languages*, pages 43–53, Baltimore, Maryland, USA, June. Association for Computational Linguistics.

Balthasar Bickel, Sabine Stoll, Martin Gaenszle, Novel Kishor Rai, Elena Lieven, Goma Banjade, Toya Nath Bhatta, Netra Paudyal, Judith Pettigrew, Ichchha P. Rai, and Manoj Rai. 2004-2015. Audiovisual corpus of the chintang language, including a longitudinal corpus of language acquisition by six children. DOBES Archive, `http://www.mpi.nl/DOBES`.

Steven Bird, Florian R. Hanke, Oliver Adams, and Haejoong Lee. 2014. Aikuma: A mobile app for collaborative language documentation. In *Proceedings of the 2014 Workshop on the Use of Computational Methods in the Study of Endangered Languages*, pages 1–5, Baltimore, Maryland, USA, June. Association for Computational Linguistics.

Chris Collins. 1997. Argument sharing in serial verb constructions. *Linguistic Inquiry*, 28:461–497.

Joel Dunham, Gina Cook, and Joshua Horner. 2014. Lingsync & the online linguistic database: New models for the collection and management of data for language communities, linguists and language learners. In *Proceedings of the 2014 Workshop on the Use of Computational Methods in the Study of Endangered Languages*, pages 24–33, Baltimore, Maryland, USA, June. Association for Computational Linguistics.

Dan Garrette and Jason Baldridge. 2013. Learning a part-of-speech tagger from two hours of annotation. In *Proceedings of the 2013 Conference of the North American Chapter of the Association for Computational Linguistics: Human Language Technologies*, pages 138–147. Association for Computational Linguistics.

Andrea Gesmundo and Tanja Samardžić. 2012. Lemmatisation as a tagging task. In *Proceedings of the 50th Annual Meeting of the Association for Computational Linguistics (Volume 2: Short Papers)*, pages 368–372, Jeju Island, Korea, July. Association for Computational Linguistics.

Andrea Gesmundo. 2011. Bidirectional Sequence Classification for Tagging Tasks with Guided Learning. In *Proceedings of TALN 2011*.

R. Florian Hanke and Steven Bird. 2013. Large-scale text collection for unwritten languages. In *Proceedings of the Sixth International Joint Conference on Natural Language Processing*, pages 1134–1138. Asian Federation of Natural Language Processing.

Yves Scherrer and Benoît Sagot. 2014. A language-independent and fully unsupervised approach to lexicon induction and part-of-speech tagging for closely related languages. In *Proceedings of the Ninth International Conference on Language Resources and Evaluation (LREC-2014)*. European Language Resources Association (ELRA).

Yves Scherrer. 2014. Unsupervised adaptation of supervised part-of-speech taggers for closely related languages. In *First Workshop on Applying NLP Tools to Similar Languages, Varieties and Dialects (VarDial)*, Dublin, Ireland. Association for Computational Linguistics.

Conor Snoek, Dorothy Thunder, Kaidi Lõo, Antti Arppe, Jordan Lachler, Sjur Moshagen, and Trond Trosterud. 2014. Modeling the noun morphology of plains cree. In *Proceedings of the 2014 Workshop on the Use of Computational Methods in the Study of Endangered Languages*, pages 34–42, Baltimore, Maryland, USA, June. Association for Computational Linguistics.

Sabine Stoll, Taras Zakharko, Steven Moran, Robert Schikowski, and Balthasar Bickel. 2015. Syntactic mixing across generations in an environment of community-wide bilingualism. *Frontiers in Psychology*, 6(82).

Morgan Ulinski, Anusha Balakrishnan, Daniel Bauer, Bob Coyne, Julia Hirschberg, and Owen Rambow. 2014. Documenting endangered languages with the wordseye linguistics tool. In *Proceedings of the 2014 Workshop on the Use of Computational Methods in the Study of Endangered Languages*, pages 6–14, Baltimore, Maryland, USA, June. Association for Computational Linguistics.

David Yarowsky, Grace Ngai, and Richard Wicentowski. 2001. Inducing multilingual text analysis tools via robust projection across aligned corpora. In *Proceedings of the 1st international conference Human Language Technology*, pages 161–168, San Diego, CA. Association for Computational Linguistics.

Enriching Digitized Medieval Manuscripts: Linking Image, Text and Lexical Knowledge

Aitor Arronte Álvarez
Center for Language and Technology
University of Hawaii
arronte@hawaii.edu

Abstract

This paper describes an on-going project of transcribing and annotating digitized manuscripts of medieval Spanish with paleographic and lexical information. We link lexical units from the manuscripts with the Multilingual Central Repository (MCR), making terms retrievable by any of the languages that integrate MCR. The goal of the project is twofold: creating a paleographic knowledge base from digitized medieval facsimiles, that will allow paleographers, philologist, historical linguist, and humanities scholars in general, to analyze and retrieve graphemic, lexical and textual information from historical documents; and on the other hand, developing machine readable documents that will link image representations of graphemic and lexical units in a facsimile with Linked Open Data resources. This paper concentrates on the encoding and cross-linking procedures.

1 Introduction

In recent years, historical documents have been massively digitized and published online in openly available databases, gathering much of the attention of the Digital Humanities community. As a result, large collections of historical handwriting online databases have emerged such as Pares[1], paleographic resources like DigiPal[2], citizen scholar projects (Deciphering Secrets: Unlocking the Manuscripts of Medieval Spain[3]) and digital paleography learning tools (Spanish Paleography Digital Teaching and Learning Tool[4]). In this context, computerized tools have become part of the toolkit of the current humanities scholar.

Most of the research in the computational analysis of digitized historical handwritten documents, has concentrated in its paleographic analysis: the deciphering, dating, and description of ancient manuscripts (Wolf, et. al, 2011; Hassner, et. al, 2013). In this paper, we describe an ongoing project for encoding digitized medieval Spanish manuscripts from the 13th, 14th and early 15th centuries, and linking their content with the Multilingual Central Repository (MCR)[5] (Gonzalez-Agirre et al., 2012).

The main goal of the project is the development of an online database of digitized medieval manuscripts that will enable users to obtain graphemic and lexical information from facsimiles. Manuscripts will be fully searchable using any of the languages that integrate the MCR.

The resource will aid the paleographic understanding of medieval manuscripts as well as the linguistic and philological analysis of medieval Spanish. Also, the database can be a valuable source for computational researchers interested in the automatic processing of medieval manuscripts, since image data will be linked to text and lexical information. To our knowledge, an online resource of this type does not exist.

In this paper we concentrate on: the description of the methods for transcribing, annotating, and encoding manuscripts; the process of automatically linking their content at a lexical level with MCR entries, and for codifying these relationships in a model.

2 Encoding transcriptions of medieval manuscripts

Historical Spanish language varieties exhibit important differences not only at the syntactical and

[1] http://pares.mcu.es/
[2] http://www.digipal.eu/
[3] http://decipheringsecrets.net/
[4] http://spanishpaleographytool.org/
[5] http://adimen.si.ehu.es/web/MCR/

Proceedings of the 9th SIGHUM Workshop on Language Technology for Cultural Heritage, Social Sciences, and Humanities, pages 73–77,
Beijing, China, July 30, 2015.

morphological level, but also at the graphemic. This is due to the fact that orthographic rules in Spanish were not defined until the 18th century[6], bringing serious difficulties for the understanding of Medieval Spanish[7] manuscripts, since there is substantial variation even within documents of the same period; mostly because scribes had different handwriting styles. Medieval orthography also does not follow contemporary patterns, there is not in a strict sense, different options between graphemes, but rather a combination of factors that may explain certain solutions. As mentioned by Sánchez-Prieto (2004), medieval manuscripts should be understood following a triple correlation of factors:

1. Paleographic uses and shapes of the letters.
2. Identification of the letters.
3. Phonetic changes.

In this triple relation lies the evolution of handwriting, and may reveal important aspects of phonetic change. For that reason, handwritten medieval documents are nowadays manually transcribed with the aid of computational tools. In Figure 1, two examples of different handwriting styles from early 15th century are shown, where the grapheme "a" at the end of each word, is written in a triangular shape (for the first word "la"), and in a square shape (for the second word "buena"). In our work, we segmented the transcribed words in manuscripts using the UVic Image Markup Tool[8], which allows for the annotation and transcription of facsimiles using the Text Encoding Initiative (TEI[9]) model. We customize the markup of the TEI document to be able to codify graphemic and lexical information.

Figure 1: Early 15th century handwriting styles. The grapheme "a" is marked in a box.

TEI is de facto XML standard for the representation of texts in digital form. Following TEI guidelines, different graphemic representations are declared using the element <glyph> in the header of the document (see Figure 2). Image representations of words in the facsimile are segmented using the element <surface>, which defines a written surface as a two-dimensional coordinate space, specifying zones of interest or grouping graphic representations within that space; and the <zone> element, that defines a two dimensional area within a <surface>. The attributes @ulx, @uly, @lrx and @lry, represent respectively, the *x* and *y* values for the upper left and lower right corners of a rectangular space (see Figure 3). Declarations of graphemes are linked to the transcribed text using the element <g>, so variations of a grapheme can be identified and compared. Transcribed words are represented in the TEI document using the <w> element. We automatically generate unique xml:id for each element in the TEI document. The nested representation of words and graphemes in a facsimile is shown in Figure 4.

```
<encodingDesc>
    <charDecl>
      <glyph xml:id="a1">
       <glyphName> roman letter a with
       triangular shape</glyphName>
      <charProp>
         <locaName> entity</localName>
        <value>a1</value>
      </charProp>
      <figure>
        <graphic url="a1.png"/>
      </figure>
      </glyph>
    </charDecl>
 </encodingDesc>
```

Figure 2: Grapheme declaration in TEI document.

```
<facsimile xml:id="imtAnnotatedImage">
   <surface>
     <graphic url="DiegoHernandez.jpg"
width="902px" height="1240px"></graphic>
       <zone xml:id="imtArea_1"
ulx="298" uly="233" lrx="326" lry="253"
rend="visible"></zone>
        <zone xml:id="imtArea_2"
ulx="326" uly="234" lrx="343" lry="251"
rend="visible"></zone>
        <zone xml:id="imtArea_3"
ulx="344" uly="237" lrx="393" lry="254"
rend="visible"></zone>
         <zone xml:id="imtArea_4"
ulx="345" uly="233" lrx="391" lry="252"
rend="visible"></zone>
         <zone xml:id="imtArea_5"
ulx="363" uly="238" lrx="372" lry="251"
rend="visible"></zone>
```

[6] The Royal Spanish Academy published the first orthographic rules in 1726, as part of the first volume of the Diccionario de Autoridades.

[7] Medieval Spanish is an early form of Spanish that ranges from the 10th to the 15th century, as it is considered by most scholars.

[8] http://tapor.uvic.ca/~mholmes/image_markup/index.php

[9] http://www.tei-c.org/index.xml. TEI is an XML-based file format for exchanging text.

```
    </surface>
  </facsimile>
```

Figure 3: TEI representation of image segments in a facsimile.

```
<body>
  <div xml:id="imtImageAnnotations">
    <s xml:lang="spa">
     <w xml:id="ms1_w_6" cor-
resp="#imtArea_1"> por</w>
      <w xml:id="ms1_w_7" cor-
resp="#imtArea_2">la</w>
      <w xml:id="ms1_w_8" cor-
resp="#imtArea_3">gr<g xml:id="ms1_g_1"
corresp="#imtArea_4"
ref="#a1">a</g>çia</w>
       <w xml:id="ms1_w_9" cor-
resp="#imtArea_5">de</w>
      </s>
  </div>
</body>
```

Figure 4: text representation of words and graphemes linked to their corresponding image segments.

3 Linking medieval manuscripts with multilingual lexical resources

In order to link image representations of words in a historical variety with a multilingual lexical database, two operations need to take place:

1. Matching the historical form of the word with its contemporary standard.
2. Codifying that relation in the document.

3.1 Mapping medieval Spanish with contemporary standard

Before the cross-linking of the transcribed words from the manuscript with MCR entries, words from medieval Spanish will need to be mapped to the standard form of contemporary Spanish. We follow the rules presented in (Sánchez-Prieto, 2004) and previous computational work on historical language varieties (Sánchez-Marco et. al, 2010).

The mapping rules used can be divided into substring rules and word rules. In Table 1 examples of the mappings using substring rules are introduced. Words that are not covered by the substring rules include graphemic variation of the type: *decaydo→decaído, fablar→hablar.*

Substring rules		
Medieval	Modern	Transformation
euo	*evo*	*nueuo→nuevo*
iua	*iva*	*dadiua→dadiva*

Table 1: substring rules

3.2 Linking terms from medieval manuscripts with MCR synsets

WordNet is a large lexical database of English (Miller, 1995), where open class words are grouped into concepts represented by synonyms (synsets) that are linked to each other by semantic relations such as hyponymy and meronymy. There are multiple wordnets for different languages, and wordnets for groups of languages like the Euro WordNet (Vossen, 1998). Wordnets have also been extended by using external lexical resources like Wiktionary (McCrae et al., 2012) or with a combination of multilingual resources (De Melo & Weikum, 2009; Bond & Foster, 2013). Also, the Portuguese wordnet incorporates non standard varieties of the language (Marrafa et al., 2011). Our goal is to link words from historical varieties of Spanish extracted from manuscripts, to synsets in MCR, in such a way that the image representation of a medieval word can be directly associated to its contemporary form or via semantic relations to a sense.

The MCR integrates wordnets in five different languages, English, Spanish, Catalan, Basque and Galician that are linked to each other via an Inter-Lingual-Index (ILI). Each of the wordnets in the MCR is aligned to the Princeton WordNet 3.0 and encoded using Lexicon Model for Ontologies (*lemon*)[10]. One of the main advantages of using *lemon* is its linguistically sound structure based on the Lexical Markup Framework (LMF), making it an ideal model for lexicons and machine-readable dictionaries in the Linked Data Cloud.

We use a Python script for linking words from historical Spanish manuscripts encoded in a TEI document with existing MCR synsets, by matching lemmas in medieval Spanish with contemporary standard. We follow the substring and word mapping rules described in the previous subsection, matching them with contemporary Spanish lemmas in MCR. This approach is imperfect, since there are medieval words that no longer exist or might have different lexical realizations. In these cases, medieval words will need to be

[10] http://lemon-model.net/

linked with synsets via the linguistic analysis of their meanings using a historical dictionary, following an approach similar to the one described in (Declerck et al., 2014). Also, we should note that PoS-taggers of standard contemporary Spanish used in a historical variety context, perform below state of the art taggers (Sánchez-Marco et. al, 2011), which makes manual verification an unavoidable step.

In order to represent the semantic linking of the words in the TEI document with lexical entries in the *lemon* model of the MCR, we need to extend our initial TEI representation with pointing mechanisms associated to the TEI <relation> element. In Figure 5 we show how semantic relationships can be established between words in the manuscripts and external lexical resources.

```
<relation
 ref="http://www.lemon-
 model.net/lemon#formVariant"
 active="#ms1_w_8"
passive =" mcr:spa-gracia-n#Sense-
04840715-n "/>

<relation
 ref="http://wordnet-
rdf.princeton.edu/ontology#translation"
 active="http://wordnet-
rdf.princeton.edu/wn30/14458181-n"
 passive="#ms1_w_8"/>
```

Figure 5: semantic annotations to external resources.

4 Next steps: sharing knowledge between manuscripts

In the encoding presented in this paper, manuscripts are annotated, codified, and linked to external lexical resources. Even though several paleographic and graphemic relations are established implicitly in the markup of the TEI document, this representation of a manuscript does not provide semantic relationships beyond the ones defined at a lexical level. In order to share paleographic knowledge with other open resources across the web, following Linked Open Data principles (Chiarcos et. al, 2011), a paleographic ontology for medieval Spanish documents needs to be develop. The ontology should capture relationships within a given document, between different manuscripts in a collection and between different collections. Allographs, glyphs, ligatures, word and common name abbreviations, contractions, acronyms, numbers and dates variations in notation should be defined at an ontological level. More general relationships and document data such as typology (legal, church, private document, etc), style, place of origin, manuscript collection, archive, author and year of the transcription, will also be included in the ontology.

Since we are dealing with cultural heritage materials, existing ontologies such as the Functional Requirements for Bibliographic Records (FRBR), CIDOC Conceptual Reference Model (CIDOC CRM), and more directly related to our work, the General Ontology for Linguistic Description (GOLD), already define the terminology and some of the relationships that can be found in medieval manuscripts; in these cases classes can be directly imported and reused. In some other cases, classes may need to be created to define specific graphemic objects and paleographic relationships that are not defined in the existing ontologies.

In the TEI representation described in this paper, unique ids are given to lexical and graphemic units, allowing for the automatic creation of URIs that can be used for external resources to link to it. The RDF annotation can be done following the example given in Figure 5 using the element <relation> and the relationships defined in the paleographic ontology.

At a lexical level, semantic relations are established in the TEI document via external resources. Even though lexical ontologies such as *lemon,* and to some extent WordNet, define linguistic relationships between lexical units, they may not be specific enough to describe the different relationships of a language with its historical varieties. Future steps in the project should consider adding such detailed linguistic relationships.

5 Conclusions

In this paper we described the first steps towards the creation of an online resource of digitized medieval Spanish manuscripts, where graphemic, lexical and textual information can be retrieved directly from facsimiles. We have shown and demonstrated a method for transcribing and encoding in TEI P5 image data from manuscripts. We have described also how medieval Spanish can be linked to its contemporary standard and to the rest of the languages that integrate MCR, making manuscript terms retrievable using any of these languages. Next steps in the project include: developing a paleographic ontology of medieval Spanish, extending semantic annotations at a lexical level incorporating historical varieties relationships, building a web interface, and making data available in the cloud.

References

Bond, F., & Foster, R. (2013). Linking and Extending an Open Multilingual Wordnet. *ACL, 1*, pp. 1352-1362.

Chiarcos, C., Hellmann, S., & Nordhoff, S. (2011). Towards a Linguistic Linked Open Data cloud: The Open Linguistics Working Group. *52* (3), 245-275.

De Melo, G., & Weikum, G. (2009). Towards a universal wordnet by learning from combined evidence. *Proceedings of the 18th ACM conference on Information and knowledge management* (pp. 513-522). ACM.

Declerck, T., Wand-Vogt, E., Mörth, K., & Resch, C. (2014). Towards a Unified Approach for Publishing Regional and Historical Language Resources on the Linked Data Framework. *CCURL 2014: Collaboration and Computing for Under-Resourced Languages in the Linked Open Data, 17.*

Gonzalez-Agirre, A., Laparra, E., & Rigau, G. (2012). Multilingual Central Repository version 3.0. *LREC*, (pp. 2525-2529).

Hassner, T., Rehbein, M., Stokes, P., & Wolf, L. (2013). Computation and Palaeography: Potentials and Limits. *Dagstuhl Manifestos , 2* (1), 14-35.

Marrafa, P., Amaro, P., & Mendes, S. (2011). WordNet. PT global: extending WordNet. PT to Portuguese varieties. *Proceedings of the First Workshop on Algorithms and Resources for Modelling of Dialects and Language Varieties* (pp. 70-74). Association for Computational Linguistics.

McCrae, J., Montiel-Ponsoda, E., & Cimiano, P. (2012). Integrating WordNet and Wiktionary with lemon. In *Linked Data in Linguistics* (pp. 25-34). Berlin, Heidelberg: Springer.

Miller, G. (1995). WordNet: a lexical database for English. *Communications of the ACM , 38* (11), 39-41.

Sánchez-Marco, C., Fontana, J., Domingo, J., & Boleda Torrent, G. (2010). *Annotation and representation of a diachronic corpus of Spanish.*

Sánchez-Marco, C., Boleda, G., & Padró, L. (2011). Extending the tool, or how to annotate historical language varieties. In *Proceedings of the 5th ACL-HLT workshop on language technology for cultural heritage, social sciences, and humanities* (pp. 1-9). Association for Computational Linguistics.

Sánchez-Prieto, P. (2004). *La normalización del castellano escrito en el siglo XIII. Los caracteres de la lengua: grafías y fonemas.*

Vossen, P. (1998). *A multilingual database with lexical semantic networks.* Dordrecht: Kluwer Academic Publishers.

Wolf, L., Potikha, L., Dershowitz, N., Shweka, R., & Choueka, Y. (2011). Computerized paleography: tools for historical manuscripts. *18th IEEE International Conference on Image Processing (ICIP)* (pp. 3545-3548). IEEE.

A preliminary study on similarity-preserving digital book identifiers

Klemo Vladimir[1], Marin Silic[1], Nenad Romic[2], Goran Delac[1], and Sinisa Srbljic[1]

[1]University of Zagreb, Faculty of Electrical Engineering and Computing
Consumer Computing Lab, Unska 3, 10000 Zagreb, Croatia
{klemo.vladimir, marin.silic, goran.delac, sinisa.srbljic}@fer.hr

[2]Leuphana Universität Lüneburg, DCRL Digital Cultures Research Lab
Am Sande 5, 21335 Lüneburg, Germany
ki.ber@kom.uni.st

Abstract

Due to proliferation of digital publishing, e-book catalogs are abundant but noisy and unstructured. Tools for the digital librarian rely on ISBN, metadata embedded into digital files (without accepted standard) and cryptographic hash functions for the identification of coderivative or near-duplicate content. However, unreliability of metadata and sensitivity of hashing to even smallest changes prevents efficient detection of coderivative or similar digital books. Focus of the study are books with many versions that differ in certain amount of OCR errors and have a number of sentence-length variations. Identification of similar books is performed using small-sized fingerprints that can be easily shared and compared. We created synthetic datasets to evaluate fingerprinting accuracy while providing standard precision and recall measurements.

1 Introduction

The need and then creation of a system to identify every particular book in an archive or repository has a long history. An invention and iterative development of a card catalog, as we know it today, a universal discrete machine which stores, processes and transfers data took several centuries (Krajewski, 2011). However, only in late 1960s, when computer technology began to become an important part of trade, publishers came up with a standardized numeric identifier describing (only) a geographical or language area, publisher and a specific edition and title of the book.

It's hard to imagine a book today which is not prepared and processed as a digital file before it gets published. Still, the unique book identifier in use is created by (and for) bureaucracy and as a consequence it only reflects book's context related to commerce - nothing else (ISBN Information, 2015).

Today's available digital books are coming from many different sources: comprehensive scanning projects like the Internet archive or the National Library of Norway, community driven repositories like Library Genesis, Aaaaarg.org, Monoskop.org, Ubu.com or commercial providers like Amazon, Google or Apple.

There is contextual information already embedded in the content of every digital book which could improve and optimize file storage (detection of duplicates), network transfer (detection of network peers), classification, topic clustering, language analysis and more. We envision a different kind of digital book identifier which will embed and carry much more of its relevant context than what is the case with existing ones.

In this paper we present a feasibility study of using locality sensitive hashing for construction of similarity-preserving digital book identifiers. In order to evaluate the suggested approach, we have constructed a comprehensive dataset that contains highly similar book entries[1]. Proposed identifiers can be used in practice for scalable comparison of books, retrieval of near-duplicate books or as an index for metadata provisioning services that tolerate different e-book formats, imperfect metadata or minor changes on text itself.

The rest of the paper is organized as follows. Next section gives an overview of related work. Section 3 describes construction and structure of the dataset used in the experiments. Implementation and characteristics of similarity preserving fingerprinting are presented in Section 4. Section 5 presents and discusses experimental results. Fi-

[1]Dataset and code available at http://ccl.fer.hr/ds/2015/readme.html

Proceedings of the 9th SIGHUM Workshop on Language Technology for Cultural Heritage, Social Sciences, and Humanities, pages 78–83,
Beijing, China, July 30, 2015.

nally, Section 6 concludes the paper and proposes future research directions.

2 Related work

A general overview of two dominant approaches for the identification of near-duplicate documents, ranking and fingerprinting, is presented in (Hoad and Zobel, 2003). The ranking relies on vector space models where documents are represented using high-dimensional vectors. Document fingerprinting is used to create compact representation of document vectors using hashing functions. A number of methods were proposed and evaluated for features of various resolutions, such as characters, words or sentences (Manber and others, 1994; Shivakumar and Garcia-Molina, 1995; Brin et al., 1995).

The dimensionality of document vectors can be reduced using locality sensitive hashing, mostly using simhash or min-hash algorithms. Min-hash (Broder, 1997) was used for large-scale detection of similar books at the page level (Spasojevic and Poncin, 2011). While min-hash uses many hash values to represent a document, having each value computed with a different hash function, simhash gives a more compact output by reducing document vectors to a small sized real-valued fingerprints (Charikar, 2002). Simhash was successfully evaluated for duplicate detection of web pages (Manku et al., 2007; Henzinger, 2006), code segments (Uddin et al., 2011), short messages (Pi et al., 2009), spam (Ho et al., 2014) and academic papers (Williams and Giles, 2013). Our contribution to the literature is in the use of simhash fingerprinting for larger texts in form of digital books.

Partial duplicates detection in large collections of scanned books was proposed in (Yalniz et al., 2011). Here, books were represented by a sequence of unique words and duplicates were identified by the longest common sub-sequence alignment. However, book representation using unique words is still to large to be useful as an identifier, e.g. for a 100k words book there are $2-3$k unique words.

Other approaches rely on hashing metadata contents only (Padmasree et al., 2006; Voß et al., 2009). Near-duplicate detection based on metadata is also well researched in the field of record linkage where matching of records that relate to the same entities from several databases is studied (Christen, 2012). However, primary motivation for this preliminary study is to derive similarity book identifier based on content, not the metadata.

3 Dataset construction

Synthetic book collections were generated to evaluate book fingerprints constructed using locality sensitive hashing. Datasets were generated by "mutating" referent, or "seed", books taken from the *Project Gutenberg* website (Project Gutenberg, 2015). We randomly sampled books from the larger collection of available books and preprocessed so that only raw text files without any additional data remain.

3.1 Synthesis methodology

For each canonical book a random number of mutations were performed. There are two main types of mutations: (1) OCR errors and (2) random text mutations.

(1) Introduction of OCR (Optical Character Recognition) errors simulates existence of multiple versions of the single book scanned and post-processed by different equipment, different software stack or different librarians. Following the previous work (Reynaert, 2011; Feng and Manmatha, 2006; Esakov et al., 1994), mutations were created by building a custom discrete distribution of basic "errors" derived from common OCR character confusions. For example, the most common character-level mistake is the insertion of space. Other included mistakes were random character insertion, replacement of a single character with another character or a number of characters, and merging of two characters into single character (e.g. `rn` $\rightarrow$ `m`). As an illustrative example, a random text *"the immortality of the soul"* with 3% character-level corruption rate (at book level) becomes *"1he immttality of th e soul"*. Character-error rates reported in the literature range from $0.5-10\%$ (Esakov et al., 1994; Yalniz et al., 2011; Abdulkader and Casey, 2009).

(2) In addition to character-level mutations, a certain amount of sentence-level mutations were introduced. Addition or removal of random sentences can simulate book annotations, bookmarks or metadata insertions performed by editors, readers or e-book authoring or reading software. Addition of new material was sourced from a random book in the collection while keeping the length of the corrupted text similar to the canonical text.

3.2 Dataset structure

We compiled two datasets by corrupting texts with different corruption rates. Smaller, *1k* dataset was used for the exploration of fingerprinting parameters. The 1k dataset was generated from the seed of 100 distinct books where another 9 versions were derived from each canonical book using mutations described in the previous section. Additionally, 1k dataset was replicated for various corruption rates.

Larger, *75k* dataset was used to evaluate quality of the generated fingerprints, as well as performance in terms on execution time. The 75k dataset (28GB uncompressed) was generated from the seed of 9k distinct books where a random number of derivatives were created in range $1-15$ with random corruption rates in range $0-5\%$.

4 Similarity preserving fingerprints

We chose to work with simhash fingerprints because of it's compactness and simplicity. In order to create a simhash fingerprint for the given book, a clear text must be extracted from the book file and converted to a set of features. Since our setting does not resemble traditional monolithic database, but rather a set of distributed libraries, our approach is not able to use *inverse document frequency* (IDF) analysis[2]. Thus, feature vector extraction is minimal and consists of identifying lower-cased terms as character n-grams and counting term occurrence.

4.1 Fingerprint computation

An arbitrary hash length n[3] is selected and n-dimensional fingerprint vector *sh* is initialized to all zeroes. In order to calculate a fingerprint, every feature in the feature vector f is hashed to a n-bit digest $h(f_i)$ using an arbitrary (cryptographic) hash function. Bit b at the position j in the computed digest $h(f_i)$ impacts the value at the same position in sh vector as follows: if b is 1, then $sh[j]$ is incremented by the weight of feature f_i; if not, then $sh[j]$ is decremented by the same weight. Weight of feature is equal to term occurrence calculated for a given feature in the feature extraction phase. The final fingerprint is calculated by reducing vector sh to a n-bit number where bit at position i is determined by the sign of the i-th element in the sh.

[2]IDF requires access to global collection

[3]We used hash lengths between 64 and 256 bits with the step of 32

4.2 Fingerprint similarity

Books that differ in small number of characters or words will have fingerprints that differ in a small number of bits. In order to illustrate this property of the simhash fingerprint, we corrupted three books of different sizes at a corruption rate in range $1-10\%$. Difference for 128-bit fingerprints (in Hamming distance) between canonical book and each corrupted version is presented in Fig. 1.

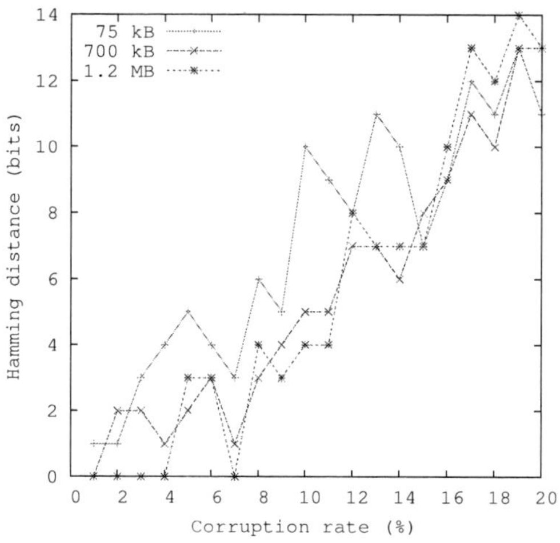

Figure 1: Impact of corruption rate on fingerprint similarity for books with different text lengths

Results show that distance between canonical and derivative texts correlates with corruption rate. Moreover, figure indicates that fingerprints of smaller books are more sensitive to text variations[4].

5 Experimental results

In this section we present and discuss evaluation methodology and results. First, we describe preliminary evaluation of the proposed method using k-means clustering on the smaller dataset. Clustering is used to confirm, in a very simple and intuitive way, that coderivative book fingerprints group (or "gravitate") well around known canonical books. In a realistic setting a number of canonical books and their distribution is unknown. Thus, we use efficient bucket-based similarity queries to

[4]We plan to address this issue in future work with the encoding of size information in the fingerprint itself

identify coderivative books on the larger dataset with variable number of coderivative books.

5.1 Fingerprint clustering

Initial feasibility test and exploration of design parameters for the proposed similarity preserving fingerprints is performed using k-means clustering on the smaller *1k* dataset. The main idea is not to identify coderivative books using clustering, but to test how well the proposed method groups books based only on distance between corresponding fingerprints. Generated book fingerprints are converted from an integer representation to a feature vector of zeros and ones. Finally, book fingerprints are clustered using k-means algorithm where the number of clusters equals the number of canonical books. Standard accuracy measures are calculated based on the difference between the obtained clusters and the gold truth cluster information.

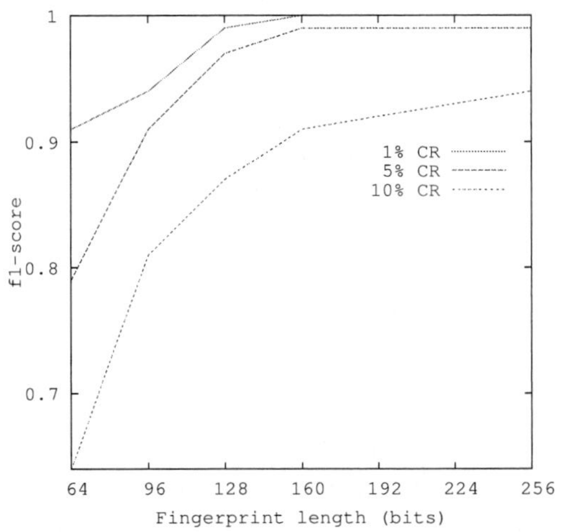

Figure 2: Clustering accuracy for different fingerprint lengths on the 1k dataset

Results for different fingerprint lengths and corruption rates are presented using F_1 score on Fig. 2. Please note that we have evaluated different n-gram lengths for feature extraction on 1k dataset, of both characters and words, and character-level approach outperformed word-level approach (also observed in (Spasojevic and Poncin, 2011)). Best results were obtained with character n-grams of size 4 (we did not include these results due to limited space). It is clear that accuracy grows as fingerprint length increases and corruption rate decreases. Results suggest that 128-bit fingerprints achieve satisfactory accuracy ($F_1 = 0.97$) for the average corruption rate of 5%.

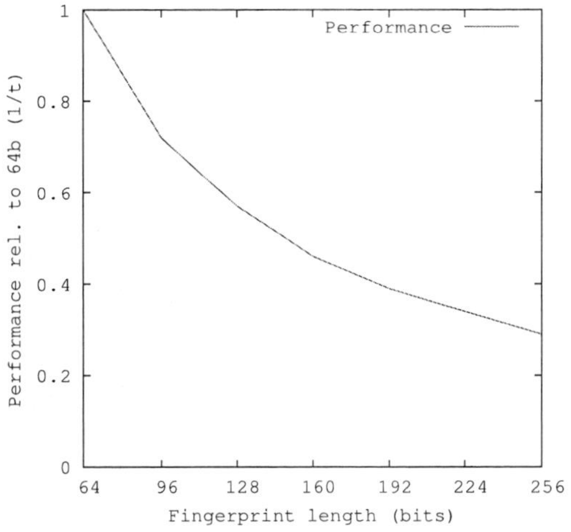

Figure 3: Performance drop for the increasing fingerprint lengths on the 1k dataset

However, note that there is a trade-off between performance and quality of results. Performance, defined as an inverse of the fingerprint generation execution time in minutes related to the 64-bit fingerprint, expectedly drops with the increase in fingerprint length (Fig. 3).

5.2 Similarity queries

In the real-world setting a number of clusters and distribution of books per cluster are unknown. Thus, evaluation of the proposed algorithm with 128-bit fingerprints is evaluated on the larger *75k* dataset that is generated with the intention to resemble real-world digital library, i.e. number of coderivative books is not fixed. In order to analyze Hamming distance thresholds for coderivative books, instead of clustering a brute-force similarity queries are run over whole dataset. That is, for every book a set of other books from the dataset is identified whose fingerprints have maximum distance of d bits. Since brute-force querying over the whole dataset has $O(n^2)$ time complexity, we have implemented a bucketing algorithm that significantly reduces execution time with minimal accuracy penalty. Fingerprints are divided into an arbitrary number of bands, and a pair of fingerprints are considered candidates for similarity only if they are identical in at least one band (Rajaraman and Ullman, 2011). Precision and recall are calculated for every query as a number of coderivative books divided by the number of returned results or number of expected results, respectively. Figure 4 presents precision and recall graphs for various d for both brute-force and bucketing versions.

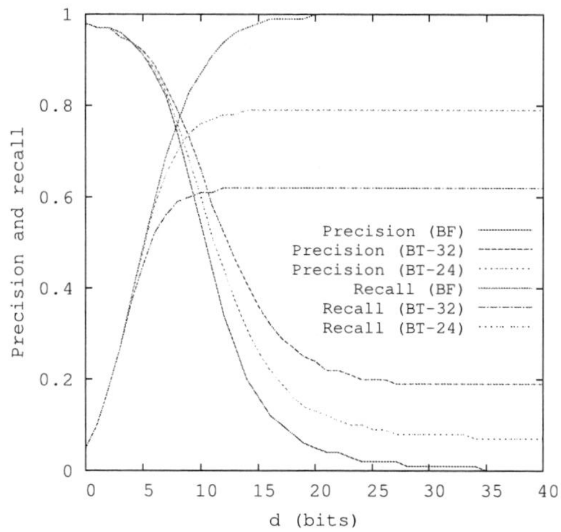

Figure 4: Precision and recall for various d on the 75k dataset for brute-force queries (BF) and bucketing (BT) algorithms

Brute-force queries over the whole dataset achieve the best F_1 score of 0.75 at $d = 7$ bits but also have worst average execution time of 29.73 minutes[5]. The bucketing version was tested with different band lengths of 24 and 32 bits, respectively. Best F_1 score for the 24-bit band was 0.73 at $d = 7$, which is tolerable (2.6% lower precision compared to brute-force) since average execution time is reduced to only 1.22 minutes. With the increased band lengths accuracy decreases but execution time significantly drops, e.g. 32-bit band version achieves F_1 of 0.67 with the execution time of only 8.55 seconds. However, note that bucketing algorithms can not achieve high recall since some candidates which are not identical in any band never get a chance to be compared. Such performance suggests that bucketing algorithms, with some implementation improvements, could be used for real-time detection of the top-k near duplicates.

[5]All the experiments were conducted on an Intel Core 2 Quad 2.66GHz CPU with 8GB of memory, running Ubuntu 14.04 LTS

6 Conclusions and future work

In conclusion, we described an application of the simhash algorithm for generation of similarity-preserving digital book fingerprints derived from the content of the book. We further evaluated our proposed method on the synthetic dataset which was generated by randomly mutating canonical books. Books were mutated at different rates with various mutations that simulate real-world noisy libraries. Preliminary results suggest that proposed techniques could be useful for the identification of coderivative books.

Traditional book identifiers, in form of ISBN numbers, embed metadata (geographical area, publisher, title etc.) and, being only 13 digits long, enable efficient transfer and computer processing. In addition to these benefits, proposed similarity-preserving fingerprints enable quick calculation of the semantic distance between any two books in the universe of all digital books. A combination of these is the apparatus for approaching chaotic world of digital file repositories in the age of the Internet. Resulting composite book identifier, comprised of both metadata (ISBN) and identifiers derived from content, could be part of future infrastructure based on peer-to-peer distributed heterogeneous network or a centralized service provided by the institutions.

In addition to composite book identifier, future explorations will include detection of different editions or translations of a single book and application of similar methods for books comprised of mostly images. Moreover, we are working on crawlers for amateur libraries and public archives with the goal of collecting a larger real-world dataset.

Acknowledgments

This work was supported in part by the Croatian science foundation through the Recommender System for Service-oriented Architecture research project and in part by Leuphana Universität Lüneburg, DCRL Digital Cultures Research Lab. The authors would like to thank Robert M. Ochshorn and Goran Glavaš for their invaluable comments and suggestions and Project Gutenberg for their book collection.

References

Ahmad Abdulkader and Mathew R Casey. 2009. Low cost correction of ocr errors using learning in a multi-engine environment. In *Document Analysis and Recognition, 2009. ICDAR'09. 10th International Conference on*, pages 576–580. IEEE.

Sergey Brin, James Davis, and Hector Garcia-Molina. 1995. Copy detection mechanisms for digital documents. In *ACM SIGMOD Record*, volume 24, pages 398–409. ACM.

Andrei Z Broder. 1997. On the resemblance and containment of documents. In *Compression and Complexity of Sequences 1997. Proceedings*, pages 21–29. IEEE.

Moses S Charikar. 2002. Similarity estimation techniques from rounding algorithms. In *Proceedings of the thiry-fourth annual ACM symposium on Theory of computing*, pages 380–388. ACM.

Peter Christen. 2012. A survey of indexing techniques for scalable record linkage and deduplication. *Knowledge and Data Engineering, IEEE Transactions on*, 24(9):1537–1555.

Jeffrey Esakov, Daniel P Lopresti, and Jonathan S Sandberg. 1994. Classification and distribution of optical character recognition errors. In *IS&T/SPIE 1994 International Symposium on Electronic Imaging: Science and Technology*, pages 204–216. International Society for Optics and Photonics.

Shaolei Feng and R Manmatha. 2006. A hierarchical, hmm-based automatic evaluation of ocr accuracy for a digital library of books. In *Digital Libraries, 2006. JCDL'06. Proceedings of the 6th ACM/IEEE-CS Joint Conference on*, pages 109–118. IEEE.

Monika Henzinger. 2006. Finding near-duplicate web pages: a large-scale evaluation of algorithms. In *Proceedings of the 29th annual international ACM SIGIR conference on Research and development in information retrieval*, pages 284–291. ACM.

Phuc-Tran Ho, Hee-Sun Kim, and Sung-Ryul Kim. 2014. Application of sim-hash algorithm and big data analysis in spam email detection system. In *Proceedings of the 2014 Conference on Research in Adaptive and Convergent Systems*, pages 242–246. ACM.

Timothy C Hoad and Justin Zobel. 2003. Methods for identifying versioned and plagiarized documents. *Journal of the American society for information science and technology*, 54(3):203–215.

ISBN Information. 2015. `http://isbn-information.com/history-of-the-isbn-system.html`. Accessed: 2015-05-05.

Markus Krajewski. 2011. *Paper machines: about cards & catalogs, 1548-1929*. MIT Press.

Udi Manber et al. 1994. Finding similar files in a large file system. In *Usenix Winter*, volume 94, pages 1–10.

Gurmeet Singh Manku, Arvind Jain, and Anish Das Sarma. 2007. Detecting near-duplicates for web crawling. In *Proceedings of the 16th international conference on World Wide Web*, pages 141–150. ACM.

L Padmasree, Vamshi Ambati, J Chandulal, M Rao, and Regional Mega Scanning Center. 2006. Signature based duplication detection in digital libraries. *Signature*, 10001011:00001100.

Bingfeng Pi, Shunkai Fu, Weilei Wang, and Song Han. 2009. Simhash-based effective and efficient detecting of near-duplicate short messages. In *Proceedings of the 2nd Symposium International Computer Science and Computational Technology*. Citeseer.

Project Gutenberg. 2015. `http://www.gutenberg.org`. Accessed: 2015-05-01.

Anand Rajaraman and Jeffrey David Ullman. 2011. *Mining of massive datasets*. Cambridge University Press.

Martin WC Reynaert. 2011. Character confusion versus focus word-based correction of spelling and ocr variants in corpora. *International Journal on Document Analysis and Recognition (IJDAR)*, 14(2):173–187.

Narayanan Shivakumar and Hector Garcia-Molina. 1995. Scam: A copy detection mechanism for digital documents.

Nemanja Spasojevic and Guillaume Poncin. 2011. Large scale page-based book similarity clustering. In *Document Analysis and Recognition (ICDAR), 2011 International Conference on*, pages 119–125. IEEE.

Md Sharif Uddin, Chanchal K Roy, Kevin A Schneider, and Abram Hindle. 2011. On the effectiveness of simhash for detecting near-miss clones in large scale software systems. In *Reverse Engineering (WCRE), 2011 18th Working Conference on*, pages 13–22. IEEE.

Jakob Voß, Hotho Andreas, and Jäschke Robert. 2009. Mapping bibliographic records with bibliographic hash keys.

Kyle Williams and C Lee Giles. 2013. Near duplicate detection in an academic digital library. In *Proceedings of the 2013 ACM symposium on Document engineering*, pages 91–94. ACM.

Ismet Zeki Yalniz, Ethem F Can, and R Manmatha. 2011. Partial duplicate detection for large book collections. In *Proceedings of the 20th ACM international conference on Information and knowledge management*, pages 469–474. ACM.

When Translation Requires Interpretation: Collaborative Computer–Assisted Translation of Ancient Texts

D. Albanesi[1], A. Bellandi[1], G. Benotto[1], G. Di Segni[2], E. Giovannetti[1]
[1] Istituto di Linguistica Computazionale, Consiglio Nazionale delle Ricerche
Via G. Moruzzi 1, 56124, Pisa - Italy
name.surname@ilc.cnr.it
[2] Istituto di Biologia Cellulare e Neurobiologia, Consiglio Nazionale delle Ricerche
Via Ramarini 32, 00015, Monterotondo (Rome) - Italy
gianfranco.disegni@cnr.it

Abstract

This paper introduces the main features of *Traduco*, a Web-based, collaborative Computer-Assisted Translation (CAT) tool developed to support the translation of ancient texts. In addition to the standard components offered by traditional CAT tools, *Traduco* includes a number of features designed to ease the translation of ancient texts, such as the Babylonian Talmud, posing specific structural, stylistic, linguistic and hermeneutical challenges.

1 Introduction

We here describe *Traduco*, a collaborative Web application designed to support the translation of ancient texts, developed in the context of a project for the translation of the Babylonian Talmud (BT) into Italian. *Traduco* extends most of the standard components of a traditional Computer–Assisted Translation (CAT) tool with specific features needed to support the translation of ancient texts such as the BT. The design and development of *Traduco* required the adoption of a multidisciplinary approach, leveraging on advances in software engineering, knowledge engineering, computational linguistics, Talmudic knowledge, Semitic linguistics and publishing. The Babylonian Talmud consists in the teachings of the Masters of Judaism in a span of six centuries, until the fifth century, and it is divided into Mishnah and Gemara. The Babylonian Talmud consists of 5422 pages. It is not a unified work but it is a collection of sayings of many different Masters, delivered in the course of several generations, partly in Hebrew and mostly in Aramaic. It has a complex layering and it is written in a concise manner, difficult to understand, using many idioms that, if translated literally, would be incomprehensible. The way in which the discussion develops is that of questions and answers, objections and attempts to reply. Many passages occur in different tractates, with or without variants. Having dealt with the translation of a literary creation of such hermeneutical complexity, richness and heterogeneity of topics as the Babylonian Talmud, *Traduco* can be easily applied to support the translation of other ancient texts and to manage other languages.

2 The *Traduco* System

Computer–Assisted Translation (CAT) tools are designed to aid in the translation of a text (Christensen and Schjoldager, 1996; Gordon, 1996; Planas, 2005; Barracchina et. al, 2009). The core technology of a CAT tool is the Translation Memory (TM), a repository that allows translators to consult and reuse past translations, primarily developed to speed up the translation process (Reinke, 2006; Somers, 2003; Koehn, 2009; O'Brien, 2006; Planas and Furuse, 1999). However, considering the nature of the texts we are working on (as the BT), the quality of the translation is much more important than the translation pace. For this reason, a system developed to support the translation of ancient texts must go beyond the standard set of functionalities offered by a traditional CAT tool. Moreover, particularly complex texts, as the BT, can require the competencies of a multiplicity of specialized users that must be able to translate the very same text in a collaborative way on a Web environment. The most used available open source CAT tools (OpenTM[1], OmegaT[2], Transolution[3], Olanto[4], MateCat[5], MASMCAT[6])

[1] http://www.opentm2.org/
[2] http://www.omegat.org/
[3] http://www.tran-solution.net/
[4] http://olanto.org/
[5] https://www.matecat.com/
[6] http://www.casmacat.eu/

Proceedings of the 9th SIGHUM Workshop on Language Technology for Cultural Heritage, Social Sciences, and Humanities, pages 84–88,
Beijing, China, July 30, 2015. ©2015 Association for Computational Linguistics and The Asian Federation of Natural Language Processing

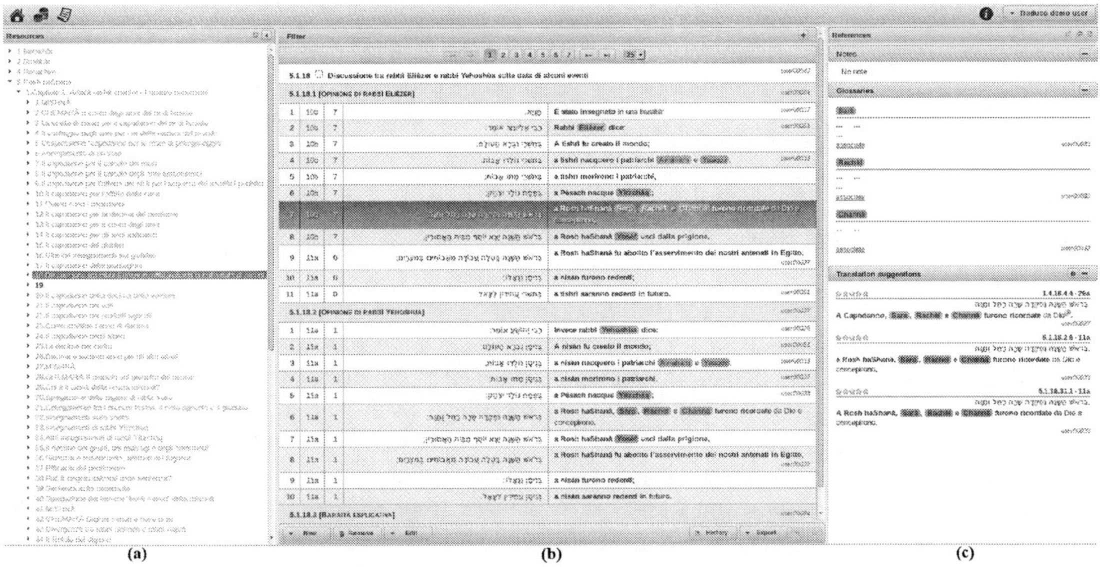

Figure 1: The main GUI of *Traduco* system. (a) hierarchical structure of the translated text; (b) translation table; (c) translation references: notes, glossaries, translation suggestions.

and even the main commercial tools (Deja Vu[7], SDL Trados[8], memoQ[9], memsource[10]) are not suitable for the collaborative translation of ancient texts (Bellandi, 2014), since they do not respond to the specific needs of those specialists. In the following, we briefly illustrate some of *Traduco*'s features specifically designed to answer to these needs. We strongly encourage to try the demo version of *Traduco*[11] (all the references have been blocked for the review process).

Manual segmentation process and hierarchical structuring.
Typically, a CAT tool automatically segments the source text into sentences. However, several different languages and dialectal variants alternate in the text of the BT, making difficult, if not impossible, to develop an automatic (statistical or pattern–based) tool able to split sentences on language transitions. In addition, to maximise the use of the TM and to reuse past translations, it is necessary to isolate the formulaic expressions scattered all over the whole text, even if they do not cover an entire sentence. *Traduco* eases the process of manual segmentation by providing the "Generate" function. Instead of translating pericope by pericope[12], a translator can insert, at once, a sequence of pericopes: a whole portion of text can be pasted inside a specific text field and split into distinct lines, each of which will be interpreted as a single pericope. To ease the translation process a rich text editor is provided with a series of buttons opening subpanels (see Figure 2). From left to right: bold (to indicate literal translations), italic (to indicate quotations from the Bible), underline (to mark Hebrew words for publishing purposes), small caps (for the Mishnah and quotations from the Mishnah), notes, semantic annotations, undo, redo, remove formatting, show HTML source, special characters (e.g. for transliterations, quotation marks, etc.), and, finally, six shortcuts for bibliographic references (e.g., Bible, Legal Code, Mishnah, etc.). Furthermore, due to the complexity of the inner structure of the BT, *Traduco* allows to hierarchically organize the translation both to preserve the structure of the source text (e.g. in the

[7]http://www.translation.net/deja_vu_x.html

[8]http://www.translationzone.com/products/sdl-trados-studio/

[9]https://www.memoq.com/get-memoq

[10]https://www.memsource.com/en

[11]Test *Traduco* at http://146.48.92.138:8082/talmud (user: traducodemo - password: traducodemo): we recommend to use Mozilla Firefox. You will also find an exhaustive use-cases guide to test the main features of the System (click on the "i" button, once logged in). Parts of data, authors, and parts of the original BT text have been clouded for privacy and rights reasons.

[12]A pericope defines a portion of text having an arbitrary length.

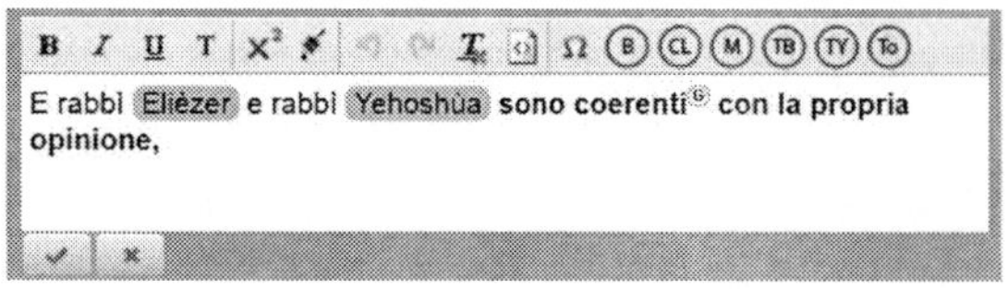

Figure 2: The rich text editor. The sentence means: "Rabbi Eliézer and Rabbi Yehoshúa are coherent with their own opinion"

case of the BT, tractates, chapters, and blocks[13]) and to add customized levels (e.g. logical units[14]).

Literal and explicative translations, notes.
An ancient writing such as the BT cannot be translated as a modern text, since a literal translation would not be intelligible to a modern reader. Therefore, a good translation of the BT requires the addition of explicative integrations within the translation, which is not merely a translation, but, to a certain extent, an interpretative commentary in itself. To do so, *Traduco* provides tools that enable to distinguish the literal part of the translation (indicated in bold) from the explicative additions of the translators/scholars. Furthermore, it allows the insertion of different types of explicative notes in the text (see Figure 2 for an example of a generic note, shown as a little "G" inside a circle, following the word "coerenti": the text of the note will be inserted in a dedicated panel in the upper right part of the interface).

Revision support: multiple user roles, versioning.
Traduco offers a multirole environment: users can either be translators, revisors, editors or administrators. Concerning revisors, they can edit translations done by translators, which, in turn, can exploit the versioning system to keep track of the history of each resource (translated pericope, note, glossary entry). Additionally, revisors can bring the translators' attention to a specific portion of translation by adding special revision notes. Finally, revisors and editors can work together to attain a more coherent, homogeneous and fluent translation of the text by comparing each translation to the ones the suggestion component shows.

[13]A block corresponds to a discussion about a homogeneous and well-defined subject.

[14]A logical unit is a part of a block with a defined logic, e.g. thesis, hypothesis, objection, question, biblical quotation, etc.

Ranking of translation suggestions.
Being a collaborative Web environment, *Traduco* can rank the translation suggestions (Vanallemeersch, 2015; Wolff, 2014) stored in the TM on the basis of several parameters, including the authoritativeness of the translator that produced the suggested translation and the tractate the suggestions belong to.

Semantic annotation and glossaries.
Since the BT translation includes discussions regarding many different fields of knowledge (jurisprudence, liturgy, ethics, rituals, philosophy, trade, medicine, astronomy, etc.), it can greatly benefit from semantic annotations, in order to provide readers with further assistance in the interpretation of the text. For the translation of the BT, *Traduco* provides a set of six predefined semantic classes: concepts, linguistic expressions, Rabbis, measures, nature, and persons. This functionality allows the creation of specialized glossaries that can be queried and browsed in a dedicated section of the system. Annotations can be done by selecting the text and then choosing one of the classes in the sub–panel opening through the paintbrush button of the editor (see Figure 2). A semantic annotation is represented with a specific colored highlighting: in Figure 2, for example, two names of Rabbis have been annotated and highlighted in gray. Each annotation can be accompanied by a free textual description (see the "Glossaries" panel on the right of Figure 1(c)), an optional transliteration and an optional Hebrew original form. A new annotation can be associated to a canonical form by referring to an existing glossary entry: it can be done with the "Associate" link at the bottom of the "Glossaries" panel. Furthermore, glossary entries can be browsed and searched in a dedicated interface, opened via the "Glossaries" button on the upper left part of the main GUI.

3 General Architecture and Technical Solutions

From the technical point of view, *Traduco* was designed as a group of independent web–based components connected by interfaces. It is based on the software design pattern known as "three–tier architecture", and it exploits Apache Tomcat v7.0 as web server. The system was implemented using

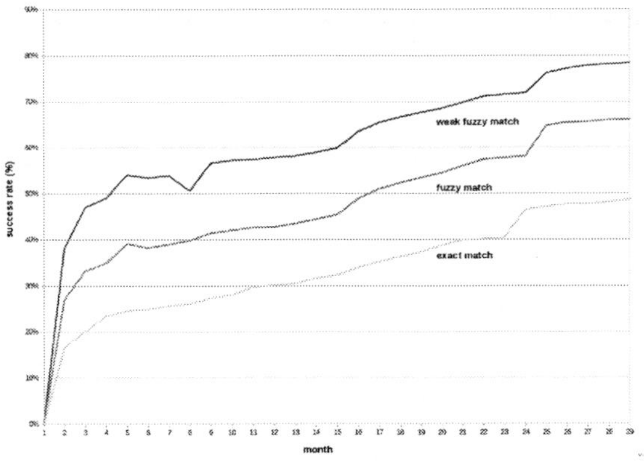

Figure 3: The TM redundancy curves w.r.t. the ranking of the similarity function ED.

the Java 2 Standard Edition (J2SE) framework, allowing, among the other things, to easily manipulate unicode characters and thus to manage other languages. Relational persistence and query services are managed by Hibernate v4.3.7 that takes care of the mapping from Java classes to the Mysql v5.0 database tables. The presentation tier has been implemented by means of JavaServer Faces (JSF). As JSF library, we used Primefaces v5.1. To accomplish the translation suggestion task, the system includes a Translation Memory (TM) designed to remember every translated portion of text, organized at the pericope level. For each pericope, the TM contains the translation, the author of the translation, and the reference to the tractate to which the pericope belongs (here called context). In order to develop a language independent component, we took account of adopting similarity measures based on edit distance, $ED(p_1, p_2)$, by considering two pericopes to be more similar when the same terms tend to appear in the same order. Given a pericope p_q of length $|p_q|$, and a distance error δ, our similarity function allows to both retrieve all pericopes in the TM (called suggestions) such that $ED(p_q, p) \leq round(|p_q|)$, and rank suggestions, not only on the basis of the ED outcome, but also on both the current context and the suggestion author. In order to take into account the lenght of the query (p_q), we considered δ as the percentage of admitted errors w.r.t. the sentences to be translated, multiplying it by the length of the query segment (Mandreoli et al., 2002). In collaboration with the translators' team, we have experimentally tuned δ to 0.7. Our similarity algorithm is based on dynamic programming, and its implementation refers to (Navarro, 2001). The inverted index data structure is the central component of our search engine indexing algorithm, for accessing the TM. The goal of our search engine implementation is to optimize the speed of the queries to provide a more efficient suggestion of the pre-existing translations. In particular, we used a record level inverted index technique, containing a list of references to pericopes for each word. In order to roughly estimate the degree of redundancy of the TM, we conducted a jackknife experiment (Wu, 2009), as reported in Figure 3. The curve labelled with "exact match" represents perfect suggestions, while the one labelled with "fuzzy match" indicates that few corrections are required to improve the suggestion. Finally, the curve labelled with "weak fuzzy match" refers, in most of the cases, to acceptable suggestions. The percentage of source segments found both verbatim and fuzzy in the memory grows logarithmically both with time and the size of the TM.

4 Conclusions and Perspectives

It is renowned that CAT techniques work best on texts that are highly repetitive, and for this reason they are mainly applied to the translation of technical manuals. They are also helpful for translating incremental changes in a previously translated document, corresponding, for example, to minor changes in a new version of a user manual. Thus, Translation Memories have not been considered appropriate for literary or creative texts. One of the novelty of our work is that of applying this kind of approach to the process of translating ancient texts. In general, these texts share common features, both from the content and the linguistic perspective. As exemplified in particular by our test bed, ancient texts can be lexically poor and repetitive by nature, they have a complex inner structure that has to be taken into account while translating, and they necessarily need annotations at various levels of granularity in order to make ancient concepts expressed in the texts understandable to contemporary readers. Such complexity also entails that, in order to be properly translated, these texts should be processed by a team of scholars with heterogeneous competences. Our system satisfy this need by introducing the idea of collaborative work to CAT and by enhancing it with tools apt to satisfy the different users competences (i.e., translators, revisors, editors).

Acknowledgments

This work has been conducted in the context of the research project TALMUD and the scientific partnership between S.c.a r.l. "Progetto Traduzione del Talmud Babilonese" and ILC-CNR and on the basis of the regulations stated in the "Protocollo dIntesa" (memorandum of understanding) between the Italian Presidency of the Council of Ministers, the Italian Ministry of Education, Universities and Research, the Union of Italian Jewish Communities, the Italian Rabbinical College and the Italian National Research Council (21/01/2011).

References

Sergio Barracchina, Oliver Bender, Francisco Casacuberta, Jorge Civera, Elsa Cubel, Shahram Khadivi, Antonio Lagarda, Hermann Ney, Jesús Tomás and Enrique Vidal. 2009. Statistical approaches to computer-assisted translation. *Computational Linguistics*, 35(1): 3-28.

Andrea Bellandi, Alessia Bellusci, Emiliano Giovannetti. 2014. *Computer Assisted Translation of Ancient Texts: the Babylonian Talmud Case Study*. In: Proceedings of the 11th International Natural Language Processing and Cognitive Systems, pp. 287-302, Venice, Italy.

Tina P. Christensen and Anne Schjoldager. 1996. Translation-memory (TM) research: what do we know and how do we know it? *Hermes, Journal of Language and Communication Studies*, 44: 89-101.

Ian Gordon. 1996. *Letting the CAT out of the bag–or was it MT?* In: Proceedings of the 8th International Conference on Translating and the Computer, Aslib, London.

Philipp Koehn. 2009. *A web-based interactive computer aided translation tool.* In: Proceedings of the ACL-IJCNLP 2009 Software Demonstrations. Association for Computational Linguistics, 2009. p. 17-20.

Federica Mandreoli, Riccardo Martoglia, and Paolo Tiberio. 2002. *Searching Similar (Sub) Sentences for Example-Based Machine Translation.* In: Atti del Decimo Convegno Nazionale su Sistemi Evoluti per Basi di Dati (SEBD). Portoferraio (Isola dÉlba), Italy.

Gonzalo Navarro. 2001. A guided tour to approximate string matching. *ACM computing surveys (CSUR)*, 33(1): 31-88.

Sharon O'Brien. 2006. Eye-tracking and translation memory matches. *Perspectives: Studies in translatology*, 14(3): 185-205.

Emmanuel Planas, Osamu Furuse. 1999. *Formalizing translation memories.* In: Machine Translation Summit VII. 1999. p. 331-339.

Emmanuel Planas. 2005. *SIMILIS Second-generation translation memory software* In: Proceedings of the 27th International Conference on Translating and the Computer, Aslib, London.

Uwe Reinke. 2006. Translation Memories *Encyclopedia of Language and Linguistics*, 61-65.

Harold L. Somers. 2003. Translation memory systems. *Benjamins Translation Library*, 35 (2003): 31-48.

Tom Vanallemeersch, Vincent Vandeghinste. 2015. *Assessing Linguistically Aware Fuzzy Matching in Translation Memories.* In: Proceedings of the 18th Annual Conference of the European Association for Machine Translation (EAMT2015), Antalya, Turkey.

Friedel Wolff, Laurette Pretorius, Paul Buitelaar. 2014. *Missed Opportunities in Translation Memory Matching.* In: Proceedings of the 9th International Conference on Language Resources and Evaluation (LREC): 4401-4406, Reykjavik, Iceland.

Jeff Chien-Fu Wu. 1986. Bootstrap and Other Resampling Methods in Regression Analysis. *The Annals of Statistics*, 14(4): 1261-1295.

Integrating Query Performance Prediction in Term Scoring for Diachronic Thesaurus

Chaya Liebeskind, Ido Dagan
Department of Computer Science
Bar-Ilan University
Ramat-Gan, Israel
liebchaya@gmail.com
dagan@cs.biu.ac.il

Abstract

A diachronic thesaurus is a lexical resource that aims to map between modern terms and their semantically related terms in earlier periods. In this paper, we investigate the task of collecting a list of relevant modern target terms for a domain-specific diachronic thesaurus. We propose a supervised learning scheme, which integrates features from two closely related fields: Terminology Extraction and Query Performance Prediction (QPP). Our method further expands modern candidate terms with ancient related terms, before assessing their corpus relevancy with QPP measures. We evaluate the empirical benefit of our method for a thesaurus for a diachronic Jewish corpus.

1 Introduction

In recent years, there has been growing interest in diachronic lexical resources, which comprise terms from different language periods. (Borin and Forsberg, 2011; Liebeskind et al., 2013; Riedl et al., 2014). These resources are mainly used for studying language change and supporting searches in historical domains, bridging the lexical gap between modern and ancient language.

In particular, we are interested in this paper in a certain type of diachronic thesaurus. It contains entries for modern terms, denoted as *target terms*. Each entry includes a list of ancient *related terms*. Beyond being a historical linguistic resource, such thesaurus is useful for supporting searches in a diachronic corpus, composed of both modern and ancient documents. For example, in our historical Jewish corpus, the modern Hebrew term for *terminal patient*[1] has only few verbatim occurrences, in modern documents, but this topic has been widely discussed in ancient periods. A domain searcher needs the diachronic thesaurus to enrich the search with ancient synonyms or related terms, such as *dying* and *living for the moment*.

Prior work on diachronic thesauri addressed the problem of collecting relevant related terms for given thesaurus entries. In this paper we focus on the complementary preceding task of collecting a relevant list of modern target terms for a diachronic thesaurus in a certain domain. As a starting point, we assume that a list of meaningful terms in the modern language is given, such as titles of Wikipedia articles. Then, our task is to automatically decide which of these *candidate terms* are likely to be relevant for the corpus domain and should be included in the thesaurus. In other words, we need to decide which of the candidate modern terms corresponds to a concept that has been discussed significantly in the diachronic domain corpus.

Our task is closely related to term scoring in the known Terminology Extraction (TE) task in NLP. The goal of corpus-based TE is to automatically extract prominent terms from a given corpus and score them for domain relevancy. In our setting, since all the target terms are modern, we avoid extracting them from the diachronic corpus of modern and ancient language. Instead, we use a given candidate list and apply only the term scoring phase. As a starting point, we adopt a rich set of state-of-the-art TE scoring measures and integrate them as features in a common supervised classification approach (Foo and Merkel, 2010; Zhang et al., 2010; Loukachevitch, 2012).

Given our Information Retrieval (IR) motivation, we notice a closely related task to TE, namely Query Performance Prediction (QPP). QPP methods are designed to estimate the retrieval quality of search queries, by assessing their relevance to the text collection. Therefore, QPP scoring measures

[1] The examples in this paper refer to Hebrew terms that were literally translated.

Proceedings of the 9th SIGHUM Workshop on Language Technology for Cultural Heritage, Social Sciences, and Humanities, pages 89–94,
Beijing, China, July 30, 2015.

seem to be potentially suitable also for our terminology scoring task, by considering the candidate term as a search query. Some of the QPP measures are indeed similar in nature to the TE methods, analyzing the distribution of the query terms within the collection. However, some of the QPP methods have different IR-biased characteristics and may provide a marginal contribution. Therefore, we adopted them as additional features for our classifier and indeed observed a performance increase.

Most of the QPP methods prioritize query terms with high frequency in the corpus. However, in a diachronic corpus, such criterion may sometimes be problematic. A modern target term might appear only in few modern documents, while being referred to, via ancient terminology, also in ancient documents. Therefore, we would like our prediction measure to be aware of these ancient documents as well. Following a particular QPP measure (Zhou and Croft, 2007), we address this problem through Query Expansion (QE). Accordingly, our method first expands the query containing the modern candidate term, then calculates the QPP scores of the expanded query and then utilizes them as scoring features. Combining the baseline features with our expansion-based QPP features yields additional improvement in the classification results.

2 Term Scoring Measures

This section reviews common measures developed for Terminology Extraction (Section 2.1) and for Query Performance Prediction (Section 2.2). Table 1 lists those measures that were considered as features in our system, as described in Section 3.

2.1 Terminology Extraction

Terminology Extraction (TE) methods aim to identify terms that are frequently used in a specific domain. Typically, linguistic processors (e.g. POS tagger, phrase chunker) are used to filter out stop words and restrict candidate terms to nouns or noun phrases. Then, statistical measures are used to rank the candidate terms. There are two main terminological properties that the statistical measures identify: *unithood* and *termhood*. Measures that express unithood indicate the collocation strength of units that comprise a single term. Measures that express termhood indicate the statistical prominence of the term in the target domain corpus. For our task, we focus on the second property, since the candidates are taken from a key-list of terms whose coherence in the language is already known. Measures expressing termhood are based either on frequency in the target corpus (1, 2, 3, 4, 9, 11, 12, 13)[2], or on comparison with frequency in a reference background corpus (8, 14, 16). Recently, approaches which combine both unithood and termhood were investigated as well (7, 8, 15, 16).

2.2 Query Performance Prediction

Query Performance Prediction (QPP) aims to estimate the quality of answers that a search system would return in response to a particular query. Statistical QPP methods are categorized into two types: pre-retrieval methods, analyzing the distribution of the query term within the document collection; and post-retrieval methods, additionally analyzing the search results. Some of the pre-retrieval methods are similar to TE methods based on the same term frequency statistics.

Pre-retrieval methods measure various properties of the query: specificity (17, 18, 24, 25), similarity to the corpus (19), coherence of the documents containing the query terms (26), variance of the query terms' weights over the documents containing it (20); and relatedness, as good performance is expected when the query terms co-occur frequently in the collection (21).

Post-retrieval methods are usually more complex, where the top search results are retrieved and analyzed. They are categorized into three main paradigms: clarity-based methods (28), robustness-based methods (22) and score distribution based methods (23, 29).

We pay special attention to two post-retrieval QPP methods; *Query Feedback* (22) and *Clarity* (23). The Clarity method measures the coherence of the query's search results with respect to the corpus. It is defined as the KL divergence between a language model induced from the result list and that induced from the corpus. The Query Feedback method measures the robustness of the query's results to query perturbations. It models retrieval as a communication channel. The input is the query, the channel is the search system, and the set of results is the noisy output of the channel. A new query is generated from the list of search

[2]The numbers in parentheses correspond to the numbers in Table 1.

Terminology Extraction measures			
1	Term Frequency (TF)	9	Relative Frequency
2	Document Frequency	10	N-gram Length
3	Residual Inverse Document Frequency (Manning and Schütze, 1999)	11	TF-Inverse Document Frequency (TF-IDF) (Witten et al., 1999)
4	Average Term frequency	12	Term Contribution (Liu et al., 2003)
5	Term Variance (Liu et al., 2005)	13	Term Variance Quality (Liu et al., 2005)
6	TF-Disjoint Corpora Frequency (Lopes et al., 2012)	14	Weirdness (Ahmad et al., 1999)
7	C-value (Frantzi and Ananiadou, 1999)	15	NC-value (Frantzi and Ananiadou, 1999)
8	Glossex (Kozakov et al., 2004)	16	TermExtractor (Sclano and Velardi, 2007)
Query Performance Prediction measures			
17	Average IDF (He and Ounis, 2004)	24	Average ICTF (Inverse collection term frequency) (Plachouras et al., 2004)
18	Query Scope (He and Ounis, 2004)	25	Simplified Clarity Score (He and Ounis, 2004)
19	Similarity Collection Query (Zhao et al., 2008)	26	Query Coherence (He et al., 2008)
20	Average Variance (Zhao et al., 2008)	27	Average Entropy (Cristina, 2013)
21	Term Relatedness (Hauff et al., 2008)	28	Clarity (Cronen-Townsend et al., 2002)
22	Query Feedback (Zhou and Croft, 2007)	29	Normalized Query Commitment (Shtok et al., 2009)
23	Weighted Information Gain (Zhou and Croft, 2007)		

Table 1: Prior art measures considered in our work

results, taking the terms with maximal contribution to the Clarity score, and then a second list of results is retrieved for that second query. The overlap between the two lists is the robustness score. Our suggested method was inspired by the Query Feedback measure, as detailed in the next section.

3 Integrated Term Scoring

We adopt the supervised framework for TE (Foo and Merkel, 2010; Zhang et al., 2010; Loukachevitch, 2012), considering each candidate target term as a learning instance. For each candidate, we calculate a set of features over which learning and classification are performed. The classification predicts which candidates are suitable as target terms for the diachronic thesaurus. Our baseline system (*TE*) includes state-of-the-art TE measures as features, listed in the upper part of Table 1.

Next, we introduce two system variants that integrate QPP measures as additional features. The first system, *TE-QPP*$_{Term}$, applies the QPP measures to the candidate term as the query. All QPP measures, listed in the lower part of Table 1, are utilized except for the Query Feedback measure (22) (see below). To verify which QPP features are actually beneficial for terminology scoring, we measure the marginal contribution of each feature via ablation tests in 10-fold cross validation over the training data (see Section 4.1). Features which did not yield marginal contribution were not included[3].

The two systems, described so far, rely on corpus occurrences of the original candidate term, prioritizing relatively frequent terms. In a diachronic corpus, however, a candidate term might be rare in its original modern form, yet frequently referred to by archaic forms. Therefore, we adopt a query expansion strategy based on Pseudo Relevance Feedback, which expands a query based on analyzing the top retrieved documents. In our setting, this approach takes advantage of a typical property of modern documents in a diachronic corpus, namely their temporally-mixed language. Often, modern documents in a diachronic domain include ancient terms that were either preserved in modern language or appear as citations. Therefore, an expanded query of a modern term, which retrieves only modern documents, is likely to pick some of these ancient terms as well. Thus, the expanded query would likely retrieve both modern and ancient documents and would allow QPP measures to evaluate the query relevance across periods.

Therefore, our second integrated system, *TE-QPP*$_{QE}$, utilizes the Pseudo Relevance Feedback Query Expansion approach to expand our modern candidate with topically-related terms. First, similarly to the Query Feedback measure (measure (22) in the lower part of Table 1), we expand the candidate by adding terms with maximal contribution (top 5, in our experiments) to the Clarity score (Section 2.2). Then, we calculate all QPP measures for the expanded query. Since the expan-

[3]Removed features from *TE-QPP*$_{Term}$: 17, 19, 22, 23, 24, 25.

sions that we extract from the top retrieved documents typically include ancient terms as well, the new scores may better express the relevancy of the candidate's topic across the diachronic corpus. We also performed feature selection, as done for the first system[4].

4 Evaluation

4.1 Evaluation Setting

We applied our method to the diachronic corpus is the Responsa project Hebrew corpus[5]. The Responsa corpus includes rabbinic case-law rulings which represent the historical-sociological milieu of real-life situations, collected over more than a thousand years, from the 11th century until today. The corpus consists of 81,993 documents, and was used for previous NLP and IR research (Choueka et al., 1971; Choueka et al., 1987; HaCohen-Kerner et al., 2008; Liebeskind et al., 2012; Zohar et al., 2013; Liebeskind et al., 2013).

The candidate target terms for our classification task were taken from the publicly available key-list of Hebrew Wikipedia entries[6]. Since many of these tens of thousands entries, such as person names and place names, were not suitable as target terms, we first filtered them by Hebrew Named Entity Recognition[7] and manually. Then, a list of approximately 5000 candidate target terms was manually annotated by two domain experts. The experts decided which of the candidates corresponds to a concept that has been discussed significantly in our diachronic domain corpus. Only candidates that the annotators agreed on their annotation were retained, and then balanced for equal number of positive and negative examples. Consequently, the balanced training and test sets contain 500 and 200 candidates, respectively.

For classification, Weka's[8] Support Vector Machine supervised classifier with polynomial kernel was used. We train the classifier with our training set and measure the accuracy on the test set.

4.2 Results

Table 2 compares the classification performance of our baseline (*TE*) and integrated systems, (*TE-QPP*$_{Term}$) and (*TE-QPP*$_{QE}$), proposed in Section 3.

[4]Removed features from *TE-QPP*$_{QE}$: 20, 21, 22, 26.
[5]http://www.biu.ac.il/jh/Responsa/
[6]http://he.wikipedia.org/wiki/
[7]http://www.cs.bgu.ac.il/ nlpproj/hebrewNER/
[8]http://www.cs.waikato.ac.nz/ml/weka/

Feature Set	Accuracy (%)
TE	61.5
TE-QPP$_{Term}$	65
TE-QPP$_{QE}$	**66.5**

Table 2: Comparison of system performance

In general, additional QPP features increase the classification accuracy. Even though the improvement of the term-based QPP over the baseline is not statistically significant according to the McNemar's test (McNemar, 1947), on our diachronic corpus it seems to help. Yet, when the QPP score is measured over the expanded candidate, and ancient documents are utilized, the performance increase is more notable (5 points) and the improvement over the baseline is statistically significant according to the McNemar's test with $p<0.05$.

We analyzed the false negative classifications of the baseline that were classified correctly by the QE-based configuration. We found that their expanded forms contain ancient terms that help the system making the right decision. For example, the Hebrew target term for *slippers* was expanded by the ancient expression corresponding to *made of leather*. This is a useful expansion since in the ancient documents slippers are discussed in the context of fasts, as in two of the Jewish fasts wearing leather shoes is forbidden and people wear cloth-made slippers.

5 Conclusions and Future Work

We introduced a method that combines features from two closely related tasks, terminology extraction and query performance prediction, to solve the task of target terms selection for a diachronic thesaurus. In our diachronic setting, we showed that enriching TE measures with QPP measures, particularly when calculated on expanded candidates, significantly improves performance. Our results suggest that it may be worth investigating this integrated approach also for other terminology extraction and QPP settings.

We plan to further explore the suggested method by utilizing additional query expansion algorithms. In particular, to avoid expanding queries for which expansion degrade retrieval performance, we plan to investigate the selective query expansion approach (Cronen-Townsend et al., 2004).

References

Khurshid Ahmad, Lee Gillam, and Lena Tostevin. 1999. University of surrey participation in trec8: Weirdness indexing for logical document extrapolation and retrieval (wilder). In *Proceedings of the eighth Text REtrieval Conference, TREC 1999*.

Lars Borin and Markus Forsberg. 2011. A diachronic computational lexical resource for 800 years of swedish. In Caroline Sporleder, Antal van den Bosch, and Kalliopi Zervanou, editors, *Language Technology for Cultural Heritage*, Theory and Applications of Natural Language Processing, pages 41–61. Springer Berlin Heidelberg.

Yaacov Choueka, M. Cohen, J. Dueck, Aviezri S. Fraenkel, and M. Slae. 1971. Full text document retrieval: Hebrew legal texts. In *Proceedings of the International ACM SIGIR conference on Information Storage and Retrieval, SIGIR 1971*, pages 61–79.

Yaacov Choueka, Aviezri S. Fraenkel, Shmuel T. Klein, and E. Segal. 1987. Improved techniques for processing queries in full-text systems. In *Proceedings of the 10th Annual International ACM SIGIR Conference on Research and Development in Information Retrieval, SIGIR 1987*, pages 306–315, New Orleans, USA. ACM.

Haiduc Sonia Cristina. 2013. *Supporting Text Retrieval Query Formulation In Software Engineering*. Ph.D. thesis, Wayne State University.

Steve Cronen-Townsend, Yun Zhou, and W. Bruce Croft. 2002. Predicting query performance. In *Proceedings of the 25th Annual International ACM SIGIR Conference on Research and Development in Information Retrieval*, SIGIR 2002, pages 299–306, New York, NY, USA. ACM.

Steve Cronen-Townsend, Yun Zhou, and W. Bruce Croft. 2004. A framework for selective query expansion. In *Proceedings of the Thirteenth ACM International Conference on Information and Knowledge Management*, CIKM 2004, pages 236–237, New York, NY, USA. ACM.

Jody Foo and Magnus Merkel. 2010. Using machine learning to perform automatic term recognition. In *Proceedings of the LREC 2010 Workshop on Methods for automatic acquisition of Language Resources and their evaluation methods*, pages 49–54.

Katerina T Frantzi and Sophia Ananiadou. 1999. The c-value/nc-value domain-independent method for multi-word term extraction. *Journal of Natural Language Processing*, 6(3):145–179.

Yaakov HaCohen-Kerner, Ariel Kass, and Ariel Peretz. 2008. Combined one sense disambiguation of abbreviations. In *Proceedings of ACL 2008: HLT, Short Papers*, pages 61–64.

Claudia Hauff, Djoerd Hiemstra, and Franciska de Jong. 2008. A survey of pre-retrieval query performance predictors. In *Proceedings of the 17th ACM Conference on Information and Knowledge Management*, CIKM 2008, pages 1419–1420, New York, NY, USA. ACM.

Ben He and Iadh Ounis. 2004. Inferring query performance using pre-retrieval predictors. In Alberto Apostolico and Massimo Melucci, editors, *String Processing and Information Retrieval*, volume 3246 of *Lecture Notes in Computer Science*, pages 43–54. Springer Berlin Heidelberg.

Jiyin He, Martha Larson, and Maarten de Rijke. 2008. Using coherence-based measures to predict query difficulty. In Craig Macdonald, Iadh Ounis, Vassilis Plachouras, Ian Ruthven, and RyenW. White, editors, *Advances in Information Retrieval*, volume 4956 of *Lecture Notes in Computer Science*, pages 689–694. Springer Berlin Heidelberg.

L Kozakov, Y Park, T Fin, Y Drissi, N Doganata, and T Confino. 2004. Glossary extraction and knowledge in large organisations via semantic web technologies. In *Proceedings of the 6th International Semantic Web Conference and he 2nd Asian Semantic Web Conference (Se-mantic Web Challenge Track)*.

Chaya Liebeskind, Ido Dagan, and Jonathan Schler. 2012. Statistical thesaurus construction for a morphologically rich language. In **SEM 2012: The First Joint Conference on Lexical and Computational Semantics*, pages 59–64, Montréal, Canada, 7-8 June. Association for Computational Linguistics.

Chaya Liebeskind, Ido Dagan, and Jonathan Schler. 2013. Semi-automatic construction of cross-period thesaurus. In *Proceedings of the 7th Workshop on Language Technology for Cultural Heritage, Social Sciences, and Humanities*, pages 29–35, Sofia, Bulgaria, August. Association for Computational Linguistics.

Tao Liu, Shengping Liu, Zheng Chen, and Wei-Ying Ma. 2003. An evaluation on feature selection for text clustering. In *Proceedings of the Twentieth International Conference on Machine Learning, ICML 2003*, volume 3, pages 488–495.

Luying Liu, Jianchu Kang, Jing Yu, and Zhongliang Wang. 2005. A comparative study on unsupervised feature selection methods for text clustering. In *Natural Language Processing and Knowledge Engineering, 2005. IEEE NLP-KE 2005*, pages 597–601, Oct.

Lucelene Lopes, Paulo Fernandes, and Renata Vieira. 2012. Domain term relevance through tf-dcf. *ICAI–International Conference in Artificial Inteligence*, pages 1–7.

Natalia Loukachevitch. 2012. Automatic term recognition needs multiple evidence. In Nicoletta Calzolari (Conference Chair), Khalid Choukri, Thierry

Declerck, Mehmet Ugur Dogan, Bente Maegaard, Joseph Mariani, Asuncion Moreno, Jan Odijk, and Stelios Piperidis, editors, *Proceedings of the Eight International Conference on Language Resources and Evaluation, LREC 2012*, Istanbul, Turkey, May. European Language Resources Association (ELRA).

Christopher D. Manning and Hinrich Schütze. 1999. *Foundations of Statistical Natural Language Processing*. MIT Press, Cambridge, MA, USA.

Quinn McNemar. 1947. Note on the sampling error of the difference between correlated proportions or percentages. *Psychometrika*, 12(2):153–157.

Vassilis Plachouras, Ben He, and Iadh Ounis. 2004. University of glasgow at trec 2004: Experiments in web, robust, and terabyte tracks with terrier. In *Proceedings of the Thirteenth Text REtrieval Conference, TREC 2004*.

Martin Riedl, Richard Steuer, and Chris Biemann. 2014. Distributed distributional similarities of google books over the centuries. In *Proceedings of the Ninth International Conference on Language Resources and Evaluation, LREC 2014*, pages 1401–1405, Reykjavik, Iceland.

Francesco Sclano and Paola Velardi. 2007. Termextractor: a web application to learn the shared terminology of emergent web communities. In *Proceedings of the 3rd International Conference on Interoperability for Enterprise Software and Applications, I-ESA 2007*, Funchal (Madeira Island), Portugal, March.

Anna Shtok, Oren Kurland, and David Carmel. 2009. Predicting query performance by query-drift estimation. In Leif Azzopardi, Gabriella Kazai, Stephen Robertson, Stefan Rger, Milad Shokouhi, Dawei Song, and Emine Yilmaz, editors, *Advances in Information Retrieval Theory*, volume 5766 of *Lecture Notes in Computer Science*, pages 305–312. Springer Berlin Heidelberg.

Ian H. Witten, Alistair Moffat, and Timothy C. Bell. 1999. *Managing Gigabytes (2Nd Ed.): Compressing and Indexing Documents and Images*. Morgan Kaufmann Publishers Inc., San Francisco, CA, USA.

Xing Zhang, Yan Song, and A.C. Fang. 2010. Term recognition using conditional random fields. In *Natural Language Processing and Knowledge Engineering, NLP-KE 2010*, pages 1–6, Aug.

Ying Zhao, Falk Scholer, and Yohannes Tsegay. 2008. Effective pre-retrieval query performance prediction using similarity and variability evidence. In Craig Macdonald, Iadh Ounis, Vassilis Plachouras, Ian Ruthven, and RyenW. White, editors, *Advances in Information Retrieval*, volume 4956 of *Lecture Notes in Computer Science*, pages 52–64. Springer Berlin Heidelberg.

Yun Zhou and W. Bruce Croft. 2007. Query performance prediction in web search environments. In *Proceedings of the 30th Annual International ACM SIGIR Conference on Research and Development in Information Retrieval*, SIGIR 2007, pages 543–550, New York, NY, USA. ACM.

Hadas Zohar, Chaya Liebeskind, Jonathan Schler, and Ido Dagan. 2013. Automatic thesaurus construction for cross generation corpus. *Journal on Computing and Cultural Heritage (JOCCH)*, 6(1):4:1–4:19, April.

Minoan linguistic resources: The Linear A Digital Corpus

Tommaso Petrolito[⊙] **Ruggero Petrolito**[⊙] **Grégoire Winterstein**[⊖] and **Francesco Perono Cacciafoco**[⊕⊙]
[⊙] Filologia Letteratura e Linguistica, **University of Pisa**, Italy
[⊖]Linguistics and Modern Language Studies, **The Hong Kong Institute of Education**, Hong Kong
[⊕]Linguistics and Multilingual Studies, **Nanyang Technological University**, Singapore
tommasouni@gmail.com, ruggero.petrolito@gmail.com,
gregoire@ied.edu.hk, fcacciafoco@ntu.edu.sg

Abstract

This paper describes the Linear A/Minoan digital corpus and the approaches we applied to develop it.

We aim to set up a suitable study resource for Linear A and Minoan.

Firstly we start by introducing Linear A and Minoan in order to make it clear why we should develop a digital marked up corpus of the existing Linear A transcriptions.

Secondly we list and describe some of the existing resources about Linear A: Linear A documents (seals, statuettes, vessels etc.), the traditional encoding systems (standard code numbers referring to distinct symbols), a Linear A font, and the newest (released on June 16th 2014) Unicode Standard Characters set for Linear A.

Thirdly we explain our choice concerning the data format: why we decided to digitize the Linear A resources; why we decided to convert all the transcriptions in standard Unicode characters; why we decided to use an XML format; why we decided to implement the TEI-EpiDoc DTD.

Lastly we describe: the developing process (from the data collection to the issues we faced and the solving strategies); a new font we developed (synchronized with the Unicode Characters Set) in order to make the data readable even on systems that are not updated. Finally, we discuss the corpus we developed in a Cultural Heritage preservation perspective and suggest some future works.

1 Introduction to Linear A and Minoan

Linear A is the script used by the Minoan Civilization (Cotterell, 1980) from 2500 to 1450 BC.

Writing system	Time span
Cretan Hieroglyphic	2100 – 1700 BC
Linear A	2500 – 1450 BC
Linear B	1450 – 1200 BC

Table 1: Time spans of Cretan Hieroglyphic, Linear A and Linear B.

The Minoan Civilization arose on the island of Crete in the Aegean Sea during the Bronze Age. Minoan ruins and artifacts have been found mainly in Crete but also in other Greek islands and in mainland Greece, in Bulgaria, in Turkey and in Israel.

Linear A is not used anymore and, even after decades of studies (it was discovered by Sir Arthur Evans around 1900 (Evans, 1909)), it still remains undeciphered.

All the assumptions and hypotheses made about Linear A and Minoan (its underlying language) are mainly based on the comparison with the well known Linear B, the famous child system originated by Linear A. In fact, Linear B was fully deciphered during the 1950s by Michael Ventris [1] and was found to encode an ancient Greek dialect used by the Mycenaean civilization.

Archaeologist Arthur Evans named the script 'Linear' because it consisted just of lines inscribed in clay (Robinson, 2009) while, in the same period (as shown in Table 1), Cretan hieroglyphs were more pictographic and three-dimensional .

Even if many symbols are shared by both Linear A and Linear B, it has not been possible to find intelligible words within inscriptions in Linear A by applying Linear B segmentation and phonemes.

Linear A consists of hundreds of symbols probably having syllabic, ideographic, and semantic values. Many of the Linear A symbols that are

[1] http://www.cam.ac.uk/research/news/cracking-the-code-the-decipherment-of-linear-b-60-years-on

Proceedings of the 9th SIGHUM Workshop on Language Technology for Cultural Heritage, Social Sciences, and Humanities, pages 95–104, Beijing, China, July 30, 2015.

Text	𐀓𐀛𐀱
Phonetic Value	*KU-NI-SU*
Possible Meaning	*Knossos*

Table 2: Example of John G. Younger's deciphering attempt.

found in Linear B (81 in total) are assumed to have syllabic values, while the remaining are assumed to be logograms.

There have been several attempts to decipher Linear A and the Minoan Language. We can divide the underlying hypotheses in six groups: Greek-like language (Nagy, 1963), distinct Indo-European branch (Owens, 1999), Anatolian language close to Luwian (Palmer, 1958), archaic form of Phoenician (Dietrich and Loretz, 2001), Indo-Iranian (Faure, 1998) and Etruscan-like language (Giulio M. Facchetti and Negri, 2003).

There is also an interesting attempt (Younger, 2000b) to decipher single words, specifically toponyms, by applying Linear B phonetic values to the symbols shared by both Linear A and Linear B and following the assumption that toponyms are much more likely to survive as loans in Mycenaean Greek (written in Linear B); we show an example of this approach in Table 2.

In the next sections we describe the available existing resources concerning Linear A and the Linear A Digital Corpus: why and how we developed it.

2 Linear A available resources

Even if Linear A and Linear B were discovered more than one century ago, Linear A has not been deciphered yet. Nevertheless, many scholars worked on collecting and organizing all the available data in order to study and to decipher the script and the language.

Probably due to the fact that only historical linguists, philologists and archaeologists attempted to collect and organize all the existing data, nowadays a rich and well organized digital corpus is still not available.

In this section we describe all the available Linear A resources, including both physical documents and digital data.

ID	Type of Support
default	tablets (page, bars, lames)
Wa	noduli
Wb	sealings
Wc	roundels
Za	stone vessels
Zb	clay vessels
Zc	inked inscriptions
Zd	graffiti
Ze	architecture
Zf	metal objects
Zg	stone objects

Table 3: Indexed types of support (Younger, 2000e).

2.1 Linear A documents

Linear A was written on a variety of media, such as stone offering tables, gold and silver hair pins, and pots (inked and inscribed).

The clay documents consist of tablets, roundels, and sealings (one-hole, two-hole, and flat-based).

Roundels are related to a "conveyance of a commodity, either within the central administration or between the central administration and an external party" (Palmer, 1995; Schoep, 2002). The roundel is the record of this transaction that stays within the central administration as the commodity moves out of the transacting bureau (Hallager, 1996). Two-hole sealings probably dangled from commodities brought into the center; one-hole sealings apparently dangled from papyrus/-parchment documents; flat-based sealings (themselves never inscribed) were pressed against the twine that secured papyrus/parchment documents (Younger, 2000g; Schoep, 2002) as shown by photographs (Müller, 1999), (Müller, 2002) of the imprints that survive on the underside of flat-based sealings.

There are 1,427 Linear A documents containing 7,362-7,396 signs, much less than the quantity of data we have for Linear B (more than 4,600 documents containing 57,398 signs) (Younger, 2000f).

2.2 Godart and Olivier's Collection of Linear A Inscriptions

There is a complete and organized collection of Linear A documents on a paper corpus, the **GORILA** Louis **G**odart and Jean-Pierre **O**livier, ***R**ecueil des **i**nscriptions en **L**inéaire **A*** (Godart and Olivier, 1976).

Unicode	GORILA	Pope&Raison	Syllable
10600	AB01	L30	DA
10601	AB02	L22	RO
10602	AB03	L2	PA

Table 4: Excerpt of John G. Younger's transcription systems conversion table extended with the Unicode codes.

Godart and Olivier have indexed the documents by original location and type of support, following the Raison–Pope Index (Raison and Pope, 1971).

For example, the document **AP Za 1** is from **AP** = *Apodoulou* and the support type is **Za** = *stone vessels* as shown in Table 3.

Younger (2000h) provides a map with all the Cretan sites and one with all the Greek non-Cretan sites (Younger, 2000i).

Godart and Olivier also provide referential data about conservation places (mainly museums), and periodization (for example: **EM II** = *Second Early Minoan*).

Since 1976, this has been the main source of data and point of reference about Linear A documents and it has set up the basis for further studies. Even recent corpora, such as the *Corpus transnuméré du linéaire A* (Raison and Pope, 1994), always refer to GORILA precise volumes and pages describing each document.

2.3 John G. Younger's website

Younger (2000j) has published a website that is the best digital resource available (there is another interesting project, never completed, on Yannis Deliyannis's website[2]). It collects most of the existing inscriptions (taking GORILA as main source of data and point of reference) transcribed as Linear B phonetic values (like the *KU-NI-SU* transcription above).

The transcriptions are kept up to date and a complete restructuring in June 2015 has been announced (Younger, 2000j).

2.4 GORILA symbols catalogue

Many transcription systems have been defined.

The first one has been proposed by Raison and Pope (1971) and uses a string composed by one or two characters (*Lm*, *L* or *Lc* depending on the symbol, respectively metric, phonetic or compound) followed by a number, for example: *L2*.

[2]http://y.deliyannis.free.fr/linearA/

This system has been widely used by many scholars such as David Woodley Packard (president of the Packard Humanities Institute[3]), Colin Renfrew and Richard Janko (Packard, 1974; Renfrew, 1977; Janko, 1982).

The second one, used in the GORILA collection (Godart and Olivier, 1976) and on John G. Younger's website, consists of a string composed by one or two characters (*AB* if the symbol is shared by Linear A and Linear B, *A* if the symbol is only used in Linear A) followed by a number and eventually other alphabetical characters (due to *addenda* and *corrigenda* to earlier versions), for example: *AB03*.

Many scholars transcribe the symbols shared by Linear A and B with the assumed phonetical/syllabic transcription. This syllabic transcription is based on the corresponding Linear B phonetic values. Younger (2000a) provides a conversion table of Pope and Raison's transcription system, GORILA's transcription system and his own phonetic/syllabic transcription system.

Developing our corpus, we worked mainly on Younger's syllabic and GORILA transcriptions, because the Unicode Linear A encoding is broadly based on the GORILA catalogue, which is also the basic set of characters used in decipherment efforts[4]. We provide an example of different transcriptions for the same symbol in Table 4. As can be noticed, the Unicode encoding is based on the GORILA transcription system.

2.5 Linear A Font

The best Linear A Font available is `LA.ttf`, released by D.W. Borgdorff[5] in 2004.

In this font some arbitrary Unicode positions for Latin characters are mapped to Linear A symbols.

On one hand this allows the user to type Linear A symbols directly by pressing the keys on the keyboard; on the other hand, only transliterations can be produced. The text eventually typed internally will be a series of Latin characters.

It should be remarked that this font would not be useful to make readable a Linear A corpus that is non-translittered and encoded in Unicode.

[3]http://www.packhum.org/

[4]http://www.unicode.org/versions/Unicode7.0.0/ch08.pdf

[5]http://www.fontineed.com/author/D.W.\%20Borgdorff

2.6 Unicode Linear A Characters Set

On June 16th 2014, Version 7.0 of Unicode standard was released[6], adding 2,834 new characters and including, finally, the Linear A character set.

Linear A block has been set in the range 10600–1077F and the order mainly follows GORILA's one[7], as seen in Table 4.

This Unicode Set covers simple signs, vase shapes, complex signs, complex signs with vase shapes, fractions and compound fractions.

This is a resource that opens, for the first time, the possibility to develop a Linear A digital corpus not consisting of a transliteration or alternative transcription.

3 Corpus data format

Many scholars have faced the issues for data curation and considered various possibilities.

Among all the possible solutions, we chose to develop the Linear A Digital Corpus as a collection of TEI-EpiDoc XML documents.

In this section we explain why.

3.1 Why Digital?

Many epigraphic corpora have begun to be digitalized; there are many reasons to do so.

A digital corpus can include several representations of the inscriptions (Mahoney, 2007):

- pictures of the original document;
- pictures of drawings or transcriptions made by hand simplifying the document;
- diplomatic transcriptions;
- edited texts;
- translations;
- commentaries.

Building a database is enough to get much richer features than the ones a paper corpus would provide. The most visible feature of an epigraphic database is its utility as an *Index Universalis* (Gómez Pantoja and Álvarez, 2011); unlike hand-made indexes, there is no need to constrain the number of available search-keys.

Needless to say, the opportunity to have the data available also on the web is valuable.

[6] `http://blog.unicode.org/2014/06/announcing-unicode-standard-version-70.html`

[7] `http://www.unicode.org/versions/Unicode7.0.0/ch08.pdf`

3.2 Why Unicode?

Text processing must also take into account the writing systems represented in the corpus.

If the corpus consists of inscriptions written in the Latin alphabet, then the writing system of the inscriptions is the same as that of the Western European modern languages used for meta-data, translations, and commentaries.

In our case, unluckily, we have to deal with Linear A, so we need to find a way to represent our text.

Scholars objected to epigraphic databases on the ground of its poor graphic ability to represent non-Latin writing systems (García Barriocanal et al., 2011).

This led to the use of non-standard fonts in some databases which probed to be a bad move, compromising overall compatibility and system upgrading.

This approach is appealing because if the corpus needs to be printed, sooner or later fonts will be a need in all cases.

The font-based solution assumes that all the software involved can recognize font-change markers. Unluckily, some Database Management Systems (DMSs) do not allow changes of font within a text field and some export or interchange formats lose font information.

When the scripts of the corpus are all supported, which will be the case for any script still used by a living language, Unicode is a better approach. Despite Minoan not being a living language, Linear A is finally part of the Unicode 7.0 Character Code Charts [8] but some sign groups conventionally interpreted as numbers have no Unicode representation.

3.3 Why XML?

Until not so long ago, markup systems have always involved special typographical symbols in the text—brackets, underdots, and so on.

Some epigraphers see XML as a natural transformation of what they have always done, with all the additional benefits that come from standardization within the community.

There is a growing consensus that XML is the best way to encode text.

Some corpora may also use the typographical marks of the Leiden system, which has the advan-

[8] `http://www.unicode.org/charts/`

```
<glyph xml:id="n5">
  <glyphName>
    Number 5
  </glyphName>
  <mapping type="standardized">
    5
  </mapping>
</glyph>
```

Figure 1: Example XML declaration of a glyph with no Unicode representation.

tage of being entirely familiar to the epigraphers who create and maintain the corpus.

Unfortunately, the special brackets, underdots, and other typographical devices may not be supported by the character set of the computer system to be used.

A key incentive for using XML is the ability to exchange data with other projects.

It is convenient to be able to divide the information in many layers: cataloging, annotating, commenting and editing the inscriptions.

In some cases, merging different layers from different projects could be a need (for example when each of these projects is focused on a specific layer, for which provides the best quality), as a consequence the resulting data should be in compatible forms.

If the projects use the same Document Type Definition (DTD), in the same way, this is relatively easy.

While corpora that store their texts as word-processor files with Leiden markup can also share data, they must agree explicitly on the details of text layout, file formats, and character encodings.

With XML, it is possible to define either elements or entities for unsupported characters.

This feature is particularly interesting in our case, giving a solution for the numbers representation (Linear A numbers, except for fractions, have no Unicode representation). Suppose you want to mark up the sign group , conventionally interpreted as the number 5, in the XML. As specified in the TEI DTD, this could be expressed as `<g ref="#n5"/>`, where the element `g` indicates a glyph, or a non-standard character and the attribute value points to the element `glyph`, which contains information about the specific glyph. An example is given in Figure 1.

Alternatively, the project might define an entity to represent this character.

Either way, the XML text notes that there is the Linear A number 5, and the later rendering of the text for display or printing can substitute the appropriate character in a known font, a picture of the character, or even a numeral from a different system. Such approaches assume that tools are available for these conversions; some application, transformation, or stylesheet must have a way to know how to interpret the given element or entity.

The usage of XML provides two advantages: in first place, it makes possible the encoding of the characters that occur in the text (as shown above); in second place, it's really useful for encoding meta-information.

3.4 Why EpiDoc?

If a project decides to use XML, the most appropriate DTD (or schema) to be used needs to be chosen. As in every other humanities discipline, the basic question is whether to use a general DTD, like the TEI, or to write a project-specific one. Some projects need DTDs that are extremely specific to the types of inscriptions they are dealing with, instead other projects prefer to rely on existing, widely used DTDs.

Mahoney (2007) has deeply analyzed all the digitization issues, taking into account all the advantages and disadvantages of different approaches; her conclusion is that it's best to use **EpiDoc**[9] an XML encoding tool that could be also used to write structured documents compliant with the TEI standard[10].

The EpiDoc DTD is the TEI, with a few epigraphically oriented customizations made using the standard TEI mechanisms. Rather than writing a DTD for epigraphy from scratch, the EpiDoc group uses the TEI because TEI has already addressed many of the taxonomic and semantic challenges faced by epigraphers, because the TEI-using community can provide a wide range of best-practice examples and guiding expertise, and because existing tooling built around TEI could easily lead to early and effective presentation and use of TEI-encoded epigraphic texts (Mahoney, 2007).

The TEI and EpiDoc approaches have already been adopted by several epigraphic projects (Bodard, 2009), such as the Dêmos project (Furman

[9] `http://www.tei-c.org/Activities/Projects/ep01.xml`

[10] `http://www.tei-c.org/index.xml`

University) and the corpus of Macedonian and Thracian inscriptions being compiled at KERA, the Research Center for Greek and Roman Antiquity at Athens (Mahoney, 2007).

Also other scholars evaluate EpiDoc as a suitable choice. Felle (2011) compares the EAGLE (Electronic Archive of Greek and Latin Epigraphy[11]) project with the EpiDoc existing resources, viewing these resources as different but complementary.

Álvarez et al. (2010) and Gómez Pantoja and Álvarez (2011) discuss the possibility of sharing Epigraphic Information as EpiDoc-based Linked Data and describe how they implemented a relational-to-linked data solution for the Hispania Epigraphica database.

Cayless (2003) evaluates EpiDoc as a relevant digital tool for Epigraphy allowing for a uniform representation of epigraphic metadata.

The EpiDoc guidelines are emerging as one standard for digital epigraphy with the TEI.

EpiDoc is not the only possible way to use the TEI for epigraphic texts but the tools, documentation, and examples[12] make it a good environment for new digitization projects as ours.

3.5 EpiDoc structure

An EpiDoc document is structured as a standard TEI document with the `teiHeader` element including some initial `Desc` sections (`fileDesc`, `encodingDesc`, `profileDesc`, `revisionDesc`, etc) containing metadata, general information and descriptions (here we annotated place, period, kind of support and specific objects/fragments IDs). An interesting use of `encodingDesc` is shown in Figure 1 above: the `gliph` element has to be defined inside its parent element `charDecl` and its grandparent element `encodingDesc`.

The `teiHeader` element is followed by the `text` element including the `body` element composed by a series of unnumbered `<div>`s, distinguished by their `type` attributes (we show an example of the Epidoc `<div>` element in Figure 2).

Typical divisions might include:

- text itself (`type="edition"`);
- translation (`type="translation"`);
- description (`type="description"`;
- commentary (`type="commentary"`);
- historical information(`type="history"`);
- bibliography (`type="bibliography"`).

```
<div lang="minoan"
     n="text"
     type="edition"
     part="N"
     sample="complete"
     org="uniform">
  <head lang="eng">Edition</head>
  <cb rend="front" n="HM 1673"/>
  <ab part="N">
    <lb n="1"/>
    <w part="N">[illegible]</w>
    <space dim="horizontal"
           extent="1em"
           unit="character"/>
    <w part="N">[illegible]</w>
    <lb n="2"/>
    <w part="N">[illegible]</w>
    <g ref="#n5"/>
    <w part="N">[illegible]</w>
    <lb n="3"/>
    <w part="N">[illegible]</w>
    <g ref="#n12"/>
    <w part="N">[illegible]</w>
    <lb n="4"/>
    <w part="N">[illegible]</w>
    <g ref="#n6"/>
    <lb n="5"/>
    <w part="N">[illegible]</w>
    <lb n="6"/>
    <g ref="#n4"/>
    <w part="N">[illegible]</w>
    <supplied reason="damage">
      [illegible]
    </supplied>
    <gap extent="2em"
         reason="lost"
         unit="character"
         dim="right"/>
  </ab>
</div>
```

Figure 2: Example of the Epidoc `<div>` element with `type="edition"`.

The EpiDoc DTD introduces a finite set of possible values for the type of a `<div>`, so that there

[11] http://www.eagle-eagle.it/

[12] http://wiki.tei-c.org/index.php/Samples_of_TEI_texts

is a clear distinction between sections covering different aspects, such as the commentary, the description or the archaeological history.

One advantage of structured markup is that editors can encode more information about how certain a particular feature is. The date of an inscription, for example, can be encoded as a range of possible dates. EpiDoc includes the TEI `<certainty>` element and the cert attribute to encourage editors to say whether or not they are completely confident of a given reading. After some discussion, the EpiDoc community (Mahoney, 2007) decided that certainty should be expressed as a yes-or-no value: either the editor is certain of the reading, or not. Gradual certainty is too complicated to manage and is best explained in the commentary.

4 Developing the Linear A Corpus

The hope that computational approaches could help decipher Linear A, along with the evident lack of rich digital resources in this field, led us to develop this new resource. In this section we describe which issues we faced and which solving strategies we used.

4.1 Data Collection

Luckily the existence of Younger's website and GORILA volumes, together with the Raison–Pope Index, made possible a semi-automatic collection process, starting from syllabic transcriptions taken from Younger's website (with his permission), converting them in Unicode strings through Python scripts and acquiring all the metadata provided in Younger's transcriptions (location and support IDs, conservation place, periodization etc.).

Younger's resources on his website consist of two HTML pages, one containing inscriptions from Haghia Triada (that is the richest location in terms of documents found there) (Younger, 2000k) and the other containing documents from all the other locations (Younger, 2000l).

Younger's transcriptions are well enriched with metadata. The metadata convey the same information found in GORILA, including the Raison–Pope Index, plus some additional description of the support (this was not necessary in GORILA volumes, where the transcriptions are shown just next to the documents pictures) and the reference to the specific GORILA volume and pages.

4.2 Segmentation Issues

When working on ancient writing systems, segmentation issues are expected to come up. John G. Younger explains (Younger, 2000c) that in Linear A separation is mainly indicated in two ways: first, by associating sign groups with numbers or logograms, thereby implying a separation; second, by placing a dot between two sign groups, thereby explicitly separating the sign groups or between a sign group and some other sign like a transaction sign or a logogram. Younger also explains that in texts that employ a string of sign groups, dots are used to separate them and this practice is most notable on non-bureaucratic texts and especially in religious texts.

On his website, Younger also covers the hyphenization issue (Younger, 2000d), explaining that in some cases we find a split across lines and the reason may involve separating prefixes from base words (the root of a sign group) or base words from their suffixes. As Younger points out, this hypothesis would require evidence showing that affixes are involved. The hyphenization issue is more complex to solve because a 'neutral' resource should avoid transcriptions implying a well known segmentation for Linear A sign groups. In Younger's transcriptions, split sign groups are reunified in order to make it clearer when a known sign group is there. Instead, our digital collection keeps the text as it is on the document, all the information about interpretations of such kind can be stored separately.

4.3 Obtaining Unicode transcriptions

We managed to obtain Unicode encoded transcriptions by automatically converting Younger's phonetic transcriptions to GORILA transcriptions (manually checked against GORILA volumes) and then by automatically converting GORILA transcriptions to Unicode codes and printing them as Unicode characters (UTF-8 encoding). In order to create the syllables-to-GORILA and the GORILA-to-Unicode dictionaries, we took into account Younger's conversion table mentioned in Subsection 2.4 and the official Unicode documentation (containing explicit Unicode-to-GORILA mapping information). All these processing steps have been implemented through Python scripts.

4.4 XML annotation

Once collected the whole corpus encoded in Unicode, we automatically added part of the XML annotation through a python script. These documents have been later manually corrected and completed, checking against GORILA volumes.

4.5 A new Linear A font

Before the Unicode 7.0 release, there was no way to visualize Unicode characters in the range 10600–1077F. Even now, systems that are not updated may have trouble to visualize those characters. Some implementations for Unicode support in certain contexts (for example for LaTeX's output) are not always up-to-date, so it is not obvious that the fonts for the most recent characters sets are available. We decided to develop a new Linear A font, solving the main issue found in `LA.ttf` (wrong Unicode positions). Starting from the official Unicode documentation, we created a set of symbols graphically similar to the official ones and aligned them to the right Unicode positions. We decided to name the font `John_Younger.ttf` to show our appreciation for Younger's work. He made the results of GORILA available to a wider public on digital media; this is the same goal we want to pursue by developing and distributing this font. We released the font file at the following URL: `http://openfontlibrary.org/en/font/john-younger`.

5 The Linear A Digital Corpus as cultural resource

As stated by European Commission (2015) and UNESCO (2003), the meaning of the notion of *cultural heritage* does not apply just to material objects and works of art, but also to 'intangible cultural heritage', as traditions and creative expressions. In this perspective, linguistic corpora fit perfectly this definition; in fact, they contain information about tradition, knowledge and lifestyle of a certain culture.

Despite the fact that the Minoan language has not yet been deciphered, we know that the Linear A corpus provides interesting information concerning economy, commerce and religion.

As mentioned in Subsection 2.1, Schoep (2002) made a critical assessment of the Linear A tablets and their role in the administrative process, studying the physical supports.

Ruth Palmer (1995) made a deep study of commodities distributions (listing precise quantities and places) among Minoan centers, even without a full understanding of documents contents. As Palmer points out, 'the ideograms for basic commodities, and the formats of the Linear A texts are similar enough to their Linear B counterparts to allow valid comparison of the types and amounts of commodities which appear in specific contexts'. So, it's possible to have 'an idea of the focus of the economy' and of 'the scale and complexity of the transactions'. From the linear A tablets, we can infer information about the resources management and administration system of Minoan centers.

Van den Kerkhof and Rem (2007) analyzed the Minoan libation formulas: religious inscriptions on cups, ladles and tables that were used in the offerings of oil and other powerful drinks at dawn. The priestesses that carried out the Minoan libation ritual used all kinds of utensils, and they often inscribed their sacred formulas onto these objects. Around thirty of these texts have survived (whole or in part) on libation tables, ladles and vases, written in various kinds of handwriting. Transcripts of these religious inscriptions are available from Consani et al. (1999) and from John G. Younger (2000m) on his website. As noticed by Duhoux (1989) the Minoan libation formulas have a fixed structure with variable elements. In fact, some studies (Davis, 2014) about Minoan syntax have been made by observing the sign groups order found in these regular formulas. More importantly, the presence of olive-like ideograms could tell us that the Minoans used olive oil for libation (Van den Kerkhof and Rem, 2007). Beyond all these parts of the Minoan cultural heritage already available, a huge part is preserved there too: the Minoan language, with its hidden stories reflecting the life of a civilization. We hope that our contribution can be useful to the community and that the Minoan, in its digital form, may finally be deciphered through computational approaches.

6 Future Work

We are working on XSL style sheets in order to create suitable HTML pages. All the data will be freely available and published at the following URL: `http://ling.ied.edu.HK/~gregoire/lineara`. A further step will be developing a web interface to annotate, and dynamically enrich the corpus information.

References

Fernando Luis Álvarez, Elena García Barriocanal, and Joaquín L. Gómez Pantoja. 2010. Sharing Epigraphic Information as Linked Data. In *Metadata and Semantic Research*, pages 222–234. Springer.

Gabriel Bodard. 2009. EpiDoc: Epigraphic documents in XML for publication and interchange. *Latin on Stone: Epigraphic Research and Electronic Archives, Roman Studies: Interdisciplinary Approaches, forthcoming*.

Hugh Cayless. 2003. Tools for Digital Epigraphy. *Proc. of the Association for Computing in the Humanities/Association for Literary and Linguistic Computing, Athens GA*.

Carlo Consani, Mario Negri, Francesco Aspesi, and Cristina Lembo. 1999. Testi minoici trascritti. *Rome: CNR–Istituto per gli studi micenei ed egeo-anatolici*.

Arthur Cotterell. 1980. *The Minoan World*. Charles Scribner's Sons.

Brent Davis. 2014. Syntax in Linear A: The Word-Order of the 'Libation Formula'. *Kadmos*, 52, Issue 1.

Manfried Dietrich and Oswald Loretz. 2001. *In memoriam Cyrus H. Gordon:*. Ugarit-Forschungen. Ugarit-Verlag. `https://books.google.it/books?id=tlrvMQEACAAJ`.

Yves Duhoux. 1989. Le Linéaire A: problèmes de Déchiffrement in Problems in Decipherment. *Bibliothèque des Cahiers de l'Institut de Linguistique de Louvain*, 49:59–119.

European Commission, 2015. *Supporting cultural heritage - European Commission*. `http://ec.europa.eu/culture/policy/culture-policies/cultural-heritage_en.htm`.

Arthur John Evans. 1909. Scripta minoa, vol. I. *Oxford: Clarendon Press*, I.

Paul Faure. 1998. 8. La Marle (Hubert), Linéaire A. La première écriture syllabique de Crète. Vol. 1: Essai de lecture; Vol. 2: éléments de grammaire. *Revue des Études Grecques*, 111(1):339–340.

Antonio Enrico Felle. 2011. Esperienze diverse e complementari nel trattamento digitale delle fonti epigrafiche: il caso di EAGLE ed EpiDoc. *Diritto romano e scienze antichistiche nell'era digitale. Convegno di studio (Firenze, 12-13 settembre 2011)*, pages 47–54.

Elena García Barriocanal, Zeynel Cebeci, Aydín Öztürk, and MehmetC. Okur. 2011. *Metadata and Semantic Research: 5th International Conference, MTSR 2011, Izmir, Turkey, October 12-14, 2011. Proceedings*. Communications in Computer and Information Science. Springer. `https://books.google.it/books/about/Metadata_and_Semantic_Research.html?id=ydHP9iZRsdoC&hl=en`.

Giulio M. Facchetti and Mario Negri. 2003. *Creta minoica: sulle tracce delle più antiche scritture d'Europa*. LS Olschki.

Louis Godart and Jean Pierre Olivier. 1976. *Recueil des inscriptions en linéaire A*. Librairie Orientaliste Paul Geuthner.

Joaquín L. Gómez Pantoja and Fernando Luis Álvarez. 2011. From relational databases to Linked Data in Epigraphy: Hispania Epigraphica Online, Elena García Barriocanal, Zeynel Cebeci, Mehmet C. Okur and Aydín Öztürk (eds.), Metadata and Semantic Research (Proceedings of the 5th International Conference, MTSR 2011, Izmir, Turkey, October 12-14, 2011). *Communications in Computer and Information Science*, 240.

Erik Hallager. 1996. *The Minoan roundel and other sealed documents in the neopalatial Linear A administration*, volume 14. Université de Liège, Histoire de l'art et archéologie de la Grèce antique.

Richard Janko. 1982. A stone object inscribed in Linear A from Ayios Stephanos, Laconia. *Kadmos*, 21(2):97–100.

Anne Mahoney. 2007. Electronic Textual Editing: Epigraphy. *TEI-Text Encoding Initiatives*. `http://www.tei-c.org/About/Archive_new/ETE/Preview/mahoney.xml`.

Walter Müller. 1999. Die Tonplomben und andere gestempelte Tonobjekte. *I. Pini (ed.), Iraklion Archaeologisches Museum, Teil 6, Die Siegelabrücke von Aj. Triada und anderen Zentral- und Ostkretischen Fundorten. CMS (Corpus der Minoischen und Mykenischen Siegel) II,6. Berlin*, pages 339–400.

Walter Müller. 2002. Untersuchungen zur Typologie, Funktion und Verbreitung der Tonplomben von Knossos. *I. Pini (ed.), Iraklion Archäologisches Museum, Teil 8, Die Siegelabrücke von Knossos. CMS (Corpus der Minoischen und Mykenischen Siegel) II,8. Berlin*, pages 24–93.

Gregory Nagy. 1963. Greek-like Elements in Linear A. *Greek, Roman, and Byzantine Studies*, 4(4):181–211.

Gareth Owens. 1999. The structure of the Minoan language. *Journal of Indo-European Studies*, 27(1-2):15–55.

David W. Packard. 1974. *Minoan Linear A*. University of California Press. `https://books.google.it/books?id=vax3kwoscWQC`.

Leonard Robert Palmer. 1958. Luvian and Linear A. *Transactions of the Philological Society*, 57(1):75–100.

Ruth Palmer. 1995. Linear A commodities: a comparison of resources. *POLITEIA. Society and State in the Aegean Bronze Age, Aegaeum*, 13:133–156.

Jacques Raison and Maurice Pope. 1971. *Index du linéaire A.*, volume 41 of *Incunabula Graeca*. Edizioni dell'Ateneo. https://books.google.it/books?id=Nl0eYAAACAAJ.

Jacques Raison and Maurice Pope. 1994. *Corpus transnuméré du linéaire A*. BCILL (Louvain-la-Neuve). Isd. https://books.google.it/books?id=TbgcAQAAIAAJ.

Colin Renfrew. 1977. A Linear A tablet fragment from Phylakopi in Melos.(with a note on the inscription by William C. Brice). *Kadmos*, 16(2):111–119.

Andrew Robinson. 2009. *Writing and script: a very short introduction*. Oxford University Press.

Ilse Schoep. 2002. The administration of neopalatial Crete: a critical assessment of the Linear A tablets and their role in the administrative process. *Minos: Revista de filología egea*, (17):1–230.

UNESCO, 2003. *What is meant by "cultural heritage"?* http://www.unesco.org/culture/ich/index.php?lg=EN&pg=00022.

Astrid Van den Kerkhof and Peter Rem. 2007. The Minoan libation formulas.

John G. Younger. 2000a. Linear A texts in phonetic Transcription: 1. List of Linked Files, Concordance: Raison-Pope-GORILA signs (a Microsoft Word document). http://www.people.ku.edu/~jyounger/LinearA/RAISON-GORILA_SIGNS.doc.

John G. Younger. 2000b. Linear A texts in Phonetic Transcription: 10c. Place Names. http://www.people.ku.edu/~jyounger/LinearA/#10c.

John G. Younger. 2000c. Linear A texts in Phonetic Transcription: 16. Word Separation. http://people.ku.edu/~jyounger/LinearA/#16.

John G. Younger. 2000d. Linear A texts in Phonetic Transcription: 17. Hyphenization. http://people.ku.edu/~jyounger/LinearA/#17.

John G. Younger. 2000e. Linear A texts in phonetic Transcription: 4. Conventions (bibliographical, epigraphical). http://people.ku.edu/~jyounger/LinearA/#4.

John G. Younger. 2000f. Linear A texts in Phonetic Transcription: 5. Basic Statistics. http://www.people.ku.edu/~jyounger/LinearA/#5.

John G. Younger. 2000g. Linear A texts in Phonetic Transcription: 7c. The Documents. http://people.ku.edu/~jyounger/LinearA/#7.

John G. Younger. 2000h. Linear A Texts in Phonetic Transcription: A map of Crete showing the location of the cretan sites. http://people.ku.edu/~jyounger/pix/LinearA_Crete.jpg.

John G. Younger. 2000i. Linear A Texts in Phonetic Transcription: A map of Greece showing the location of the greek sites outside Crete. http://people.ku.edu/~jyounger/pix/LinearA_Greece.jpg.

John G. Younger. 2000j. Linear A texts in phonetic Transcription: Homepage. http://www.people.ku.edu/~jyounger/LinearA/.

John G. Younger. 2000k. Linear A texts in phonetic Transcription: HT (Haghia Triada). http://people.ku.edu/~jyounger/LinearA/HTtexts.html.

John G. Younger. 2000l. Linear A texts in phonetic Transcription: Other Texts (not Haghia Triada). http://people.ku.edu/~jyounger/LinearA/misctexts.html.

John G. Younger. 2000m. Linear A Texts in Phonetic Transcription: Presumably Religious Inscriptions. http://www.people.ku.edu/~jyounger/LinearA/religioustexts.html.

Lexicon-assisted tagging and lemmatization in Latin: A comparison of six taggers and two lemmatization methods

Steffen Eger
Text Technology Lab
Universität Frankfurt

Tim vor der Brück
Text Technology Lab
Universität Frankfurt

Alexander Mehler
Text Technology Lab
Universität Frankfurt

{steeger,vorderbr,mehler}@em.uni-frankfurt.de

Abstract

We present a survey of tagging accuracies — concerning part-of-speech and full morphological tagging — for several taggers based on a corpus for medieval church Latin (see www.comphistsem.org). The best tagger in our sample, Lapos, has a PoS tagging accuracy of close to 96% and an overall tagging accuracy (including full morphological tagging) of about 85%. When we 'intersect' the taggers with our lexicon, the latter score increases to almost 91% for Lapos. A conservative assessment of lemmatization accuracy on our data estimates a score of 93-94% for a lexicon-based lemmatization strategy and a score of 94-95% for lemmatizing via trained lemmatizers.

1 Introduction

Part-of-speech (PoS) tagging is a standard task in natural language processing (NLP) in which the goal is to assign each word in a sentence its (possibly complex) part-of-speech label. While part-of-speech tagging for English is well-researched, morphologically rich languages like some Slavic languages or classical languages such as ancient Greek or Latin have received considerably less attention. Often-cited problems for the latter class of languages include relatively free word-order and a high degree of inflectional variability, leading to data sparseness problems.

In this work, we survey tagging accuracies (part-of-speech as well as full morphological tagging) for several part-of-speech taggers based on a corpus of Latin texts.

The *corpus*, which was built as part of the *Computational Historical Semantics* (CompHistSem) project[1], comprises about 15 500 sentences as exemplified in Table 1. The aim of CompHistSem is to develop an historical semantics based on medieval Latin texts that allows for fine-grained analyses of word meanings starting from richly annotated corpora. The application scenario of the current study is to meet this annotation requirement by means of open access tools.

Our corpus is based on the capitularies, the amalarius corpus as partly available via the Patrologia Latina[2] and three further texts from the MGH[3] corpus (Visio Baronti, Vita Adelphii, Vita Amandi). Each token of the corpus has been manually annotated with a reference to an associated lexicon entry as described below (cf. Mehler et al. (2015)). In this way, full morphological features are available for all tokens. Our *lexicon* has been compiled from several sources such as LemLat and from rule-based lexical expanders. We describe its composition in more depth in Section 2.

The *taggers* we survey include three relatively new taggers (Lapos, Mate, and the Stanford tagger) as well as two taggers originating in an earlier tagging tradition (TnT, TreeTagger). In addition, we report results for two tagger variants available in the OpenNLP package. All taggers are trained on our corpus. In accordance with Moore's law describing scientific/technological progress over time, we find that more recent tagger classes substantially outperform their predecessor generation. The best tagger in our sample, Lapos, has a PoS tagging accuracy of close to 96% and an overall tagging accuracy (including full morphological tagging) of about 85%. When we 'intersect' the taggers with our lexicon, the latter score increases to almost 91% for Lapos. Concerning lemmatization, we lemmatize words on the basis of the taggers' outputs. We employ two dif-

[1] www.comphistsem.org

[2] http://patristica.net/latina

[3] MGH is the acronym of Monumenta Germaniae Historica, the German Central Institute for Middle Age research (deutsches Zentralinstitut zur Erforschung des Mittelalters).

Proceedings of the 9th SIGHUM Workshop on Language Technology for Cultural Heritage, Social Sciences, and Humanities, pages 105–113,
Beijing, China, July 30, 2015.

Form	Lemma	PoS-tag	Sub.-cats.
Ex	ex	AP	
frugibus	frux	NN	gender=f, case=abl. number=pl
terrae	terra	NN	gender=f, case=gen. number=sg,
corpus	corpus	NN	gender=n, case=nom. number=sg,
nostrum	noster	PRO	gender=n, case=nom. number=sg,
sustentatur	sustento	V	number=sg, person=3 mood=ind, voice=pass. tense=present

Table 1: Sample sentence ('from the fruits of the earth our body is sustained') in our corpus and its annotation.

ferent lemmatization strategies: we either look up the current lemma in the lexicon given the word form as well as the predicted tag information (lexicon-based lemmatization) or we lemmatize on the basis of statistical lemmatizers/string transducers trained on our corpus. A conservative assessment of lemmatization accuracy estimates a score of 93-94% for the lexicon-based strategy and a score of 94-95% for the trained lemmatizers.

This work is structured as follows. Section 2 describes our lexicon. Section 3 outlines related work, on part-of-speech tagging and resources for Latin. Section 4 describes our lemmatization module and Section 5 the tagging systems we survey. In Section 6, we outline results and we conclude in Section 7.

2 Lexicon

Our lexicon named Collex.LA (Mehler et al., 2015) consists both of manually created lexicon entries as well as of automatically extracted entries from several freely available Web resources, in particular AGFL (Koster and Verbruggen, 2002), LemLat (Passerotti, 2004), Perseus Digital Library (Smith et al., 2000), Whitaker word list[4], Thomisticum[5] (Busa, 1980; McGilivray et al., 2009), Ramminger word list[6], and several others. In total it consists of 8 347 062 word forms, 119 595 lemmas and 104 905 superlemmas.[7] A superlemma is a special kind of lemma that unifies several writing variants. The lexicon distribution over different parts of speech is given in Table 2. Each lexicon entry consists of word form, part-of-speech, and lemma. Depending on the part-of-speech of the entry, additional grammatical features can be provided. For instance, each verb entry contains its mood, voice, number, person, verb type (transitive or intransitive), tense and the conjugation class. Pronouns are annotated with a pronoun type that further differentiates pronouns into demonstrative, interrogative, personal, reflexive, relative, possessive, indefinite, intensive, and correlative pronouns. Analogously, additional grammatical features are provided for nouns, adverbs and adjectives. In total, there are currently 17 different grammatical features defined. Our lexicon can be accessed via the website `collex.hucompute.org`.

3 Related work

PoS tagging is a long-standing NLP task and (modern) classical approaches to solving it include Hidden Markov models, conditional random fields (CRFs), averaged perceptrons, structured SVMs, and max margin Markov networks (Nguyen and Guo, 2007). For highly inflectional languages, the problem of large tagsets arises, which leads to serious data sparsity issues, besides tractability problems. Tufis (1999) addresses this via a multi-stage tagging approach in which tagging is initially performed with a reduced tagset. Müller et al. (2013) show that even higher-order CRFs can be used for large tagsets when approximations are employed. Boros et al. (2013) use feed forward neural networks, which can arguably better smooth probabilities, for this problem. In a non-contextual task setting, Toutanova and Cherry (2009) show that, for morphologically rich languages, *lemmatization* and part-of-speech tagging may mutually

[4]URL: `http://archives.nd.edu/whitaker/dictpage.htm`

[5]URL: `http://www.corpusthomisticum.org/tl.html`

[6]`http://www.neulatein.de`

[7]The lexicon is currently extended by additionally exploring the Latin Wiktionary as a resource.

Part-of-speech	#Word forms	#Lemmas	#Superlemmas
verb (V)	4 646 369	11 556	8 666
adjective (ADJ)	2 693 333	24 020	21 155
normal noun (NN)	654 194	40 906	34 096
anthroponym (NP)	229 299	26 241	25 898
named entity (NE)	68 276	5 387	4 821
adverb (ADV)	40 771	10 625	9 594
pronoun (PRO)	6 377	139	113
ordinal number (ORD)	3 349	116	87
cardinal number (NUM)	1 835	104	75
distributive number (DIST)	1 216	44	44
foreign material (FM)	1 023	91	32
conjunction (CON)	383	122	103
preposition (AP)	341	104	87
interjection (ITJ)	199	110	109
non word (XY)	69	14	14
particle (PTC)	28	16	11

Table 2: Distribution of the lexicon entries over the different parts of speech.

inform each other. Lee et al. (2011) show that tagging and *dependency parsing* may mutually inform each other in such a setup, too.

Concerning lexical resources for Latin, to our knowledge, there are concurrently three freely available resources for Latin: Perseus (Smith et al., 2000; Bamman and Crane, 2007), Proiel (Haug and Jøhndal, 2008), and the Index Thomisticus (IT) (Busa, 1980; McGilivray et al., 2009). Perseus and Proiel cover the more classical Latin era, while IT focuses on the writings of Thomas Aquinas. All resources indicate lemma and various part-of-speech information for its tokens. IT in addition provides dependency information. Concerning size, Perseus is the smallest resource with roughly 3 500 sentences, and Proiel and IT each contain about 13 000–14 000 Latin sentences.

4 Lemmatization

On our corpus, we learn a character-level string transducer as a component model of our tagger. This lemmatizer is trained on pairs of strings $(\mathbf{x}, \mathbf{y})$ where $\mathbf{x}$ is a full form (e.g., *amavisse* 'have loved') and $\mathbf{y}$ its corresponding lemma (e.g., *amo* 'love'). Learning a statistical lemmatizer has the advantage that it can cope with OOV words and may adapt to the distribution of the corpus. Our lemmatization module is LemmaGen (Juršič et al., 2010). LemmaGen learns 'if-then' rules from $(\mathbf{x}, \mathbf{y})$ pairs as indicated. To transduce/lemmatize a new input form, rules (and their exceptions) are ordered, and the first condition that is satisfied fires the corresponding rule.

5 Part-of-speech taggers

Here, we briefly sketch the taggers we survey in Section 6. All taggers outlined are language-independent and general-purpose taggers.

The **TreeTagger** (Schmid, 1994) implements a tagger based on decision trees. Despite its simple architecture, it seems to enjoy considerable popularity up until recently. Concurrently, two freely available TreeTagger taggers for Latin are available.[8] **TnT** (Brants, 2000) implements a trigram Hidden Markov tagger with a module for handling unknown words. It has been shown to perform similarly well as maximum entropy models. **Lapos** (Tsuruoka et al., 2011) is a 'history based' tagging model (this model class subsumes maximum entropy Markov model) incorporating a lookahead mechanism into its decision-making process. It has been reported to be competitive with globally optimized models such as CRFs and structured perceptrons. **Mate** (Bohnet and Nivre, 2012) implements a transition based system for joint part-of-speech tagging and dependency parsing reported to exhibit high performance for richly

[8] See `http://www.cis.uni-muenchen.de/~schmid/tools/TreeTagger/`.

inflected languages, where there may be considerable dependence between morphology and syntax, as well as for more configurational languages like English. The **OpenNLPTagger** is an official Apache project and provides three different tagging methods: *maximum entropy*, *perceptron* and *perceptron sequence* (cf. (Ratnaparkhi, 1996; Collins, 2002)) for maximum/perceptron based entropy tagging). We evaluated the maximum entropy and the perceptron approach.[9]

The **Stanford tagger** (Toutanova et al., 2003) implements a bidirectional log-linear model that makes broad use of lexical features. The implementation lets the user specifically activate and deactivate desired features.

We use default parametrizations for all taggers[10] and trained all taggers on a random sample of our data of about 14 000 sentences and test them on the remainder of about 1 500 sentences.

6 Results

6.1 Tagging

Contrary to some of our related work, we view the morphological tagging problem for Latin as a multi-label tagging problem in which each tagging task (PoS, case, gender, etc.) is handled *independently*. To compensate for this naïvety, we subsequently 'intersect' the resulting tag decisions with our lexicon, which considerably improves performance, as we show.

Table 3 shows accuracies (fraction of correctly tagged words) on each tagging subtask. The almost consistently best tagger is Lapos, with a slight margin over Mate and the Stanford tagger. TnT's and particularly OpenNLP's and the TreeTagger's performance are substantially worse. For example, overall tagging accuracy (indicating the probability that a system is jointly correct on *all* subtasks) of Lapos is about 2.9% higher than that of TnT and about 6.6% higher than that of the TreeTagger. When we 'intersect' the taggers' outputs with our lexicon — i.e., we retrieve the closest lexicon classification for the input form in question if the form is in the lexicon[11] — all performance values increase substantially, on the order of about 5-6 percentage points (see Table 3). Individual increases (for Lapos) for each subtask are outlined in Table 5.[12]

Figure 1 shows the learning curve (accuracy as a function of training set size) for the three selected taggers Lapos, Mate, and the TreeTagger for the category 'PoS' (similar curves for the other tagging subtasks). Apparently, the more recent tagger generation generalizes substantially better than the older approaches, exhibiting much higher accuracies especially at small training set sizes.

6.2 Lemmatization

Lemma accuracy is indicated in Table 4. As we mentioned, we employ two lemmatization strategies based on the taggers' outputs: either the lemma is retrieved from the lexicon given the predicted part-of-speech and the morphological tags. Alternatively, we train LemmaGen string transducers as outlined in Section 4, one for each part-of-speech. Once the taggers have predicted a part-of-speech we apply the corresponding lemmatizer for this word-class. Note that both strategies tendentially imply a loss of accuracy due to errors committed in a previous step, viz., tagging; however, even a falsely tagged form may receive correct lemmatization, e.g., when tag mismatch is between 'neighboring' parts-of-speech such as noun and proper noun. We find that, across the different taggers, lemma accuracy is about 93-94% for the lexicon based strategy and about 94-95% for the learned lemmatizers. Scores for the lexicon are lower, e.g., because the lexicon can simply not store all sorts of lemma information (e.g., numbers such as '75', '76', etc.), which is an instance of the OOV problem.[13] Moreover, the lexicon tends to suffer more strongly from free lemma variations (e.g., *honos* and *honor* as equivalent alternatives). In contrast, the learned lemmatizers can adapt to the actual form-lemma distribution in the respective corpus. Due to the free variation problem as indicated and since we also count lower/upper-

[9] Unfortunately, the documentation of these methods is not very detailed, which leaves the methodology of the tagger rather unclear. The application of the *sequence perceptron* method led to an exception during the training phase. Therefore, this method could not be evaluated.

[10] For the Stanford tagger, we include the features bidirectional5words, allwordshapes(-1,1), generic, words(-2,2), suffix(8), biwords(-1,1).

[11] We measure closeness in terms of the number of matching categories.

[12] We note that a simple majority vote additionally slightly increases performance values. Integrating in this way Lapos, Mate and the Stanford Tagger leads to a PoS accuracy of 95.97%; adding TnT leads to 95.94%; finally, integrating all systems leads to 95.88%.

[13] E.g., for Lapos, adding a rule for numbers increases accuracy to 94.61% for the lexicon-based lemmatization.

	Lapos	TnT	Mate	TreeTagger	Stanford	OpenNLP	
						Max.Entr	Perceptron
PoS	**95.86**	95.16	95.67	92.00	95.55	93.83	92.92
case	**94.64**	92.86	94.56	88.17	94.58	90.71	90.23
degree	**97.55**	97.09	97.40	92.40	97.30	95.55	94.52
gender	**96.09**	95.35	95.84	90.64	95.83	93.81	92.57
mood	**98.28**	97.73	98.13	93.33	98.12	96.04	94.55
number	97.19	96.90	97.04	95.16	**97.23**	95.52	94.92
person	99.25	98.87	**99.27**	94.07	99.18	97.51	95.64
tense	**98.53**	98.17	98.41	93.60	98.43	96.68	95.34
voice	**98.79**	98.52	98.74	94.43	98.67	97.95	96.93
OVERALL	**85.03**	82.63	84.25	79.71	84.35	78.16	75.87
OVERALL+LEX	**90.74**	88.33	90.55	86.38	90.29	84.58	84.03

Table 3: Tag accuracies in % for different systems and different categories.

case differences as errors, the reported numbers may be seen as conservative estimates of lemma accuracy.

Cat.	Acc.	Increase
PoS	96.10	+0.25
case	94.79	+0.15
degree	97.85	+0.30
gender	96.40	+0.32
mood	98.71	+0.47
number	97.89	+0.72
person	99.45	+0.20
tense	98.90	+0.37
voice	99.10	+0.31

Table 5: Tag accuracies in % for Lapos+Lexicon. The column 'Increase' indicates the increase over not consulting the lexicon.

6.3 Error analysis

Table 6 shows a fine-grained precision and recall analysis for Lapos, across each of the possible part-of-speech labels in our tagset (for the category 'PoS'), indicating that among the frequent parts-of-speech particularly adjectives (ADJ) and proper names (NE and NP) are hard to classify.

Table 7 shows the agreements in PoS prediction for the taggers of our test scenario. The agreement between the best-performing taggers Mate and Lapos is very high (98%), while the agreement of the low performing taggers to all other taggers is rather low (mostly below 95%). This is the case even when the latter taggers are compared among each other, which indicates that they commit quite different types of errors.

PoS	Precision	Recall	F_1
NN	95.89	95.50	95.69
V	96.81	96.61	96.71
CON	98.30	97.17	97.73
PRO	98.05	96.22	97.13
$,	100.00	100.00	100.00
AP	98.38	95.33	96.83
ADJ	83.95	88.07	85.96
$.	100.00	100.00	100.00
ADV	88.59	93.91	91.17
NUM	97.00	97.59	97.29
NP	92.87	84.49	88.48
NE	67.56	82.41	74.25
$(	100.00	98.22	99.10
FM	80.89	94.77	87.28
ORD	82.29	75.23	78.60
ITJ	78.26	100.00	87.80
XY	73.33	84.61	78.57
PTC	0.00	0.00	0.00
DIST	33.33	100.00	50.00

Table 6: Precision, recall and F_1 measure across the possible PoS tags in our corpus. PoS ordered by corpus frequency.

	Lapos	TnT	Mate	TreeTagger	Stanford
Lexicon	93.87	93.74	**93.90**	93.49	93.85
LemmaGen	**95.30**	94.85	95.06	94.74	94.99

Table 4: Lemma accuracy in % for 5 selected taggers based on either lexicon-based lemmatization or using the learned LemmaGen transducer.

	Lapos	TnT	Mate	Tree-Tagger	Stanford	OpenNLP Max.Entr	OpenNLP Perceptron
Lapos	100	97	98	94	98	96	94
TnT	97	100	97	95	97	96	94
Mate	98	97	100	93	97	95	94
Tree-Tagger	94	95	93	100	93	92	91
Stanford	98	97	97	93	100	95	94
Op.NLP/MaxEntr.	96	96	95	92	95	100	95
Op.NLP/Perceptron	94	94	94	91	94	95	100

Table 7: Agreement of different taggers in %.

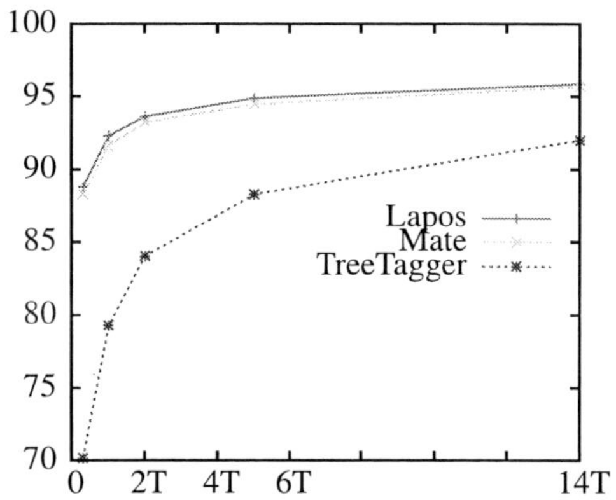

Figure 1: Accuracy as a function of training set size (300, 1000, 2000, and 5000 sentences) for Lapos, Mate, and the TreeTagger.

Our evaluation showed that in 98.90% of the cases at least one of the taggers predicted the correct part-of-speech (oracle prediction), indicating that a tagger combination could theoretically lead to accuracy values far above the 95.86% of the best performing system Lapos.

We further investigate the distribution of errors common to all taggers, shown in Figure 2.

Our analysis shows that prepositions are often confused with adverbs, because several Latin word forms can be prepositions in one context and adverbs in another. Since a preposition is almost always attached to a noun, and an adverb almost always to a verb, one possible approach to overcome this problem could be to estimate attachment probabilities of words by analyzing large Latin corpora.

A further common error is that the part-of-speech tags for nouns, adjectives and pronouns are frequently confounded by the taggers, since the associated word endings are similar and quite a few word forms are homographs with both an adjective and noun reading. In addition, the word order in Latin is relatively free. Thus, an adjective can follow or precede the modified noun, which impedes a disambiguation by statistical context analysis.

Verbs are sometimes erroneously classified as nouns, due the fact that gerund forms, annotated as verbs in the corpus, can syntactically function as nouns and have strong ending similarity with nouns.

Analogously to PoS tagging, errors in morphological tagging can occur, if the same word form can be associated to different morphological feature values of the same type, which is the case for quite a lot word forms in ablative and dative as well as for word forms in accusative and nominative plural.

Finally, some words in our corpus are annotated inconsistently. For example, ordinal numbers are sometimes tagged as adjective instead with the tag ORD that is actually intended for such numbers.

6.4 Comparison with other work

Several other papers document PoS tagging accuracies for Latin corpora. For example, Bamman

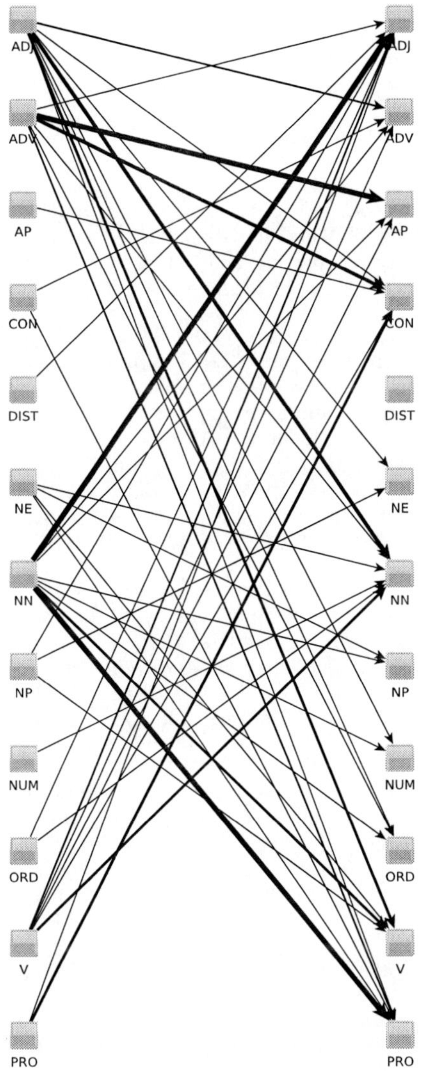

Figure 2: A bipartite graph showing the distribution of errors common to all taggers. The partition with the correct parts-of-speech are on the left side of the figure while the erroneously predicted parts of speech are displayed on the right side. The thickness of an arrow leading from the correct part-of-speech to the incorrectly predicted part-of-speech is proportional to the number of times that such an error was made by the taggers.

and Crane (2008) report a PoS tagging accuracy of 95.11% and full morphological analysis accuracy of 83.10% for the TreeTagger on Perseus. Passarotti (2010) indicates numbers of 96.75% and 89.90%, respectively, on the IT data base using an HMM-based tagger. Lee et al. (2011) introduce a joint model for morphological disambiguation and dependency parsing, achieving a PoS accuracy of 94.50% on Perseus. Müller and Schütze (2015) give a best result of 88.40% for full morphological analysis on Proiel, using a second-order CRF and features firing on the suggestions of a morphological analyzer. Of course, none of these results are directly comparable — not only because different variants of Latin are considered but also because training set sizes and annotation standards differ across corpora. For instance, while Perseus has 12 different PoS labels, our corpus has 19, making PoS tagging a priori more difficult on our corpus in this respect, irrespective of which tagging technology is employed.

7 Conclusion

We have presented a comparative study of taggers for preprocessing (medieval church) Latin. More specifically, we applied six different part-of-speech taggers to our data and surveyed their performance. This showed that the accuracy values of recent taggers barely differ on our data and take values tightly below 96% for part of speech and around 90% for full lexicon-supported morphological tagging on our test corpus. We showed that consolidating the taggers' outputs with our lexicon can substantially increase full morphological tagging performance, indicating the value of our lexical resource for addressing the problem of rich morphology in Latin. We also surveyed lemma prediction accuracy based on the taggers' outputs and found it to be on the order of around 93-94% for a lexicon-based strategy and on the order of around 94-95% for learned string transducers. Finally, we conducted a detailed error analysis that showed that all of the taggers had problems to disambiguate between prepositions and adverbs as well as between nouns and adjectives. We hope that our survey may serve as a guideline for other researchers. In future work, we intend to investigate how our results generalize to other variants of Latin. Moreover, all trained taggers presented here are made available via the website `https://prepro.hucompute.org/`. This also concerns our training corpus that will be made available in a way that respects copyright while allowing taggers to be trained thereon.

References

David Bamman and Gregory Crane. 2007. The latin dependency treebank in a cultural heritage digital library. In *Proceedings of the Second Workshop on Language Technology for Cultural Heritage Data (LaTeCH 2007)*, pages 33–40, Prague. Association for Computational Linguistics.

David Bamman and Gregory Crane. 2008. Building a dynamic lexicon from a digital library. In *Proceedings of the 8th ACM/IEEE-CS joint conference on Digital libraries*, JCDL '08, pages 11–20, New York, NY, USA. ACM.

Bernd Bohnet and Joakim Nivre. 2012. A transition-based system for joint part-of-speech tagging and labeled non-projective dependency parsing. In *Proceedings of the 2012 Joint Conference on Empirical Methods in Natural Language Processing and Computational Natural Language Learning*, pages 1455–1465, Jeju Island, Korea, July. Association for Computational Linguistics.

Tiberiu Boros, Radu Ion, and Dan Tufis. 2013. Large tagset labeling using feed forward neural networks. case study on romanian language. In *Proceedings of the 51st Annual Meeting of the Association for Computational Linguistics (Volume 1: Long Papers)*, pages 692–700. Association for Computational Linguistics.

Thorsten Brants. 2000. Tnt: A statistical part-of-speech tagger. In *Proceedings of the Sixth Conference on Applied Natural Language Processing*, ANLC '00, pages 224–231, Stroudsburg, PA, USA. Association for Computational Linguistics.

R. Busa. 1980. The annals of humanities computing: The index thomisticus. *Computers and the Humanities*, 14:83–90.

Michael Collins. 2002. Discriminative training methods for hidden markov models: Theory and experiments with perceptron algorithms. In *Proceedings of the Conference on Empirical Methods in Natural Language Processing (EMNLP)*, Stroudsburg, Pennsylvania.

Dag Trygve Truslew Haug and Marius Jøhndal. 2008. Creating a parallel treebank of the old indo-european bible translations. In *Proceedings of the Sixth International Language Resources and Evaluation (LREC'08)*.

Matjaž Juršič, Igor Mozetič, and Nada Lavrač. 2010. LemmaGen: Multilingual lemmatisation with induced ripple-down rules. *Journal of Universal Computer Science*, 16:1190–1214.

Cornelis H.A. Koster and E. Verbruggen. 2002. The agfl grammar work lab. In *Proceedings of FREENIX/Usenix*, pages 13–18.

John Lee, Jason Naradowsky, and David A. Smith. 2011. A discriminative model for joint morphological disambiguation and dependency parsing. In *Proceedings of the 49th Annual Meeting of the Association for Computational Linguistics: Human Language Technologies - Volume 1*, HLT '11, pages 885–894, Stroudsburg, PA, USA. Association for Computational Linguistics.

Barbary McGilivray, Marco Passarotti, and Paolo Ruffolo. 2009. The index thomisticus treebank project: Annotation, parsing and valency lexicon. *Traitement Automatique des Langues*, 50(2).

Alexander Mehler, Tim vor der Brück, Rüdiger Gleim, and Tim Geelhaar. 2015. Towards a network model of the coreness of texts: An experiment in classifying latin texts sing the TTLab Latin tagger. In Chris Biemann and Alexander Mehler, editors, *Text Mining: From Ontology Learning to Automated text Processing Applications*, Theory and Applications of Natural Language Processing, pages 87–112. Springer, Berlin/New York.

Thomas Müller and Hinrich Schütze. 2015. Robust morphological tagging with word representations. In *Proceedings of the 2015 Conference of the North American Chapter of the Association for Computational Linguistics: Human Language Technologies*, pages 526–536, Denver, Colorado, May–June. Association for Computational Linguistics.

Thomas Müller, Helmut Schmid, and Hinrich Schütze. 2013. Efficient higher-order CRFs for morphological tagging. In *Proceedings of the 2013 Conference on Empirical Methods in Natural Language Processing*, pages 322–332, Seattle, Washington, USA, October. Association for Computational Linguistics.

Nam Nguyen and Yunsong Guo. 2007. Comparisons of sequence labeling algorithms and extensions. In *Proceedings of the 24th international conference on Machine learning*, ICML '07, pages 681–688, New York, NY, USA. ACM.

Marco Passarotti. 2010. Leaving behind the less-resourced status. the case of Latin through the experience of the Index Thomisticus Treebank. In Kepa Sarasola, Francis M. Tyers, and Mikel L. Forcada, editors, *7th SaLTMiL Workshop on Creation and use of basic lexical resources for less-resourced languages*, pages 27–32.

Marco Passerotti. 2004. Development and perspectives of the latin morphological analyser lemlat. *Linguistica Computazionale*, 20–21.

Adwait Ratnaparkhi. 1996. A maximum entropy model for part-of-speech tagging. In *Proceedings of the 1st Conference on Empirical Methods in Natural Language Processing (EMNLP)*, Philadelphia, Pennsylvania.

Helmut Schmid. 1994. Probabilistic part-of-speech tagging using decision trees. In *International Conference on New Methods in Language Processing*, pages 44–49, Manchester, UK.

David A. Smith, Jeffrey A. Rydberg-Cox, and Gregory R. Crane. 2000. The perseus project: a digital library for the humanities. *Literary and Linguist Computing*, 15(1).

Kristina Toutanova and Colin Cherry. 2009. A global model for joint lemmatization and part-of-speech prediction. In *Proceedings of the Joint Conference of the 47th Annual Meeting of the ACL and the 4th International Joint Conference on Natural Language Processing of the AFNLP: Volume 1 - Volume 1*, ACL '09, pages 486–494, Stroudsburg, Pennsylvania. Association for Computational Linguistics.

Kristina Toutanova, Dan Klein, Christopher D. Manning, and Yoram Singer. 2003. Feature-rich part-of-speech tagging with a cyclic dependency network. In *Proceedings of the 2003 Conference of the North American Chapter of the Association for Computational Linguistics on Human Language Technology - Volume 1*, NAACL '03, pages 173–180, Stroudsburg, PA, USA. Association for Computational Linguistics.

Yoshimasa Tsuruoka, Yusuke Miyao, and Jun'ichi Kazama. 2011. Learning with lookahead: Can history-based models rival globally optimized models? In *Proceedings of the Fifteenth Conference on Computational Natural Language Learning*, CoNLL '11, pages 238–246, Stroudsburg, PA, USA. Association for Computational Linguistics.

Dan Tufis. 1999. Tiered tagging and combined language models classifiers. In Vclav Matousek, Pavel Mautner, Jana Ocelkov, and Petr Sojka, editors, *TSD*, volume 1692 of *Lecture Notes in Computer Science*, pages 28–33. Springer.

Author Index

Association for Computational Linguistics
209 N. Eighth Street
Stroudsburg, Pennsylvania 18360

ISBN 978-1-5108-0944-4

CURRAN ASSOCIATES INC.
proceedings.com